C000150502

PROPERTY TH

Property, or property rights, remains one of the most central elements in moral, legal and political thought. It figures centrally in the work of figures as various as Grotius, Locke, Hume, Smith, Hegel and Kant. This collection of essays brings fresh perspective on property theory, from both legal and political theoretical perspectives, and is essential reading for anyone interested in the nature of property. Edited by two of the world's leading theorists of property, James Penner and Michael Otsuka, this volume brings together essays that consider, amongst other topics, property and public law, the importance of legal forms in property theory, whether use or exclusion are most essential to our understanding of property, distributive justice, Lockean and Grotian theories, the common ownership of the earth and Confucian ideas of property.

JAMES PENNER is Kwa Geok Choo Professor of Property Law and Vice Dean for Research in the Faculty of Law, National University of Singapore, and a barrister of Lincoln's Inn. Professor Penner has written extensively on the law of trusts, private law more generally, and the philosophy of law, with special interests in the philosophical foundations of the common law, legal reasoning and property theory. He is the author of *The Idea of Property in Law*, which won the SPTL first prize for outstanding legal scholarship (now renamed the SLS Birks Prize). He edited (with Henry S. Smith) *The Philosophical Foundations of Property Law* (2013) and is author of *Property Rights: A Re-examination* (forthcoming).

MICHAEL OTSUKA is a professor in the Department of Philosophy, Logic and Scientific Method at the London School of Economics. His research interests encompass political philosophy, political economy and normative ethics. He is the author of *Libertarianism without Inequality* (2003), in which he explores the relations among self-ownership, world-ownership and equality from a Lockean left-libertarian perspective.

PROPERTY THEORY

Legal and Political Perspectives

Edited by

JAMES PENNER

National University of Singapore

MICHAEL OTSUKA

London School of Economics

CAMBRIDGE
UNIVERSITY PRESS

CAMBRIDGE
UNIVERSITY PRESS

University Printing House, Cambridge CB2 8BS, United Kingdom

One Liberty Plaza, 20th Floor, New York, NY 10006, USA

477 Williamstown Road, Port Melbourne, VIC 3207, Australia

314–321, 3rd Floor, Plot 3, Splendor Forum, Jasola District Centre, New Delhi – 110025, India

79 Anson Road, #06-04/06, Singapore 079906

Cambridge University Press is part of the University of Cambridge.

It furthers the University's mission by disseminating knowledge in the pursuit of education, learning, and research at the highest international levels of excellence.

www.cambridge.org
Information on this title: www.cambridge.org/9781108422420
DOI: 10.1017/9781108500043

First published 2018

Printed and bound in Great Britain by Clays Ltd, Elcograf S.p.A.

A catalogue record for this publication is available from the British Library.

Library of Congress Cataloging-in-Publication Data

Names: Penner, J. E. (James E.), editor. | Otsuka, Michael, editor.
Title: Property theory : legal and political perspectives / edited by James Penner, National University of Singapore [and] Michael Otsuka, London School of Economics.
Description: Cambridge, United Kingdom ; New York, NY, USA : Cambridge University Press, 2018.
Identifiers: LCCN 2018011057| ISBN 9781108422420 (hardback) | ISBN 9781108436687 (paperback)
Subjects: LCSH: Right of property. | BISAC: LAW / Property.
Classification: LCC K721.5 .P795 2018 | DDC 346.04/32—dc23
LC record available at https://lccn.loc.gov/2018011057

ISBN 978-1-108-42242-0 Hardback
ISBN 978-1-108-43668-7 Paperback

CONTENTS

CONTRIBUTORS

LISA M. AUSTIN Professor of Law at the University of Toronto

NORMAN P. HO Associate Professor of Law at the School of Transnational Law, Peking University

LARISSA KATZ Associate Professor and Canada Research Chair in Private Law Theory at the Faculty of Law, University of Toronto

CHRISTOPHER M. NEWMAN Associate Professor of Law at the Scalia Law School, George Mason University

JOHAN OLSTHOORN Assistant Professor in the Department of Political Science, University of Amsterdam and Postdoctoral Fellow of the Research Foundation Flanders (FWO) KU Leuven

MICHAEL OTSUKA Professor of Philosophy at the London School of Economics

JAMES PENNER Kwa Geok Choo Professor of Property Law at the National University of Singapore

NICHOLAS SAGE Assistant Professor of Law at the London School of Economics

JAMES Y. STERN Associate Professor of Law at William & Mary Law School

PREFACE

The theoretical consideration of property, and associated concepts such as possession and first acquisition, have long featured in legal and political philosophy, from the voluminous right- and left-libertarian literature which takes 'self-ownership' to be central, to the foundational positioning of property rights in the political theories of figures as diverse as Grotius, Locke, Hume, Smith, Hegel and Kant. The essays collected here show the continuing vigor of scholarship in this area.

On the legal theoretical side of the ledger, our first four essays bring pressure to bear on several popular ideas which have tended to shape the discourse in this area. Lisa Austin's essay challenges the notion that property is, for the most part, shaped by private law considerations, pointing out the way private law doctrine is shot through with public law considerations. Larissa Katz's essay reveals the relevance of property 'forms', like the trust, arguing that any Hohfeldian analysis which discounts the importance of such forms undermines our ability to reason about interpersonal relations that property law promotes and protects. For their parts, both James Stern and Christopher Newman interrogate in different ways the recent emphasis many scholars have placed on the right to exclude as the hallmark of the right to private property. Stern chips away at this thought by examining what the right to exclude does and does not achieve in explaining various elements of legal doctrine. Relatedly, but from a different angle, Newman argues that the use of property, or the right to use property, stands as a better essential or defining element of property rights than does the right to exclude.

Turning to political perspectives on property theory, the chapter by Nicholas Sage considers the justice of the original acquisition of property rights and contends that theorists have overcomplicated this issue, proffering accounts of acquisition that overlook a more parsimonious and illuminating account focused on respect for choice. The next three essays, by Michael Otsuka, James Penner and Norman Ho, each explore a different dimension of John Locke's continuing grip on our understanding of property and the considerations that make property a just institution, if it is. Otsuka defends an egalitarian version of the Lockean 'enough and as good' proviso and argues that recent attempts to downplay its contemporary relevance fail to succeed. Penner, by contrast, focuses on Locke's spoilation proviso and attributes a theory of justice in exchange to Locke to argue that scarcity in land does not lead, necessarily, to distributive injustice. Ho examines two Confucian writers, each of whom considered the nature of property rights, to show parallels with, but also distinctions between, their thought and Locke's. Our final chapter, by Johan Olsthoorn, explores Grotius's conception of property and questions the uses to which it can be put in the modern era, taking long-standing questions about the idea of 'the common ownership' of the earth as its focus.

We commend these essays to our readers and trust they will find them as intellectually stimulating as we have throughout the process of our editorship.

The editors and contributors would like to acknowledge the support of the National University of Singapore Centre for Legal Theory for hosting the workshop at which these chapters were first presented, and the generous financial support provided by the Singapore Ministry of Education in the form of Academic Research Fund (Tier 1) Research Grant No. R-241-000-141-112. We are also exceptionally grateful to Kim Hughes, Gemma Smith, Laura Blake and Geetha Williams at Cambridge University Press, and to Li Zhongsheng for editorial assistance.

James Penner and Michael Otsuka

1

The Public Nature of Private Property

LISA M. AUSTIN

1.1 Introduction

The idea that private law is a distinct normative category is not self-evidently true. One might think that it is a useful shorthand, or a pragmatic category, that brings together tort, contract, property and unjust enrichment for useful comparisons, but not one that can sustain a general principled distinction from other areas of law that we might call "public." And critics have launched various arguments that (to the extent that the distinctiveness claim involves insulating the private law from the "public" ends of political community, however these might be conceived) the claim is both descriptively false and normatively undesirable. The so-called autonomy of the private law can easily align with a conservative account of the autonomy of the self-regulating market, and its claims to be free of political regulation.

However, the idea that private law is a distinct normative category is also not self-evidently false. What the critical views often disregard is the important focus that the distinctiveness claims brings to questions of what I would call legal architecture – legal doctrine and the relationships between legal doctrines. The label "private law" points us to useful structural features of the legal areas it marks out for comparison, and many have claimed that these structures call for an "internal" perspective and cannot be fully understood (or even understood at all) if only looked at in relation to the external "public" ends that they might be thought to achieve.

In this chapter I examine one prominent version of the distinctiveness claim – the corrective justice position as expounded by Ernest Weinrib – and discuss it in relation to private property. By private property I mean the idea of private ownership and its associated doctrines. According to

In addition to the editors and contributors to this volume, I would like to thank Alan Brudner, Hanoch Dagan, Avihay Dorfman, Roy Kreitner, Ernest J. Weinrib, and the participants of the Private Law Theory Workshop at Tel Aviv University and the North American Private Law Theory Workshop for their very helpful comments on earlier versions of this chapter. All errors and misunderstandings remain mine.

Weinrib's view, corrective justice characterizes private law and distributive justice characterizes public law. But Weinrib's account also adds, as a secondary matter, a public dimension to private law adjudication. This is what he calls the "omnilateral" perspective, which ensures that the interpretation and enforcement of private rights are public. My argument is that Weinrib's account of the priority of the structure of corrective justice over the omnilaterality of public institutions gets things backwards in relation to private property. The basic structure of property is not correlativity, but omnilaterality. Property is public through and through.

But this does not mean that ownership, or the rest of property law, is a matter of distributive justice rather than corrective justice. In focusing on these forms of justice as providing the distinction between "private" and "public" law we risk ignoring the fact that *both* are connected by being "law" and that law is inherently public. The publicness of property is not about justice at all, but about the nature of law and the formal properties of law. Ownership is a *legal* relation between persons in relation to things. Its further relationship to various ideas of justice is secondary and, I will argue, it can (but does not necessarily) point toward both corrective and distributive justice considerations. The extent to which these are taken up are constrained by ideas of law and not the other way around.

I then draw several implications from this account. First, I agree that there is a formal structure to private property but that this is best understood through the idea of law and omnilaterality, rather than through the forms of justice. Second, law is intrinsically related to justice. Although this does not necessarily lead to any particular form of justice it does lead to a legal concern for the avoidance of injustice. Third, both legislation and the "public policy" considerations that might be drawn from it are not marginal to the core of private property, but central to it in a variety of ways.

1.2 The Corrective Justice Account

Weinrib's basic corrective justice account of private law is familiar to many private law theorists.[1] I will only briefly provide its main contours here in order to highlight both how Weinrib understands the relationship between correlativity and omnilaterality, and how he understands the relationship between adjudication and legislation. His account places both omnilaterality and legislation on the periphery of private law, which, I will argue, provides a distorted view of private property. Although I shall

[1] See Weinrib 1995, 2012.

here focus on Weinrib's account, the critique to follow has, I think, wider application – it should raise questions for any account of property which limits property's normative significance to corrective, or commutative, justice accounts of private law.

According to Weinrib, "[p]rivate law is a publicly rightful set of norms that governs the legal relations between parties."[2] This is further split into two sets of ideas – the norms associated with the legal relations between parties and the norms associated with "public rightfulness." The latter refers to "law's public institutions of adjudication and enforcement."[3] The first refers to the relations that are fully intelligible apart from these public institutions – with philosophical state of nature stories understood as heuristic devices that can help illuminate such relations.[4]

It is this first aspect, the normative relations between parties, which is characterized by corrective justice. Corrective justice looks to the relationship between two parties – the plaintiff and defendant – as the doer and sufferer of the same injustice, and is bipolar. In contrast, distributive justice looks to the relationship between more than two parties in terms of some distributive criterion. As Weinrib argues, "in principle no limit exists for the number of persons who can be compared and among whom something can be divided."[5] Similarly, corrective justice and distributive justice are concerned with different understandings, or facets, of equality. Corrective justice seeks to restore "the notional equality with which the parties enter into the transaction." In contrast, distributive justice is concerned with proportional equality, "in which all participants in the distribution receive their shares according to their respective merits under the criterion in question."[6] When dealing with private law liability, according to Weinrib, it is the role of the courts to do corrective justice, not distributive justice. Distributive justice lies in the realm of political judgment, and is for the legislature. The legislature may even decide to do away with private law in a particular area and replace it with something else, like a public insurance scheme for accidents instead of tort law. However, what neither institution should do is mix forms.

This is not to say that corrective justice theorists like Weinrib deny the place of distributive justice within a just legal system. Weinrib even concedes that the systematic operation of private law rights, and in particular

[2] Weinrib 2011.
[3] Weinrib 2011, p. 192.
[4] Weinrib 2011, p. 195.
[5] Weinrib 2012, p. 19.
[6] Weinrib 2012, p. 16.

private property, can lead to conditions of dependency for some individuals.[7] This generates a duty on the state to mitigate these circumstances of dependency but does not, for Weinrib, mean that private law should incorporate any concern for such dependency. As he argues, "The distributive considerations cannot be backed up into the corrective justice stage, because those considerations are not correlatively structured and therefore cannot fairly and coherently figure within private law."[8] Distributive justice is the realm of legislation and administration, not private law adjudication.

Corrective justice is a structural, not substantive principle. To fill in the substantive nature of private law liability, Weinrib takes up Kant's analysis of rights as deriving "from an analysis of how the action of one person can be consistent with the equal freedom of another."[9]

To this basic picture, Weinrib adds the dimension of "public right." The problem with the state of nature, which Weinrib takes to illuminate the nature of private law norms, lies with the "interpretation and enforcement" of private law's correlative rights. Without public institutions, the problem of unilateralism looms large.[10] But through the courts, the state becomes related to the litigants in a manner quite different from the bilateral relationship of plaintiff and defendant. As Weinrib outlines, "the relationship among members of the state is omnilateral, linking everyone to everyone else."[11] In adjudication, the court combines both the omnilateral and bilateral dimensions "by projecting its own omnilateral authority onto the parties' bilateral relationship" and in doing so making its judgment a norm for all citizens.[12] In the standard case, according to Weinrib, public right merely adds the dimensions of publicness and systematicity to private law, allowing private law to be expressed through public institutions but leaving the internal logic of private law otherwise intact.[13] In fact, to think that one cannot think about a right outside the public institutions that enforce it is to make what Kant calls "a common fault of experts on right."[14]

Occasionally, however, public right can modify the basic private law relationships through the demands of publicity and systematicity. When it does this, "the judgment of public right should vary the result that would

[7] Weinrib, "Distributive Justice" on file with author. See also Weinrib 2012, p. 263.
[8] Weinrib 2012, p. 25.
[9] Weinrib 2011, p. 195. See also Ripstein 2009.
[10] Weinrib 2011, p. 195.
[11] Weinrib 2011, p. 196.
[12] Weinrib 2011.
[13] Weinrib 2011, p. 198.
[14] Weinrib 2011, p. 201, citing Kant 1996, 6: p. 297.

follow from the internal logic of the basic categories only to the extent necessary to achieve publicness."[15] Weinrib makes a similar claim with respect to systematicity – there are times when this can operate to modify private right but only to the extent necessary to achieve systematicity.

For Weinrib, then, the idea of "public rightfulness" that is part of private law is not at all an idea of distributive justice, but a response to the problem of unilateralism in the interpretation and enforcement of private rights. The omnilateral perspective that is relevant to private law, in a kind of second-stage analysis, involves the ideas of publicity and systematicity, not distribution of benefits.

There are three conclusions regarding private property and public values that one can draw from this account. First, as a private law doctrine property should be conceived in terms of the correlativity that is at the heart of corrective justice and this can be understood independently of the public institutions needed to interpret and enforce it. Second, these public institutions bring a public perspective to bear when engaged in interpretation and enforcement and in doing so bring an additional set of public norms. These norms can occasionally modify the basic corrective justice picture of property but only at the margins as a second step. Third, adjudication through courts is the central institutional structure for private law whereas legislation is the central institutional structure for public law. Although statutes can figure in the private law, they do so at the margins. Moreover, distributive justice should be accomplished through legislation and not by private law adjudication.

In what follows I argue that this basic picture is wrong on all three counts. The idea of omnilaterality is actually *central* to understanding property. It is the use of correlative-based liability (such as the tort of trespass) that is secondary to the basic omnilateral structure of ownership. Second, it is this omnilateral perspective that can show how some distributive justice concerns can sometimes legitimately factor into private law adjudication. Third, legislation is central rather than marginal to an understanding of private property, and can also serve as the basis for bringing "public policy" norms into private law adjudication.

1.3 What's Justice Got to Do with It?

The basic problem with the corrective justice account of private law, when applied to private property, is that it attempts to shoehorn ownership into

[15] Weinrib 2011, p. 202.

a bilateral relationship. Such an account is unable to account for the central features of ownership, such as its general and impersonal nature. It also inverts the relationship between law and justice: ownership does not primarily participate in a form of justice (corrective justice) that is then made consistent with the demands of a legal system's public institutions (the role of omnilaterality) but instead is primarily a legal relation that is then oriented toward justice (in many different forms, including corrective justice).

It bears noting that the corrective justice account outlined is defended as one that takes the practice of law as we find it and then "enquires into its structure, its presuppositions, and the internal connections among its more pervasive features" in order to determine what conceptions are implicit in the practice that reveal the law as a unified and rational practice.[16] However, the practice of private property as we find it shows that its structure and presuppositions are not well illuminated through the idea of bilaterality.

Consider the foundational doctrine of possession in the common law. That things be owned, rather than unowned, and that the rules be clear on the ground so as to prevent disorderliness and violence, are clear themes that run through judicial reasoning about possession. This is not a matter of bilateral relations or corrective justice. But it also is not about distributive justice. Instead, this is about protecting the security of possession in order to safeguard public order and civil peace.[17] This is also the case when courts are asked to find exceptions to legal rules protecting possession. It is not ideas of fairness between parties that courts advert to, but very basic law and order concerns.[18]

We can contrast being subject to law with being subject to violence. As Robin West points out, one important role of law is the prevention of private violence and private law is an important means of accomplishing this.[19] So we might think of private property as a regime of law, rather than violence, in relation to how individuals interact regarding places and things. There are many different possible forms for a regime of law regarding places and things and they can be distinguished through how they deal with the question of authority in relation to places and things. Private property is one way of dealing with authority. It grants "private" authority in relation to places and things, in contrast to other more "public" forms of authority, but it still does so within a framework of law.

[16] Weinrib 2011, p. 193.
[17] Emerich 2014, p. 30.
[18] See e.g., *London Borough of Southwark* v. *William*, [1971] 2 All ER 175.
[19] West 2001.

Private in this sense does not mean pre-institutional. Nor does it imply any kind of conceptual priority of this form of authority over others: it is descriptive rather than normative. The question of authority over places and things can, and has been, answered in many different ways and private ownership is simply one form of answer. We do not need to determine whether it is the best answer, or even a justifiable answer in any particular context, to understand the way in which it provides an answer.

Although private property is about private authority, it remains fundamentally a legal relation. To adopt Weinrib's Kantian terminology, meant to characterize the public perspective brought about by entry into a civil condition, it is omnilateral. If a bilateral relationship is between two individuals, an omnilateral relationship is a relationship that connects everyone to everyone else. Private property is not bilateral but is a way of connecting everyone to everyone else.

Consider this in the context of the standard trilogy of basic core ownership entitlements: the right to exclusive control, the privilege to use the thing owned, and the power to alienate. The right to exclusive control looks bilateral, in that it is most often vindicated through trespass liability rules that connect a plaintiff and a defendant in the way corrective justice theorists describe as the basic form of private law liability. However, property theorists clearly and correctly point out that ownership is characterized by a generality and impersonality that requires explanation.[20] An owner has a right against the trespasser but there is nothing special about that owner being a particular individual; the trespasser owes an obligation to whomever the owner happens to be and does not need to know anything about that owner. There is also nothing special about the particular trespasser's obligation to "keep off" – this is an obligation held by everyone who is not the owner of the land. So even though there is a bilateral relation between a plaintiff and a defendant, it is more accurate to characterize this relationship in general terms. We could say that the owner (whoever that might be) has a right against the nonowner (everyone else).

This generality and impersonality is the reason that alienability is possible. If obligations are owed to the owner *qua* owner then it does not matter who the particular owner is. Different people may become owners without changing the normative position of the others who owe these obligations. This, in turn, generates some of the distinctive doctrines of private property. For example, restrictive covenants are obligations between owners that bind owners *qua* owners – which is why they can "run with the

[20] Penner 2000, p. 23; Merrill and Smith 2001b.

land" and obligate subsequent purchasers who were not party to the original agreement. For a valid restrictive covenant, there is nothing about the identity of a particular owner that is relevant to understand the obligation imposed. Or take the case of adverse possession. The clock for a successful adverse possession claim is not reset when the owner sells the disputed land to another purchaser because the particular identity of the owner is entirely irrelevant to the relationship between the owner (whoever that might be) and the adverse possessor.

An owner's privilege to use property is also general rather than the expression of a particular individual's subjective will. There is no legal protection for my desire to make a specific use of my property. I can keep others from using my property through the law of trespass. I can protect my specific uses against interference from my neighbor's specific uses through the law of nuisance but that simply expresses the need to protect and accommodate each individual's privilege to use property in general.

The generality and impersonality of ownership is due to the fact that it is an omnilateral relation, linking everyone to everyone else. In recent work, Weinrib partially agrees with this. He argues that ownership can be understood independently of the civil condition but that *acquisition* depends on the move from the state of nature to the civil condition.[21] That is, property can be thought about in the state of nature in terms of the correlative structure of corrective justice but nobody can actually have any property until we enter a civil condition; the omnilateral perspective is needed to make my possession the ground of an obligation held by all others. It is difficult to see how this is true if the basic structure of ownership as a claim between an owner and all non-owners is unavailable without the very kind of systematicity that Weinrib claims only comes with the move to a civil condition. However, even if the Kantian story holds that it is only acquisition that depends upon the omnilateral perspective, this leaves so much of private property doctrine on the other side of bilateral relations that it calls into question the claim that corrective justice best describes the law as we find it.

If private property is primarily a legal relation then what is its relationship to different forms of justice, whether corrective justice, distributive justice, or some other conception of justice? We can understand many features of law quite independently of any notion of justice. For example, many discussions of the rule of law stress the formal principles of legality, perhaps given their most canonical expression by Lon Fuller: generality, publicity, non-retroactivity, clarity, noncontradiction, possibility of

[21] See Weinrib, "Ownership" (on file with author).

compliance, stability, and congruence between official action and declared rule.[22] Weinrib's account of omnilaterality – which I take to be another expression of the rule of law – emphasizes the idea of a relation of each to each as well as ideas of publicity and systematicity. Although many of these ideas look formal and empty of substance, most lawyers are familiar with the way in which seemingly formal and procedural requirements can yield substantive doctrines.[23]

However, even if we start from a position that emphasizes the form(s) of law rather than the forms of justice, there is a very basic sense in which law and justice are intrinsically linked. As Waldron helpfully argues, law stands in the name of the public and is oriented to ideas of public good:

> We recognize institutions as part of a legal system when they orient themselves in their public presence to the good of the community – in other words, to issues of justice and the common good that transcend the self-interest of the powerful. It strains our ordinary concept of law to apply it to norms that address matters of personal or partial concern, or to institutions that make no pretense to operate in the name of the whole community, presenting themselves as oriented instead to the benefit of the individuals who control them.[24]

We could say that law is public in a much deeper sense than is sometimes acknowledged in rule of law discussions that emphasize the "publicity" requirement for legal norms. Law represents the public point of view in a very basic way and this must mean that it is not merely an instrument to any end but must be an instrument toward some end that is cognizable as "just."

This need not commit anyone to take sides with a more natural law approach to the rule of law against a more positivist one. Raz famously argued that the rule of law was of only instrumental value – it made law good as an instrument but did not ensure the goodness of any ends achieved through law.[25] This is true in one sense, but deeply misleading. It is true in the sense that the basic idea of the rule of law does not require that law promote any particular view of the common good, or of justice, and so the rule of law will not ensure conformity with any such view. But this is misleading in the sense that it suggests that law is not concerned with justice. We should say instead that the rule of law demands that the law have such a public aim in general. And even if that means that the rule of law does not aim at any particular end of justice, it does imply that the

22 Fuller 1969.
23 For and account of how this works with property law, see Austin 2014a.
24 Waldron 2008.
25 Raz 1977.

rule of law is concerned with avoiding injustice. This is consistent with an instrumental account of law – although it is also consistent with normative accounts of law as well – as the argument is that law might be a tool but it is one that must be used in the right way, which is a tool that promotes a public perspective.[26] The rule of law ensures that law remains an instrument of public, rather than private, authority.

Several important implications follow from taking the form of law as primary in understanding private property and the form of justice as secondary. First, a concern for avoiding injustice can lead courts to take into consideration factors that overlap with specific accounts of justice, including distributive justice. For example, private law in many of its core areas is about protecting an individual's ability to seek her private ends. There are many different accounts of why such practices might be thought consistent with some idea of justice or the common good. However, if this ability to seek one's own personal end becomes an instrument for the private domination of another then law ceases to be public in the deep sense outlined above. One can then condemn this as unjust from a legal perspective without needing to necessarily develop, or endorse, any particular view of justice. At the same time, such condemnation might be entirely consistent with a range of views regarding justice. There are many times that courts engage in considerations that thoughtful commentators point to as examples of courts endorsing views of justice and public policy that are really framed in this more negative sense of the avoidance of injustice.[27]

Second, there might be many different ways in which an omnilateral perspective, linking each to each, can be realized in practice but different institutions will have different competencies. Consider the role of precedent, which Weinrib understands in omnilateral terms. Even if a court is considering the seeming bilateral relationship between a plaintiff and a defendant, it must also situate this relation within the cases that have come before and understand that any decision on the present facts must also function as a precedent for similarly situated plaintiffs and defendants in the future. The case, as law, connects all plaintiffs with all defendants in a general way – which is why we care about the cases even after the individual dispute is resolved with finality for the particular plaintiff and defendant. Even though a court is setting out the law for all other members of the state in this way, those individuals are not before the court. And

[26] Austin 2014b.

[27] Many of the examples of policy offered by Stephen Waddams in his book (Waddams 2011) have this feature.

that necessarily limits what the court can take into account, as a matter of institutional competency. This is one of the reasons that Weinrib's basic claim that private law protects abstract agency works so well in general – a court can understand the implications a particular decision will have on *everyone* if it abstracts from the particularities of *all* individuals and treats them simply as abstract agents. This is even more true in the context of private property where the basic terms of the relationship and not just the operation of precedent, link everyone to everyone else. In this way we can still see a role for abstract agency but this does not come from a pre-legal substantive understanding of rights as demanded by the form of corrective justice but rather from an expression of the demands of the omnilateral perspective as given effect by courts.

Third, even if ideas of abstract agency help us to understand private law doctrine, on my account this can have no conceptual priority over the demands of the omnilateral perspective as given effect by other public institutions, such as the legislature. Weinrib contends that the demands of systematicity can sometimes lead courts to modify the more primary rights of corrective justice, but only to the limited extent necessary to deal with these demands. But there are many different potential institutional expressions of the omnilateral perspective and these different perspectives must be reconciled with one another as expressions of public values. There might be many different ways of doing so, and different arguments about their desirability, but claims to the autonomy of private law will not suffice to rule any of them off the table. Indeed, in complex legal systems, where we have many public instruments that express public values, courts might find other ways to reconcile different perspectives by taking into account "public policy" that is sufficiently clear and uncontroversial within the particular legal system.

1.4 Rethinking the Distributive Justice Critiques

To make the public nature of this account clearer, in what follows I take up two criticisms of corrective justice that focus on the degree to which private law is insulated from distributive justice concerns. I call these the "distributive foundations" and the "distributive aims" critiques. Both help us to focus on some of the limits of the corrective justice account. However, I argue that thinking that if something is not corrective justice then it must be distributive justice is to embrace a false dilemma. Omnilaterality provides an alternative structure that can better explain the underlying concerns of these distributive justice critiques.

1.4.1 *The Distributive Foundations Critique*

The first objection to the corrective justice thesis that I want to take up here is one put forward by Hanoch Dagan, which is that the correlativity of private law rests upon a distributive foundation. Because of this, he argues, "Weinrib is wrong in his claim that private law has an inner intelligibility that can be deciphered without recourse to public values."[28]

One of Dagan's central examples in this particular critique concerns Weinrib's analysis of gains-based remedies and the view of property that Weinrib adopts as central to his analysis. It is this particular locus of their dispute that I want to focus on, for my own view is that Dagan is correct in pointing to the inadequacy of Weinrib's account of property and also correct in his claim that the inner intelligibility of private law must make recourse to public values. However, he is incorrect to think that this must mean distributive justice.

Weinrib's concern is to show how gains-based remedies are intelligible within a corrective justice framework. As he argues in *Corrective Justice*, "If tort law is concerned with wrongful injury to the plaintiff, special arguments are required to explain why, as a matter of justice, the remedy should refer to the gains of the defendant."[29] The problem is to argue why the *plaintiff* is the one who may demand such damages as a matter of right and not merely receive such damages as a windfall in the service of some broader concern regarding injustice or social policy. Weinrib's solution to this problem is to first point to the fact that the most central and undisputed examples of gains-based remedies concern property rights. He then argues that a plaintiff can be entitled to the defendant's gain because the right to profit is part of the proprietor's entitlement. As Weinrib explains:

> Because property rights give proprietors the exclusive right to deal with the thing owned, including the right to profit from such dealings, gains resulting from the misappropriation of property are necessarily subject to restitution. Gains from dealings in property are as much within the entitlement of the proprietor as the property itself.[30]

This argument about the proprietor's entitlements to profits is what Dagan objects to. Property, he argues, is too contested a concept to "presuppose that *any* gains derived from property are *necessarily* within the entitlement of the property owner."[31] And: "The right to profit – itself a concept that can

[28] Dagan 1999.
[29] Weinrib 2012, p. 117.
[30] Weinrib 2012, p. 125.
[31] Dagan 1999, p. 148.

be interpreted in various ways – is not essential to property, nor is property the only type of right that can encompass this right to gain."[32] Determining the property entitlement, according to Dagan, enmeshes us in the broader social values and distributive questions from which, on Weinrib's account, private law is supposed to be detached.

I think Dagan is right to point to the idea of a "right to profit" as problematic. The "exclusive right to deal with a thing" that for Weinrib encompasses this right to profit runs together two ideas that are better kept apart – use and possession. An owner of a thing has both the privilege to use the thing and the exclusive right to control the thing. Gains-based remedies are not puzzling at all from the perspective of the right of possession: possession is protected through trespass norms and remedies for trespass are perhaps the paradigmatic example of gains-based remedies. The standard remedy for trespass is an injunction, but where damages are sought the measure of damages is the defendant's profits. However the wrong involved in trespass is not interference with a use (or profit) that the owner is entitled to, but using another's property without permission – the "without permission" violates the owner's exclusive control. The defendant's profit is a valuation of what it means for the owner to be out of exclusive control for the period of time at issue. In fact, Robert Stevens points out that actual gains-based restitutionary damages have little place in the common law; what we generally see instead are damages that substitute for the enforcement of the primary rights (like possession), or damages that measure losses consequent upon a rights infringement.[33] With trespass, we are not concerned with the gain *per se* but use this in some circumstances to substitute for what it would mean to enforce the owner's exclusive control.

Even though there are many cases where the measure of damages is rent rather than profits, courts have pointed out that the rental value of the land is simply one possible way to determine the profits.[34] If damages in the amount of rent were the presumptive remedy that would actually change the nature of the basic underlying entitlement; instead of the owner being the one entitled to decide regarding uses, other people would get to decide whether to use the resource, provided that they have paid the market price for it. This looks like a forced sale rather than the vindication of exclusive control. The remedy would not match the entitlement, but would undermine its very nature. The appropriate remedy has to match the idea that it

[32] Dagan 1999, p. 149.
[33] Stevens 2007, p. 79.
[34] See the discussion of this in *Edwards* v. *Lee's Adm'r* 265 Ky 418 (1936).

is the plaintiff alone, and not the defendant, who is entitled to determine any use of the thing. This is not about a specific entitlement to a particular use or benefit, but is about the entitlement to control, or authority, in relation to that thing.

This also provides a simpler way to explain the difference between negligence and intentional torts in relation to gains-based damages, at least with respect to property cases. Weinrib argues that gains-based damages are not appropriate for negligently harming another's property whereas they are for intentional torts because in relation to intentional torts the defendant must treat "the object as if it were his or her own." One does this "when one so directs one's attention to the object that its use or alienation can be regarded as an execution of one's purposes."[35] The simpler way to cast the difference is to say that intentional torts like trespass and conversion all deal with interferences with the owner's entitlement to control the object of property. This makes gains-based damages appropriate, for the reasons already outlined. In contrast, there are many ways of negligently harming another's property that are not cases of interference with the owner's exclusive control.

Weinrib has more recently suggested that remedies for loss of use should be understood in relation to the special status of an owner's liberty to use the thing owned and he criticizes the view that loss of use simply quantifies the injury to the owner's right of exclusive control. Such as view, according to Weinrib, fails to tie the remedy to the wrong.[36] This is a puzzling argument, for such remedies are very easily understood in relation to the nature of the wrong of interfering with exclusive control, as outlined in this chapter. It is not that the value of the lost use is part of a remedial claim-right where the claim right refers to a different type of jural relationship. Nor is it the case that the claim-right is indirectly protecting the liberty of use (although it may in fact do so). The lost use is really just a way of understanding lost control and putting a value on this. This is why there is so much controversy in such cases regarding the significance of an owner's actual or intended use.[37]

Where does this leave us? My argument has been that Dagan is correct to point to Weinrib's reliance upon a "right to profit" as involving a problematic view of property. However, nothing in my argument entails Dagan's general conclusion regarding the distributive foundations of

[35] Weinrib 2012, p. 126.

[36] See Weinrib, "Ownership" on file with author.

[37] Brownstein 1985.

corrective justice. Weinrib's account fails to explain the right to possession and how it generates gains-based remedies. But the fundamental structure of the right to possession is omnilateral. This is indeed "public" but not in the way that Dagan argues.

1.4.2 The Distributive Aims Critique

Another set of criticisms regarding the corrective justice paradigm is that the questions of interpersonal justice that animate private law cannot always be neatly separated from distributory concerns. This leads to a variety of proposals for integrating at least some distributory concerns with private law norms and adjudication. Hanoch Dagan and Avihay Dorfman argue that "horizontal justice" must take into account questions of substantive inequality between individuals.[38] Aditi Bagchi has argued that the private law should reflect a limited concern for distributive justice. She uses the idea of "imperfect social rights" to argue for an understanding of "how distributive injustice can condition individual responsibility."[39] According to her account, individuals hold imperfect social rights, which are "claims arising under the principles of distributive justice."[40] These imperfect rights do not give rise to independent claims against other individuals, but they "disallow, or at least discourage through higher pricing, conduct that would otherwise be permissible."[41] In particular, she points to situations of exploitation where "the circumstances of exploitation are the result of both the exploiter's failure to fulfill enforceable imperfect duties and a violation of the victim's imperfect rights."[42] With a similar focus on questions of power and exploitation, Orit Gan has recently advocated the view that the doctrine of promissory estoppel be enlisted to promote distributive justice goals. As she argues, "justice requires not only balancing between the promisee and the promisor but also that social considerations and public policy, such as the power dynamics between the parties, their relations, and the allocative implications should be taken into account."[43]

I want to suggest that there is another alternative to these seeming two choices of, on the one hand, mixing distributive justice and corrective justice concerns in relation to the norms of interpersonal interactions, and on

[38] Dagan and Dorfman 2016.
[39] Bagchi 2008.
[40] Bagchi 2008, p. 108.
[41] Bagchi 2008, p. 109.
[42] Bagchi 2008, p. 127.
[43] Gan 2014.

the other hand, keeping them strictly separate. Instead, one can reject the terms of the choice and think that distributive inequality has a bearing on private law without necessarily thinking that private law should itself seek to achieve some particular distribution.

There is a difference between thinking that a particular defendant should be enlisted in the project of redressing a preexisting state of inequality and thinking that a particular defendant should be prevented from using the law to exploit that preexisting state of inequality in her dealings with a particular plaintiff. The first concerns using a private law action between two individuals as a means to achieve a distributive end, and the second concerns preventing the private law from being used unjustly, as a tool of domination.

As I've argued, the latter is better conceived of in terms of the omnilateral perspective of law.[44] As I have argued elsewhere, one way to understand the rule of law is that it ensures that law remains an instrument of public, rather than private, authority. And in determining when the law is used unjustly, background facts of social, economic, and political power can be important to understanding the context and whether law is instead being used as an instrument of private domination.[45]

This concern that law not be used as a tool of private domination can accommodate some of the worries that motivate Dagan and Dorfman in relation to the effects of unequal power relationships between parties.[46] It also echoes many of Bagchi's concerns. According to Bagchi, "[t]he advantaged agent uses contract in a way that harms a disadvantaged party and the question is whether contract should be available as a tool for such exchange."[47] And although Gan's claims look like a broad invitation to enlist the courts in promoting distributive justice, her examples are actually quite similar to Bagchi's in the sense of being concerned with the misuse of power and exploitative relationships. If the consequent of need is a particular vulnerability to the actions of another and that other person takes advantage of that vulnerability while exercising rights, privileges and powers granted by the law, then such disadvantages can be normatively significant from the perspective of law itself without needing a more

[44] Weinrib has a very capacious understanding of DJ that includes human dignity and non-domination. While this might be a good reading of Kant, it starts to show the strain of shoehorning all of this into Artistotle's observations regarding the two forms of justice.

[45] For a discussion of this, using examples of proprietary estoppel and trespass claims in relation to shopping malls, see Austin 2014a.

[46] Dagan and Dorfman 2016.

[47] Bagchi 2014.

full-bodied sense of distributive justice. In giving effect to these concerns, courts ensure the public nature of the law in the sense of law not being an instrument of private domination.

1.5 Rethinking Starting Points and Institutional Roles

The previous discussion was concerned with private law adjudication and the role of distributive justice concerns within that practice. However, when thinking about private property it is not clear that adjudication should be given the centrality that corrective justice theorists call for. If the core of private law lies in bilateral relationships then courts, and private law adjudication, look like the appropriate institution to interpret and judge the norms of those relationships with legislatures playing a less significant role. But, as I have argued, private property is more primarily concerned with omnilaterality rather than bilaterality. While courts have an obvious role to play, claims to their primacy are more difficult to defend.

This claim actually accounts for the law as we find it. Legislatures play a central role in private property regimes. There are many statutes affecting property law that go to what many see are the core traditional elements of private ownership such as alienability. For example, if you own land in Ontario and wish to sell it then there are a host of statutes that determine how this can be done, including the Conveyancing and Law of Property Act, the Statute of Frauds, and the Land Titles Act. Transferring property upon death is also governed by statutes like Ontario's *Succession Law Reform Act*. If statutes are so intrinsically involved in the granting and defining of core aspects of property law, then this suggests that the legislature plays a central institutional role in property law. This role has been noted recently in the literature on the *numerus clausas* principle in property law. For example, Merrill and Smith point out that most important reforms of property law have come through statutes.[48]

In fact, history supports the view that land becomes as system of private ownership in the common law world *through public law*. Feudal land law was entirely public law and land became property in the sense we now understand it through public law reforms that had nothing to do with distributive justice. For example, the estate in fee simple is freely alienable because of the effects of the statute of *Quia Emptores* of 1290 and its abolition of the feudal practice of subinfeudation.[49] Moreover, land ownership

[48] Merrill and Smith 2000.

[49] K. Gray, *Elements of Land Law*; *Laurin* v. *Iron Ore Co. of Canada* (1977) at para. 90.

and political jurisdiction are closely tied together. As Penner observes, land ownership – more than chattel ownership – "depends on political sovereignty ... for the ability to maintain one's rights to land depends on whether the State is able to hold its territory against invaders from without or rebels from within."[50]

A corrective justice theorist might point to trespass liability as an important example where court-based adjudication protects the right of possession, a core aspect of private property. However, the on-the-ground protection of possession in many jurisdictions is more likely to occur through statutes that create public law processes. For example, many Canadian provinces have statutes that create a summary conviction offense of trespass and authorize owners, and those authorized by owners, to arrest offenders without a warrant. Such statutes are, according to the Supreme Court of Canada, the "workhorse of private security services in their patrol of the shopping malls, airports, sports stadiums and other private spaces where the public tends to congregate."[51] The Supreme Court went so far as to uphold the reasonable use of force when exercising this arrest power. It is far more likely that owners will have their possessory rights vindicated through the operation of these statutes than by bringing a tort action in court. As previously suggested, there is a strong basis in even court-based adjudication about possession that one of its key aspects is the protection of public order and civil peace. Protecting the security of possession through the creation of provincial offenses rather than civil liability discloses something central, rather than peripheral, about our legal practices regarding property.

What these examples yield is a strong note of skepticism regarding the starting point of the corrective justice account and the central place that it gives to adjudication in disclosing the central structures and features that must be accounted for in private law, if private law is to include property. We see statutes play a large role in property law, including in providing for and defining the terms of central legal powers, such as alienability. Even exclusive possession, for many a necessary core of private ownership, finds its strongest and most pervasive enforcement through statutes that define offences and allow for arrest powers, rather than depending on tort actions for trespass adjudicated through the courts.

[50] Penner 1997, p. 152.

[51] *R* v. *Asante-Mensah*, 2003 SC 38 at para. 2, referring to legislation like Ontario's *Petty Trespass Act*. These private security forces are also permitted to use reasonable force when arresting individuals under these statutes.

Because my account of institutional roles focuses on institutional competencies rather than the form of justice pursued, the fact that statutes are responsible for so many aspects of traditional property law is not puzzling at all. For one thing, property, on my account, is not something that can be understood apart from legal institutions. And at its core it is a complex relation that connects everyone to everyone else. It is not just that legislatures can, and do, perform key roles in relation to central aspects of property law; the legislatures are actually sometimes best placed to do so.

Statutes also play an important role in either limiting core property rights, or completely reimagining core property relationships. For example, some provincial trespass statutes provide that picketing (or other speech-related activities) on some types of privately owned property to which the public is admitted does not constitute a trespass.[52] In Canadian provinces, as in many other jurisdictions, residential tenancies are governed by legislation that radically departs from the common law. One way to understand this legislation is to argue that it pursues distributive justice in relation to important social activities (speech, housing), although some might argue that it requires a capacious understanding of distributive justice to capture what is at stake in some of these contexts.

A corrective justice account would not dispute the role of the legislature in pursuing such goals. The mistakes to avoid are to think that the resulting legislation is part of private law or to think that we can mix the models. So, on this account, we might say that Ontario's *Residential Tenancies Act* is a legislative ouster of private property law from a particular area of social life, certainly within the institutional role of the legislature, but not to be confused with the property law we encounter in "private law." Others might recoil from the conclusion that the landlord-tenant relationship is not part of private property law "proper" if the point of a theoretical account is to understand the central features of property institutions as they operate within our legal system. Residential tenancy legislation does not make housing "public" simply because it regulates the authority of owners. To say that the way in which a landlord buys and sells a building falls within private property proper, but that their relationship with their tenants does not, strikes some thoughtful commentators as being artificial and at odds with the practice of property it purports to illuminate.[53]

52 See e.g., Manitoba's *The Petty Trespasses Act*, s.4. This was enacted as a legislative response to *Harrison* v. *Carswell*. [1976] 2 SCR 200.

53 See e.g., Hanoch Dagan's critique in Dagan 2011.

There are other cases where statutes play a role in carving out exceptions to trespass but where there is no direct statutory authority for such exceptions. In other words, statutes inform the court's understanding of public policy concerns that get taken up to modify existing common law doctrines.[54] An example of this is the US case *State* v. *Shack*, which held that the defendants were not trespassing when they entered the land of the employer-farmer in order to provide legal and medical assistance to the migrant agricultural workers who lived and worked on the premises. In that case the judge pointed to legislation aimed at providing assistance to migrant and seasonally employed migrant workers, and some of the programs funded pursuant to that legislation, and held that "[t]hese ends would not be gained if the intended beneficiaries could be insulated from efforts to reach them." Therefore, at least on one reading of the case, we can say that the court did not aim at distributive justice so much as recognized an existing distributive justice scheme and sought to reconcile it with traditional property rights in order to give it effect. At the same time, a defender of private property might counter that if the legislature really did intend for the suspension of the possessory rights of employer-farmers in these circumstances, it could have directly provided this within the legislation. That it did not do so is evidence that it did not intend this outcome and the judicial "activism" on display in *State* v. *Shack* is an overstepping of the court's institutional role.

The corrective justice position suggests that the property-traditionalist critique of *State* v. *Shack* is likely correct. According to Weinrib, considerations of "public right" – which includes ideas of systematicity – can sometimes operate to change the basic underlying private right entitlements but only in a manner that is minimally impairing of those underlying rights. The most basic minimal impairment argument is to claim that legislation should be read to displace the more primary property right as little as possible. This would mean either holding that legislation should specifically displace the rights in question or, more broadly, holding that the position of the employer/farmer was correct in offering access to the workers but under his supervision. But the court gave stronger effect to the aims of the legislation than this:

> the employer may not deny the worker his privacy or interfere with his opportunity to live with dignity and to enjoy associations customary

[54] In some jurisdictions some changes to the traditional landlord-tenant model that secured greater security of tenure were accomplished through the courts. See Glendon 1982.

> among our citizens. These rights are too fundamental to be denied on the basis of an interest in real property and too fragile to be left to the unequal bargaining strength of the parties.

Note too that these are not necessarily distributive justice claims but speak to the values of dignity, community, and nonexploitation.[55]

On my account here there is no such basis for automatically favoring a minimal impairment argument. Courts have to act from the omnilateral, or public, view and the standard adjudicative setting means that they need to consider individuals in abstraction. Otherwise the concern is that judges will impose their own subjective sense of social policy, which would be "political" in that it lacks the imprimatur of the public perspective, and not because it pursues distributive justice. However, where there is clear evidence of public policy, and no concern that a decision to limit property rights on the basis of public policy would create potentially problematic consequences, the "political" critique does not apply.

Conclusion

This chapter has argued against the view that corrective justice provides the form of private law, while distributive justice provides the form of public law. More primary than the forms of justice is the form of law. Law is inherently public. The basic publicness of law can be expressed in many different ways, from the omnilateral perspective to the way in which the rule of law ensures that law is an instrument of public power rather than private domination. Because law is public it also aims at justice and the common good. While this does not mean that law is intrinsically concerned with any particular form of justice, it does mean that law is concerned with avoiding injustice.

This chapter has also argued that the basic structure of private property is public in this legal sense. Ownership is an omnilateral relation of each to each rather than a bilateral relation. Omnilaterality is more helpful in illuminating the structure of private property than the idea of corrective justice. It does so in relation to basic doctrinal features such as the law's deep concern for security of possession as a concern for civil peace and public order as well as the basic features of the generality and impersonality of

[55] Weinrib has recently suggested that these concerns do fit within the contours of distributive justice but that seems like a very capacious understanding of distributive justice. It is far from clear that all dignitary concerns are ones best characterized in terms of distributions. See Weinrib, "Distributive Justice" (on file with author).

ownership. It also does so in relation to the central role that statutes play in defining key aspects of property law.

Finally, this form of law rather than of justice can help us understand the role that distributive justice can play in relation to private law adjudication. Rather than an alien intrusion into the terrain of a very different form of justice, some of the basic concerns of distributive justice can find a home within adjudication in one of several ways. Because the law is concerned with avoiding injustice, which includes avoiding misuse of the law as a tool of private domination, courts can legitimately seek to prevent the law from being used to exploit a preexisting state of inequality. Another way is when courts seek to harmonize private law adjudication with "public policy" concerns as articulated in legislation or other sufficiently public documents. To say so does not unravel all claims to an "inner" perspective regarding private law in favor of functionalism, as the corrective justice account might imply, but it does call into question claims of the autonomy of private law. This is because it rejects the dichotomy between corrective justice and distributive justice as a map for "private" and "public" law and instead focuses on "law" as what unites both and is primary.

2

Legal Forms in Property Law Theory

LARISSA KATZ

2.1 Introduction

The last 75 years or so represents a concerted effort to reject formalism and to rethink private law, and property law in particular, in terms of "all things considered" moral reasoning. This was a period of ascendancy for legal realists and legal economists, who aimed to show that law is not a bounded domain of normativity with its own regulative ideals. There was, over roughly the same period, a parallel move among positivists, following Hart and Raz, to think of the morally salient bits of private law as tracking ordinary moral thinking. For these moralists, there is no distinctive way of reasoning legally about private law: we account for law's legitimate content in terms of (generic) moral reasoning.[1] The view from the other side, which I call formalism, is that there *is* a distinctively legal way of reasoning about how persons relate, given our conception of persons for the purposes of law. No self-respecting formalists thinks that legal forms are themselves *law*, with an authority that binds the administrators of or the participants in a legal system. What law there is, most people agree, is a matter of political choice. So even for the formalist, forms are not themselves law nor do forms cover all of what law treats as its subject matter.[2] Legal forms just are these available ways of reasoning about our interpersonal relations for the purposes of law. So, for example, one might say that the form or concept of a trust, in which an owner holds property for the benefit of another, frames

[1] For a contrary view, see Waldron 2008b (some reasons are such "complicated moral reasons as to create – in a sense – a normative world of their own and their distinctiveness may render any operational comparison with our familiar ideals of moral *reasoning* inapposite (e.g., duty of integrity, of concern for established expectations; of deference to democratic institutions, of treating like cases alike").

[2] Philbrick 1938. ("To every student of history, government, economics, or sociology it is a commonplace that law – not merely through its reformatory manifestations or basic refashionings, such as the statutes of a New Deal or a French Revolution or the Reception of the Corpus Juris, but by the steady restraints of its abiding forms – molds, while it fixes and preserves, society.")

a way of thinking about our relations as trustee and beneficiary that is normatively and conceptually distinct from, for example, the way in which the interpersonal relations of parties to a contract are framed.

The moralist and the formalist take themselves to be doing completely different things. Each also takes herself to be thinking about law on the only terms possible (in terms of legal or in terms of general moral reasoning). The distance between the two views seems impossible to traverse. There is an old joke about a tourist who asks a local New Englander the way to the airport. "You don't start from here," was the only reply. The moralist simply denies the formalist starting point, that we proceed from legal forms to an account of private law, and the formalist denies the moralist can achieve a theory of private law from any other starting point.

This paper takes up another possibility, that there is a common threshold question for moralist and formalist private law theory and that is as follows: how do we conceive of persons for the purposes of law and how then might persons so conceived relate in this or that context? A shared starting point in this threshold question seems an unlikely prospect: it suggests that moralism itself builds on a formalist foundation. My aim in this paper is to show that it only *seems* unlikely. There is, I will argue, a foothold for formalism in some prominent moralist approaches to private law and property law in particular. This foothold is found in Hohfeld's account of jural relations, which some important contemporary moralist approaches to private law take as their starting point. Hohfeld's schema, in which he identified matched sets of claim-rights and duties, powers and liabilities, privileges and no-rights, and their opposites, is widely understood to be an analytical account, free of moral valence.[3] Indeed, this agnosticism is what attracted moralists in the twentieth century to the Hohfeldian schema: content-free and freely configurable, and with legal relations that could be tailored to advance their preferred moral and social values.

The gist of my argument is that a Hohfeldian account of jural relations has a normative element that has been underappreciated.[4] It is not surprising that the normative edge of Hohfeld's jural relations has been

[3] Hohfeld was clearly influenced by Salmond's schema of jural relations and Salmond's view of the failings of Austin's command theory (which left no room for legal powers). Salmond unlike Hohfeld also thought that Austin failed to see an important connection between law and morality, as he "attempted to deprive the idea of law of that ethical significance which is one of its most essential elements" (Salmond 1972, p. 10). See Dickey 1972.

[4] Andrew Halpin has recently argued that what opponents and proponents of Hohfeld underappreciate is Hohfeldian neutrality as between moral commitments (e.g., utilitarian, libertarian, etc.). See Halpin 2017. Halpin is right that Hohfeldian analysis is perceived as being more friendly to what I call moralist and bundle of rights theories of property. But that is

overlooked. For Hohfeld, after all, law on its own does not give moral shape to the areas of human interaction that lawyers take private law to concern – our interactions with respect to things, our persons, and our agreements. For Hohfeld and his followers, law *is* useful as a technology for moral and political engineering, but it is no more than that; by using this battery of jural relations to implement what morality in general requires, we piece together a set of norms that allow us to lead our lives together.

My claim in this paper is that Hohfeld's account of jural relations does more than just establish a neutral technology for moral and political action: it sets out the ways that people might relate in law, given Hohfeld's conception of persons for the purposes of law.[5] Hohfeld's was emphatically a naturalistic conception of persons as physical beings responsive to force. It follows from this conception of persons that purely legal relations for Hohfeld could only be external, action-based relations between physical persons. Hohfeldian jural relations are just the available ways that persons, conceived in a minimal naturalistic way for the purposes of law, might relate. Hohfeldian jural relations are not purely conceptual and normatively neutral but rather are regulative and so form-like. That is to say, Hohfeldian analysis allows some ways of thinking about interpersonal relations and rules out others: it rules out any private law thinking that genuinely concerns roles or offices or special relationships – that conceives of us other than as natural persons relating through external action.[6] The core difference between full-blown forms (forms for formalists) and Hohfeldian forms (forms for moralists) is at bottom a difference in views about how we conceive of persons for the purposes of law.

So are we all formalists now about property law? Of course, in the ways that *really* matter to moralists today, we are not: moralists do not think legal reasoning contributes substantially to resolving moral problems about how we relate with respect to things; formalists do. And yet formalist and Hohfeldian-based moralist approaches to property have a liaison – the idea that legal forms are unavoidably regulative of the available ways of reasoning about our relations. My point in this paper is to reframe the disagreement between moralist and formalist as a disagreement about what these legal forms are and the extent to which legal forms

because Hohfeld is generally taken to be offering moralists neutral tools to advance their favored moral and political agendas. See Merrill and Smith 2001a.

5 Hohfeld 1913, 1916–17. See Merrill and Smith 2001. Contemporary positivists such as Robert Stevens and Ben McFarlane also ground their accounts of property on Hohfeldian jural relations. See e.g., McFarlane and Stevens 2010; Douglas and McFarlane 2013.

6 See Section 1.2.

are themselves sources for thinking morally about problems in our shared lives. Everyone agrees that juridical ideas run out at some point; the rest is politics. The disagreement concerns just how soon that point arrives – how normatively rich juridical ideas are.

This paper develops as follows: I begin by developing a normative rather than purely conceptual account of forms as regulating ways of thinking and reasoning about interpersonal relations. In the next part, I set out what I take to be the connection between moralist and formalist thinking about private law, the formalist foothold I find in moralist legal theory. I will argue that this foothold is in Hohfeldian jural relations. Hohfeldian jural relations are formal in the normative sense that a formalist might at least recognize if not in the end agree with: they set out how persons, as Hohfeld conceived of them for the purposes of law, could possibly relate, ruling out other ways of relating that would corrupt, or be inconsistent with *that* conception of persons.

2.2 Forms as Regulative Ideals for Property Law

What are legal forms, and what are they are for in the context of private law, and property law in particular? Forms set out the possible ways that we might relate to one another in a given domain of human interaction, given our conception of persons for the purposes of law.[7] Legal forms establish the ways of reasoning *legally* about problems arising out of our interactions with others. We are following these ways of thought – legal forms – when we say things like: a contract for purchase and sale is a good juridical reason for the transfer of rights to that thing; or that a person who assaults another must compensate her for the injury that results; or that it is for the owner exclusively to set the agenda for a thing.

A formalist explains property law in terms of its formal features – those not exhausted by its various manifestations in the positive law. This is what Savigny meant when he cautioned against confusing the "living production" of the jural relation, through judicial adjudication of disputes, with its form.[8] Closer examination, Savigny said, reveals "the logical form of a decision is merely called forth by accidental need and that it does not exhaust the essence of the matter but itself requires a deeper ground-work.

[7] Ripstein 2006, 2015; Wenar 2013 (suggesting that roles or identity figure in the nature of rights). See e.g., Smith 2014. Even the neo-realists like Hanoch Dagan, who think law does the bidding of politics, pay respect to form and structure today. See, Dagan 2011, pp. 3–4.

[8] Savigny 1867, p. 6. See also Waldron 1985 (distinguishing concepts and conceptions of property).

This we find in the jural relation ...." Formalists ask the question "what *kind* of relation are property relations and what are the forms appropriate to them" coherently enough without engaging first in the sociological inquiry that aims to make sense of the political choices that give law its fully determinate content.

We should not then expect from a formal account of private law the level of determinacy that formalists of old sometimes claimed to offer: a form does not tell us what law we have or even set down all of the law we ought to have.[9] Forms thus make sense of what the positive law does without dictating its precise content, allowing us to recognize complications where positive law miscomprehends or misuses concepts and coherence where it does not.

It is possible to imagine a legal system that ignores forms, in which, for example, personal responsibility is not predicated upon human agency, and ownership yields no authority with respect to a thing. And of course a legal system might aim to achieve much more through law than forms set out.[10] But these ways of thinking legally about how we relate to others are no less real for being underused or misused in certain times and place: law, or at least ways of legal thinking, *is* everywhere, whether enshrined in our positive laws, or not.[11]

Let me start with a simple illustration of the view that legal forms set out the available ways of thinking about how people relate with respect to things.[12] Say that the property law of my country makes it an actionable wrong for me to steal your bicycle. The law states further that a bicycle is *yours* until you transfer whatever rights you have in it to someone else. Whether or not the positive law makes it explicit, this scheme works off some understanding of what it would mean for things to belong to someone. What makes sense of the wrongfulness of your taking the bicycle is the idea that a thing might be *yours* at all. This idea of ownership regulates the way in which we relate with respect to things such that things might be *mine* or *yours*.

9 Forms are not meant to yield "right answers" to all legal questions.

10 I suppose I subscribe to formalism plus – see e.g., Governing Through Owners, an account of how the office of ownership is often repurposed to enhance effective state power. Some formalists would find very little scope for developing legal relations in nonlegal, i.e., moral or political terms. Ernie Weinrib might be in this class, when it comes to making sense of tort law. See, e.g., Weinrib 2012, especially Ch. 1, "Correlativity and Personality."

11 Barak 2006.

12 Harris makes a similar claim, on doctrinal grounds, in response to those who say that Anglo-American property law does not have an idea of ownership. See Harris 1996, Ch. 5. See also Katz 2008.

Forms play a similar role in a system of law in which it is announced that no one does wrong in riding off with unlocked bicycles in the city. In this property system, there is in fact no private ownership of bicycles in law.[13] But here too, coherent thinking about our relations with respect to bicycles presupposes some understanding of what it would mean to own one: city-dwellers' liberty to use bicycles is constituted by non-ownership on the part of anyone. Core property concepts, like ownership or possession, make sense also for these legal arrangements, where there is no private property in bicycles.

Here then is what a form is: it is a regulating concept for a given domain of human interaction. The form of property sets out the available ways of thinking about our relations with respect to things, given our conception of ourselves. The formalist identifies the forms appropriate to property law by making sense of the *kind* of relation that property law takes as its basic subject-matter. Property law does not take parent-child relations as its subject; it does not concern the claims and obligations triggered by promising; or any number of other ways we might relate to each other in law. Property law deals with our relations as they concern things.[14]

How is it that the form of property draws so much from our conceptions of ourselves? The answer is, I think, that the relation we posit between two objects must be a *possible* relation for those objects. Clearly the form of property cannot be such that, in regulating the relation between persons with respect to things, it corrupts the relata. If the regulative principles for a relation – its form – assumes the objects are other than they are, it is not a possible relation for those objects but the other objects it took them to be. It is incoherent to set out a relation between free people that by its very terms requires us to conceive of one person as unfree. Slavery, for instance, is not a relation that could hold between free persons. Similarly, our understanding of property relations must be consistent with its being a relation for *persons as we conceive of them* with respect to things.

So how do formalists today conceive of persons in making sense of property and how is property a relation for persons so conceived? There is no consensus formalist account of property relations but common to

[13] For instance, the (failed) attempt in Amsterdam (Jordan 2013). Not even locked bicycles: if it takes locking to preserve a claim, then we cannot say there is ownership – there is no authority that endures when the thing is beyond your physical control.

[14] In the first instance with tangible things, like land or chattels. Of course modern property systems encompass kinds of intangible property such as choses in action, but it is beyond the scope of this paper to consider how the latter "things" come to be treated under a property system in ways similar to the way tangible, ones are.

all is an attempt to work through the first question: how are property relations between persons (as conceived for the purposes of law) possible?[15] With a conception of person in mind, we bring into view the legal forms appropriate to property relations. The formalist project in relation to property law is characterized by its ambition and its modesty. The ambition of formalism is to carry a normative idea about persons (e.g., as free and equal agents) into law and to account for the available ways of thinking about relations between persons thus conceived as they concern things. To fulfill the ambition is to set out fully the appropriate legal forms for that kind of relation. We would fail fully to specify the available legal forms if we were to take the relata of property relations as anything *less* than persons so conceived – for instance, merely as physical forces with capacity to move themselves, objects or other people around. Of course, if one takes a view of law just as a set of controls to manage physical forces, then this view of persons for the purpose of law might be appropriate. A more ambitious liberal view of law, and so of the conception of persons for the purposes of law, rules this out.

Critics of formalism take aim at its characteristic modesty as much as at its ambition: formalism's modesty lies in its concern just to set out the basic ways of thinking legally about relations between persons with respect to things, how persons are conceived for the purposes of law. This modesty strikes some moralists as austere, even empty thinking about what are after all important human relations. Why not employ a substantively richer conception of ourselves for the purpose of some further aspect of social life; for example, family roles or workplace positions (e.g., property as a relation between spouses with respect to a thing; property as a relation between the employer and employee with respect to a thing)?[16] But this concern misses the point of legal formalism: it is not to establish all the particularities of property in positive law, nor to deny that there is place for further morality or policy-based decision-making about property. Rather, the point of formalism is to establish basically what kind of a relation property is and how that relation must be structured even to be possible as a relation between persons with respect to things. There are rich public levers for social policy, for introducing incentives and regulations that lead us to a richer set of social roles and identities. Through regulation and social policy, we may well choose to deviate from the basic forms

[15] There is thus a normative claim embedded in forms for formalists: the form of property emerges from our conception of ourselves for moral or political purposes.

[16] See generally the idea of relational justice, developed in Dagan and Dorfman 2016.

of ownership. Or we might choose to add additional rules constraining or requiring the transfer of authority in some circumstances, e.g., spousal property legislation motivated by concerns of local distributive justice and unjust enrichment. But thinking about people in terms of richer or simply other social roles in the civil society we actually have presupposes a way of thinking basically about idea of property in law as a relation between persons as conceived for the purposes of law.

2.3 Forms for Moralists

Formalists take there to be distinctive ways of reasoning legally about human relations. Can we find anything like this idea of legal reasoning in moralist thinking about private law? There is, I think, at least a foothold for formalism in moralist legal theory. To see it, we have to move beyond the surface level concepts that moralists sometimes employ to the Hohfeldian substructure of these views.

2.3.1 Conceptualism and Formalism Distinguished

In contemporary theory, it is not just the formalist who attends to legal concepts. Recently, what once defined the moralist project, a skepticism about legal concepts and a denial of distinctively legal ways of reasoning, seems to have stalled. In discrete areas of legal theory, particularly in relation to property law, there is a renewed interest in legal concepts and in structured ways of thinking about legal problems.[17] Contemporary property theory has taken up the challenge of working out the basic conceptual features of property in debates about the nature and structure of rights of ownership. Some contemporary property theorists take the view that property is a right to a thing, others say that it is a right-duty relation between person *a* and person *b*, with respect to a thing (which may or may not mirror the relation between person *a* and person *c*, *d*, *e*, etc.), and yet others say it is a relation between person *a* and the world at large, with respect to a thing. Put another way, property theory's self-set problem seems now to be to ascertain whether property is a right *in rem* or a bundle-of-rights *in personam* (those who think the former wring their hands further over what it

[17] Penner 1997, Ch. 4 (fitting a formal account of property as a right to exclude into a Razian framework; interest in using things grounds the duty of exclusion); Smith 2004 (fitting a formal account of property as a right to exclude into a Coasean account of law; law tailored to a world of transaction costs).

means for a right to be *in rem*: does it concern the thingness of property? Or does it just refer to its exigibility?).[18]

And yet this turn toward conceptualism among moralist property theorists is not in itself a turn toward formalism. Indeed, moralists about property flatten the distinction between concepts and policy by looking to general moral theory to guide both: law always aims at something beyond itself. Legal concepts for moralists, like ownership as a right to exclude, are for the most parts just shortcuts for "all things considered" moral reasoning about legal problems. For example, we may do better in arriving at utility maximizing legal rules if we stick with something like a right to exclude rather than the equally available alternative, a bundle of use-rights tailored to advance utility, case by case.[19] Or we may do better at protecting socially valuable interests in use if we deploy an exclusion strategy than if we structure rights directly in terms of use. Property concepts in new moralist property theory are instruments in service of general moral ends. Some of these ends (e.g., the interest in use) are more specifically concerned with property relations than others. But others, such as transaction-cost reduction, a concern with the design of legal rules generally, are not property-specific ends. Property concepts for moralists are in principle flexible – tied not to a normative view about the structure of the underlying relation, but rather tied to other normative principles that are independent of that underlying relation (e.g., a general principle of efficiency in designing legal rules).[20] Thus, moralists may identify concepts in property law but not connect these to the underlying relations that forms regulate. Of course, my point in this paper is that there is nonetheless a sense in which moralist property theory does have a formal element; we simply don't find that formal element in the promising conceptual turn in new private law theory.

2.3.2 Hohfeldian Jural Relations: A Normative Account

Where we do see a formalist foothold in at least some morality accounts of private law is in the Hohfeldian jural relations on which many contemporary moralist theories are implicitly but just as often explicitly based.

[18] What Austin calls "not the subject but the compass of the right" (Austin 1875, pp. 176–7).

[19] I take Merrill and Smith to accept that property is grounded in basic interest in use. See Merrill and Smith 2007.

[20] To be clear, no one suggests that information costs savings is the whole story. As Lon L. Fuller put in Fuller 1977, p. 185: "If the highest aim of a captain were to preserve his ship he would keep it in port forever" (paraphrasing Aquinas 1947, Pt I–II Q2 Art. 5).

Bundle of rights theories of property law are relational in precisely the way that Hohfeld himself had in mind. On a bundle-of-rights view, property law does not use forms like ownership or possession. What we are used to calling "ownership" is on this view actually a bundle of *in personam* use-rights, the composition and content of which varies with the context.[21] The Hohfeldian substructure of bundle of rights theories of property is well-recognized. The "bundle" is just the aggregation of rights, privileges and powers, assembled or disassembled as moral theory requires. Indeed, the appeal of a bundle-of-rights theory is that it is well-suited to an ends-driven account of law precisely because it has no fixed composition: we can build a range of morally and politically more complex structures out of these fundamental Hohfeldian jural relations. What matters to its proponents is how these various "sticks" are distributed in each interaction to yield better social or economic outcomes. It is precisely this moral flexibility that makes a bundle of rights theory just as much at home with Hayekian conservative views of property[22] as it is with the progressive views of many legal realists, and others in between.[23] The perceived atomism of Hohfeld's account of legal relations is the signature advantage of this view to its moralist proponents.

Property theorists who take a bundle-of-rights view are, it is true, mainly interested in the *bundling* aspect of the account and what this means for a more just (efficient, etc.) distribution of entitlements in society. But a bundle-of-rights account is not a form-free explication of property law.

Here's how we might understand the formality at the heart of Hohfeld. Hohfeld thought all jural relations concerned different ways in which human action is constrained, or not. (One implication of this view is that all jural relations, whether rights/duties, powers/liabilities or privileges/no-rights are on the same footing: all concern ways in which we are subject to or free from constraints on our conduct or ways in which we subject others to or free others from constraints on theirs.)[24]

This means property relations cannot be relations between persons and things: property is necessarily a concept "for two" because it is a way in which one person claims or imposes or is free from a constraint claimable by or

[21] E.g., Penner 1996.

[22] E.g., Epstein 2006. Thanks to Ben Zipursky for drawing the connection to Epstein.

[23] Many Hohfeldians are (professionally anyway) morally agnostic about property law's aims. See e.g., McFarlane and Stevens 2010.

[24] I am indebted to Henry E. Smith for emphasizing this point in University of Toronto reading group on Hohfeld in Spring 2015. See also Halpin 2017.

imposable by another.[25] And it also means that property relations are defined in terms of individual action; e.g., I have a right that you not *build that structure* on Blackacre; you have a duty *not to build that structure* on Blackacre. Or more simply, I have a right that you not cross the boundary line here and now, and you have a duty not to cross that boundary line here and now.[26]

At the heart of a Hohfeldian view of property is a claim that certain ordinary ways of thinking about property are in fact alien to the law: ideas of ownership or belonging; the subordinate nature of certain kinds of property rights (easements, profits, leases); the role and responsibility of finders – all ways of thinking about property rights that require us to go outside the jural relations that we might associate with these ideas and think about the connections among them and their place in a larger system of law. This emerges clearly in Hohfeld's treatment of two rights to exclude. The first is A's right to exclude B from Whiteacre where X has title to Whiteacre, and A has paid B $100 for B's undertaking to exclude himself. The second is A's right to exclude B from Blackacre where A owns Blackacre.[27] The two, he argued, are identical notwithstanding that we might ordinarily label one a property right and the other a contract right. All that the law of properly yields is a view of the jural relation between A and B in each context, i.e., an identical right/duty of exclusion. Contemporary Hohfeldians, like Ben McFarlane and Simon Douglas, say something similar about the identical rights to exclude of owners and possessors.[28]

A Hohfeldian approach denies anything distinctive about property relations and so anything distinctive about the place of property law in our general legal arrangements. This is consistent with Hohfeld's general pragmatic aim of promoting unity and harmony across law by reducing all of law to a common currency. It is also, I think, an extension of Hohfeld's principled objection to allowing law and legal reasoning to take over our rationality, to exceed its proper place in our moral universe. Hohfeld's reluctance to allow that law in itself is or can be purposive in a larger sense, such that property law is meant to do one thing and contract or tort law, another, is a matter of principle.[29] There is sign of both concerns, the pragmatic

[25] Fichte 2000, p. 45; Thompson 2004.

[26] This is how Ben McFarlane understands property, and it results in a leveling of ownership and subordinate rights, like a bailee's or a finder's right to possess. McFarlane 2008, pp. 9, 144 (there are multiple "owners" each with an identical right to exclude). Cf. Katz 2013, p. 202.

[27] Hohfeld 1916–17, p. 723. For Hohfeld we may distinguish property and contract for reasons of exposition. But this division is not internal to law.

[28] Douglas and McFarlane 2013.

[29] Hohfeld 1916.

and the principled, in Hohfeld's claim: "since the *purpose* of the law is to regulate the conduct of human beings, all jural relations must, *in order* to be clear and direct in their meaning, be predicated of such human beings"[30] (emphasis added). Hohfeld was emphatic that the law concerned just these discrete, external actions of natural persons.[31] Only the individual actions of physical persons could be the subject-matter of jural relations; it is never the person as a socially constructed whole.[32] Any further classification of rights in terms of special positions like ownership was at best of expository value and at worst misleading.

I have spoken about Hohfeldian "forms" as regulative ideals but I have not yet said enough about why I think these jural relations are regulative of private law interactions in anything like the way a formalist would recognize as regulative, allowing only certain ways of legal thought and ruling out others. What in other words do Hohfeldian forms leave out of private law? The conventional view of Hohfeld on jural relations is that he is just a reductionist and at root an empiricist: there is no legal problem that will not then yield jural relations in Hohfeldian form if we do enough excavating. But I think that Hohfeld's jural relations do something more than just describe what is *actually* going on in law.[33] They seem to require that law's directives *conform* to a view about private law relations and so act as regulative ideals appropriate to that view of private law relations.

All private law for Hohfeld concerns only external, action-based relations between real persons.[34] What Hohfeldian formalism rules out is the possibility that private law might *actually* concern itself with legal

[30] Hohfeld 1916–17, p. 721. In a speech to the AALS Hohfeld suggested that, in addition to pragmatic benefits, his "formal" analysis revealed that the unity and harmony of private law is only possible where we see all private law in terms of restrictions on individual, external action (Hohfeld 1914). Hohfeld's speech suggests a reform minded-lawyer, but not one who sought reform at the expense of harmony and unity of law.

[31] Hayek 1960, p. 148, citing Savigny. ("The rule whereby the indivisible border is fixed within which the being and activity of social individual obtains a secure and free sphere, is the law.")

[32] Cf. Savigny defines *obligation* as a relation of mastery over the individual act of another, that does not destroy the freedom of the whole person. He contrasts this with slavery, which is mastery over the *whole* person (Savigny 1867, p. 275).

[33] Hohfeld seems to have been influenced by some of Austin's work. See Merrill and Smith 2001b. It is not clear if he accepted the command theory of law though. According to Merrill and Smith "Both Hohfeld's and Kocourek's theories have antecedents in Austin's view about property that 'indefiniteness is of the very essence of the right; and implies that the right ... cannot be determined by exact and positive circumscription'" (Austin 1875, p. 827). See Kocourek 1920.

[34] "The only conduct of which the state can take notice by its laws *must* spring from natural persons – it cannot be derived from any abstraction." (Hohfeld 1909, 1913).

personae – roles or offices charged with certain responsibilities. (This might explain why for Hohfeldians like Robert Stevens, old equitable maxims that seem to convey information about *roles or offices* are not really part of the law of trusts at all but mere sentimental holdovers from sloppy (pre-Hohfeld) days.[35]) The law, for Hohfeld, has no business conceiving of private actors in terms of roles, offices or special relationships, since these are not reducible to "ultimate facts" concerning physical human action. Nor is there internal to private law any way to account for *connections* between what Hohfeld sees as jural relations, such as the idea that some rights (easements, mortgages, finder's rights) are premised on the existence of other rights (ownership) and are defined in terms of their subordinate nature.[36] Finally, there is no room on Hohfeld's accounts for what I will call "manner requirements" that qualify how an owner (or trustee) is to exercise her rights without recognizing in any private actor a *right* that she do so. I have in mind "duties" of loyalty in dealing with trust property[37] or principles of abuse of property rights, that ground judicial treatment of these rights (for instance, denying enforcement of a right to exclude exercised just out of spite). We cannot express such manner requirements intelligible in terms of jural relations and so are they are not ways of thinking *legally* about rights, powers or liberties at all, for Hohfeld. In this Hohfeld sounds Austinian: Austin, for instance suggests that status in the law of persons is there for the sake of exposition, a matter of expository convenience.[38]

Hohfeld may have thought that our positive law has gotten it mostly "right" and so is capable, through clear and careful explication, of being recast in terms of the kind of relation appropriate to private law, i.e., jural relations. But to the extent that the private law claims genuinely to impose requirements of loyalty, or to establish special roles or offices, or to forge a

[35] Stevens 2012.

[36] For instance, we make sense of certain requirement of easements, such as the requirement that they be consistent with rights retained by owners in the servient tenement and that they be capable of forming the subject-matter of a grant, only by seeing the relationship between ownership and easements. Similarly, finder's rights make sense as rights to possess that are subordinate to the true owner's: not just temporally later but, in terms of the *causa possessionis*, related to the office of ownership in a particular way. Finders are meant to serve as owners *pro tem*, until the absentee officeholder returns.

[37] Lionel Smith explains that a duty of loyalty is not really a "duty" at all but a requirement concerning the manner in which the right is exercised. Nonetheless is it is a *legal* requirement that gives shape to the office of trustee (Smith 2003).

[38] See Waldron 2013 (setting out Austin's view of status as a shorthand for a list of rights and contrasts it with Bentham's view of status which better reveals the normative connections among those rights in Human dignity).

hierarchy of rights in property, the law is doing precisely what it ought not to do, on a Hohfeldian view.

Private law takes only the view of persons that it must in order to construct a framework for further voluntary action – contractual or political. Precisely because of its restraint in what it counts as *legal thinking*, Hohfeldian formalism crosses the political spectrum, from libertarian theories of property (e.g., Richard Epstein) to the bundle-of-rights views of legal realists and positivists like McFarlane and Douglas. Hohfeldians might variously applaud private law's restraint for reasons of liberty (Epstein), see in its silence a call to arms (realists and critical legal scholars), or take this restraint as a feature of legality itself that conduces to greater harmony and unity in law.[39]

The upshot of Hohfeldian formalism then is that we cannot think legally about roles or offices in property law – although I think that property law presents itself as doing just that.[40] For Hohfeldians, not only does property law not use ideas like ownership; it *ought* not to. Forms are *regulative* ideals for Hohfeld because thinking about roles, special responsibilities, offices, etc. is inappropriate to the kind of relations involved. For the Hohfeldian, what this means is that legal thinking does not get us very far in understanding our overarching normative arrangements and the place of legal norms in them. For that, we have politics.

2.4 Conclusion

Formalists share a view that forms are more than just observable and even useful regularities in the positive law; they are regulative ideals suited to the kind of relations between persons that law concerns. Forms for formalists are ultimately grounded in some conception of persons and how persons thus conceived could possibly relate to others in a variety of human situations, including our interactions with respect to things in the world. Start with a different conception of persons, as Hohfeldian moralists do, and we end up with a different view of how we might relate with respect to

[39] Positivists like McFarlane and Stevens 2010, develop accounts of property with Hohfeldian underpinnings but do not themselves adopt a larger normative agenda for law in terms of social justice or efficiency, etc. For these positivists, institutional goals like coherence, workability or predictability keep the political and moral philosophers from doing a complete make-over of our law.

[40] See Katz 2008, 2012; Essert 2013. See Wenar 2013 on rights as sometimes concerned with roles and responsibilities. See Waldron 2013, p. 24 (describing Status e.g., bankrupt, infancy Waldron says that status does explain why taken together those rights make sense in terms of that status).

things, and the forms appropriate to that kind of relation. Unfortunately, as I have sought to show, the Hohfeldian perspective does away with many of the common concepts in property law, like ownership or trusteeship, which plausibly can be claimed to be just the sort of forms, reflecting important categories of interpersonal relationships, that a formalist would want to embrace.

3

What Is the Right to Exclude and Why Does It Matter?

JAMES Y. STERN

It is widely asserted that something called "the right to exclude" is central to the institution of property.[1] What the right to exclude means, however, isn't explained with precision, and as a result, various claims about exclusion in property law are not only confusing but, often enough, somewhat confused. This chapter will attend to some central questions about the right to exclude in an effort to provide a general overview of its role in property law. It ultimately concludes that although rights to exclude are an important part of property, they are not its defining or "essential" feature. At root, property is an authority structure, in which control or dominion over a defined subject matter is the basic conceptual currency. What is called "exclusion" is an important dimension of this authority, but the distinction between exclusion and other dimensions of control is in many respects unhelpful, leading to misunderstandings about the mechanics and structure of property law.

3.1 The Formal Structure of the Right to Exclude

Though the phrase is of relatively recent vintage as a descriptor of property,[2] the right to exclude is today commonplace in legal

[1] The focus of this chapter will be on doctrine and commentary within the United States, although basic claims about the nature of property are generally intended to be applicable to other legal systems.

[2] Scattered references to a "right to exclude" in connection with property appear in various pre-twentieth century texts – usually phrased in terms of a right to exclude *use or interference* by others, rather than the right to exclude others – but widespread use of the phrase as a description of property appears to coincide with the advent of legal realism. See Cohen 1927 (asserting that "the essence of private property is always the right to exclude others"); see also Int'l *News Serv.* v. *Associated Press*, 248 U.S. 215, 250 (1918) (Brandeis, J., dissenting) ("An essential element of individual property is the legal right to exclude others from enjoying it.)." Holmes referred to the right to exclude "interference" by others, which is rather different. See *White-Smith Music Pub. Co.* v. *Apollo Co.*, 209 U.S. 1, 19 (1908) (Holmes, J.,

discussions.[3] For such a wide-ranging legal idea, the concept generally bears a fairly specific meaning, although unfortunately the term is also used rather imprecisely in a number of texts. To date, it appears there has been no comprehensive statement of the constituent features of the right to exclude.[4] As a result, it seems that the idea is reasonably well understood at an intuitive level but without a clear sense of its analytic content. What follows is a description of what the right to exclude means, in hard-edged particulars.

To begin, then, the right to exclude can be redescribed as *the right to prohibit one or more persons from using a particular resource, either at all or in some category of ways.* More particularly, the right to exclude can be understood in terms of three central elements: (1) a claim-right, (2) that is negative in character, and (3) that pertains to the use of a discrete thing. This portion of the chapter will first elaborate on each of these three features and make some observations about them. It will then offer some additional comments on what the right to exclude means, and more importantly, on what it does not.

3.1.1 Three Defining Features

3.1.1.1 Claim-Rights

The word "right" can be used in at least two different senses. It can refer to the simple absence of a duty. I have the right to look at my neighbor's garden insofar as I am under no obligation to refrain from doing so, though

concurring specially); Holmes 1991 [1881]; see also Austin 1869. The phrase most commonly appeared in patent law decisions, possibly stemming from the opinion of Taney, C.J., in *Bloomer* v. *McQuewan*, 55 U.S. 539, 549 (1852), though it is worth nothing that Taney went out of his way to avoid any notion of patent rights as property. Cf. Proprietors of *Charles River Bridge* v. *Proprietors of Warren Bridge*, 36 U.S. 420, 490 (1837) (statutory monopoly). *See also Wheaton* v. *Peters*, 33 U.S. 591, 652 (1834) (copyright).

It is tempting to project the modern notion of the right to exclude onto earlier sources and thinkers, but this is generally anachronistic. Cf. Merrill 1998. For example, the right to exclude should not be equated with Blackstone's famous account of property as "sole and despotic dominion" over external things claimed "in total exclusion of the right" of anyone else (Blackstone 1765–9). Someone's *dominion* excluding someone else's *right* is quite different from an *actor* excluding another's *person*. See Stern 2017 (arguing that a hallmark of property is the principle that a valid property entitlement precludes the existence of anyone else's contradictory property entitlement).

[3] See Dukeminier 2010 (discussing view "conventional among lawyers" that "property entails a number of disparate rights – the right to possess, the right to use, the right to exclude, the right to transfer, etc.").

[4] Cf. Merrill 2014 (refining earlier account of right to exclude).

my right doesn't mean my neighbor must refrain from building a fence that blocks my view. Following Wesley Hohfeld,[5] such a legal relationship will be referred to here as a *privilege-right* (or just privilege). Alternatively, a right can refer to the position of being owed a duty by someone else. To change the facts in the hypothetical just given, if my neighbor did have a duty to avoid blocking my view, I would have a right in this second sense. An entitlement of this form will be referred to as a *claim-right*.

The right to exclude is meant to refer to a claim-right but it sounds like a privilege-right. A privilege-right is usually described in terms of some action that the right-holder undertakes, and the right "to exclude" sounds like the right-holder's entitlement to do something that could be described as excluding, such as physically remove a person from a parcel of land.[6] But what is ordinarily meant by the right to exclude isn't a right to engage in self-help or acts of what might be called de facto exclusion – like building fences,[7] emitting "exclusionary vibes,"[8] or simply consuming a resource so that others cannot do so themselves (eating an apple, for example).[9] It is not only possible but common to have property rights obliging others not to trespass while at the same time restricting the right-holder's freedom to practice self-help or other exclusionary tactics.[10] When theorists speak of the right to exclude, it is a claim-right to exclude they ordinarily have in mind – the position of being on the receiving end of another's duty to keep out.[11]

A few comments. First, as this suggests, the right to exclude can be linguistically confusing. (Indeed, as we shall see, this isn't the only way it can be so.) Second, the fact that property law involves claim-rights against others is certainly significant. Indeed, there is a good argument to be made that the existence of claim-rights is the starting point for a property system. Imagine a stream of water that anyone was allowed to use, meaning everyone has a privilege-right to use it. If this is all that anyone has – if, for example, individual users have no protection against others diverting water, polluting the stream, barricading routes of access to it, and so forth – it seems strange to speak of the users having any kind of property rights. The situation seems indistinguishable from one in which no law

[5] See Hohfeld 1923 [1913].

[6] I might also have privilege-rights to assert or waive my claim-right, but that doesn't mean the claim-right is itself a privilege-right.

[7] See Smith 2005.

[8] See Strahilevitz 2006.

[9] See Mossoff 2003.

[10] See Brandon et al. 1984.

[11] See Penner 1997, pp. 71–2. My point is about conventional usage and intended meaning but Shyamkrishna Balganesh adds a conceptual element to the argument. See Balganesh 2008.

existed at all. But suppose instead that each person has a duty not to dispossess any another or attempt to prevent others from using the stream. In this scenario, it can more plausibly be asserted that users have some kind of basic property right in the stream and the reason is because now they hold certain claim-rights against others.

Third, however, while the claim-rights comprising the right to exclude are indeed important to property law, there is nevertheless a serious danger of overemphasis. Certain accounts of property centered on the right to exclude tend to denigrate the status of privilege-rights of use by treating the right to use a resource as simply what's leftover when the right-holder isn't excluded and everyone else is.[12] This "donut" view of the use-rights[13] and the suggestion that such rights aren't property rights is conceptually mistaken. An owner of land who grants a negative easement to a neighbor, for instance, gives up some portion of her property rights, even though her right to exclude others is unchanged.[14] Similarly, if two co-owners of property conveyed to one another a property right to exclude the other, it would be quite peculiar to suppose that either held property rights equal what he or she would have held as a sole owner. And, one might add, property subject to fiduciary duties entails significant restrictions on how the property may be used, so much so that the fiduciary is said to hold one form of title to the property while the beneficiary is said to hold another. It is precisely because the right to use is understood to be part of property that the doctrine of regulatory takings law is at least plausible, for instance, or that the so-called anti-commons problem – too many people with veto rights – can be thought of as a threat *to* property, rather than simply a problem caused by it.[15]

The view that there is no right to use in property law seems to have several origins. Part of the concern with recognizing privileges as property entitlements seems to be a fear that doing so would prove too much: there are many privilege-rights pertaining to things that we don't think of as property – a passerby's privilege to observe the exterior of a building visible from a public thoroughfare, for example. This objection overlooks the basic conceptual material of property law, which deals in rights, including privilege-rights, concerning the *use* of things, where the concept of

[12] See Douglas and McFarlane 2013; Merrill 1998, p. 744.

[13] Cf. Katz 2008 (stating that in these accounts, "ownership is nothing more than the space left for the use of the thing by the owner once others are kept out").

[14] See, e.g., *S. Cal. Edison Co.* v. *Bourgerie*, 507 P.2d 964 (Cal. 1973).

[15] That property entails privilege-rights of use does not mean that any legal restriction on the use of property is conceptually at odds with property law. But see Merges et al. 2012.

"use" limited by a relatively intuitive sense of direct human interaction. It would be idiosyncratic to say that someone "used" a building by observing it from the street. Recognizing a property-holder's use-privilege, valid against others, as property would not imply that all privileges are part of the law of property any more than recognizing rights to exclude as property risks converting all claim-rights into property rights.

A related concern is the view that there is really nothing to privilege-rights because they simply reflect the natural or default legal state, indistinguishable from an absence of law altogether. But legal context matters. Because by definition one person's claim-right means another lacks a privilege, the existence of privileges can no longer be assumed as part of the backdrop once a system of claim-rights is established. A spot intentionally left unpainted in oil painting should be taken as a part of the artist's work, not simply a reversion to the raw canvas. Similarly, if duties respecting property are presumptive or typical, the absence of such duties in a given situation can be readily understood as the active product of the property system, rather than simply as an absence of law. In a state of nature, I might be free to pick an apple from a tree, but I do not live in a state of nature, and if I sell my orchard, the most salient fact is not that I can't prevent others from picking my fruit but that I am no longer free to pick it myself.

Finally, it is suggested that the right to use isn't really part of property because it doesn't do anything: It is subordinate to the police power and to the property rights of others who may own resources necessary to use whatever it is the property-holder is said to be entitled to use (complementary goods, in economics-speak). Such arguments come up most often in discussions of intellectual property, and especially patent law, where both regulatory requirements and other patent-holders' rights to related technologies can significantly limit a patent-holder's ability to produce and market the patented invention.[16] Oddly, it is frequently suggested that these features are somehow unique to intellectual property and thereby distinguish it from property in tangible objects or land, but quite plainly the right to use these other kinds of property is also limited in the same ways. Ownership of a gun doesn't entitle me to commit murder and doesn't entitle me to bullets owned by others; ownership of a parcel of land doesn't entitle me to operate a bordello and it doesn't entitle me to a right-of-way across my neighbor's land, even if my parcel is landlocked.[17] If it

[16] See discussion in Mossoff 2009 and sources collected therein.

[17] Although the common law provides certain forms of protection for landlocked owners, these protections are limited in their coverage. The doctrine of easements by necessity, for

is true that intellectual property entails only rights to exclude because it confers no right to use that would overcome either the police power or property rights of others, the same is true for property generally.

But it is not true. The right to exclude is also subject to the police power; a restaurant, for example, cannot defend against a charge of racial discrimination on the grounds that it owns its premises, any more than a patent-holder can defend against a charge of price-fixing on the grounds that has a patent. Again, the right to use is part of the fabric of property law because it entails the absence of a duty not to trespass. If Austin is the sole owner of Blackacre (or Black invention) he may be subject to regulation or unable to do much with the property because some other resource necessary to its effective exploitation is owned by someone else, but at least he will not be subject to trespass liability for use of the property as such. If Austin jointly owns the property with Bentham, he will generally be free of any duty to Bentham to refrain from using it; but even if he were not, he would at least hold a share of authority to determine the permissibility of his own use, so that he doesn't have to worry about trespass liability to some third party, Cardozo, who could have received his share instead. Simply put, within a recognized system of property making one person subject to another's right of exclude transfers a property right from the first person to the second.

3.1.1.2 Negative Claim-Rights (Duties of Abstention)

The claim-rights generated by property are generally negative – that is a major part of what the word "exclude" is meant to convey. This proposition doesn't sound in political philosophy or constitutional theory and isn't intended to describe the rights an individual may assert against a liberal state.[18] The assertion that property claim-rights are negative simply means that the duties those rights impose on other private parties are limited to

instance, is only available where the dominant (landlocked) and servient estates at one time belonged to a common grantor and the necessity existed at the time the parcels were separated. See *Restatement (Third) Of Property (Servitudes)* § 2.15 & cmt c (2000).

[18] To the extent property entails claim-rights that require officials to enforce property entitlements against others, it also entails affirmative claim-rights. Whether a property-holder actually has any such rights against the government is a matter of some debate. Cf. *Castle Rock* v. *Gonzales*, 545 U.S. 748 (2005) (holding that statutory entitlement to enforcement of restraining order is not property right for purposes of due process analysis). At any rate, such rights to government enforcement differ in kind from primary rights against other actors (including the government, in its capacity as would-be trespasser, as distinguished from its capacity as law enforcer). While it is often asserted that property depends upon the state for its existence, this is plainly overstated at best; mine-and-thine regimes develop spontaneously without any obvious enforcement mechanism in a wide range of contexts, such as the claiming of parking spots by hovering with the turn signal on. See generally

duties of abstention. In other words, property doesn't impose obligations on others to perform particular actions, only to refrain from acting in certain ways. It is this negative character that leads J. E. Penner to characterize the right to exclude as property's "formal essence."[19] While Penner insists property exists to serve our individual interests in using things, he maintains that the law secures that interest only by giving prohibitory rights against others.

This point is almost always missed.[20] For theorists like Penner, the significance of the right to exclude is that it is a right *only* to exclude.[21] It isn't meant to suggest that property is a matter of rights that are unqualified, that property treats human beings as atomistic hermits, or that property law seeks to jettison any sense of moral obligation to others.[22] The point, rather, is that property rights could conceivably entail something much stronger than they do. We could imagine a system with claim-rights to positive performance, like a duty in an agricultural village to assist in a barn-raising, but a property-holder's right to compel active assistance from others is quite atypical, even in close-knit communities like the Amish.[23] So while it might perhaps be true that property law exists to enable the proverbial Blackacre-owner to pursue her various projects in life, it does so by enabling her to require only that others keep out or exit, not that they enter or stick around to lend a hand.

This insight is important if only because it is true. While single-minded emphasis on the right to exclude can be criticized for implying that property only involves claim-rights, the basic claim-rights property law does create tend only to be negative ones. To be sure, there are some affirmative duties within what is conventionally understood as the domain of

---

Ellickson 1991. And of course property can be thought of as a system of moral rights and obligations, distinct from the commands of positive law.

19 Penner 1997, p. 71. See also Cohen 1927 (stating that "[t]he essence of private property is always the right to exclude others. The law does not guarantee me the physical or social ability of actually using what it calls mine").

20 Because of ambiguities in the language of exclusivity, statements about the negative aspect of property duties can be taken to deny the existence of privilege-rights to use a thing. Cf. Mossoff 2009 (interpreting Oliver Wendell Holmes's discussion of property as a negative right to deny the significance of use-privileges).

21 See Penner 1997, pp. 50, 73. Penner calls this a "negative liberty," which can be a bit confusing given the tendency to equate liberties with privilege-rights. The privilege-right is positive as well as negative; a property-holder may do affirmative acts. It is only the duties others bear that are negative.

22 Cf. Alexander 2009b (criticizing as "highly misleading" the "core image of property rights" in which an owner "has a right to exclude others and owes no further obligation to them").

23 See Ferrara 1993. See also Kemmis 1996.

property.[24] Such obligations, however, are relatively exceptional[25] and fit uneasily within the overall scheme of property.[26] By and large, those claim-rights conferred by the law of property are negative.

Recognizing the negative character of property duties can also shed light on property as an institution more generally. For example, I have argued elsewhere that central to the conceptual structure property law is a principle that rights must not overlap, so that, for example, two people cannot separately be the complete owner of the same resource – the owner of Blackacre can enter into binding contracts to sell the property to two different people, but the owner cannot actually convey title to both.[27] The negative structure of property rights helps facilitate this structure of mutually exclusive rights since it is easier to harmonize different negative duties with one another than it is to harmonize affirmative ones.[28] Separate duties to help Austin, Bentham, and Cardozo are far more likely to conflict with one another than separate duties simply to avoid actively harming them. It has also been argued that the negative character of property rights is consistent with the "in rem" structure of property, and more precisely, the large number of people bound by the duties that property law imposes ("the world" in traditional property-talk). It is generally harder to communicate as the number of people receiving the communication grows larger,

[24] Covenants and equitable servitudes, for example, can create duties to perform positive acts, and the beneficiaries of these duties are said to hold property rights. See Ellickson 2014; Katz 2012.

[25] This is especially so if we exclude positive duties arising from the choice to perform some particular act. A driver might be required to turn on his headlights at night, but only because she has chosen to drive in the first place. Obligations of this kind are often better characterized as limitations on a privilege-right, forbidding the performance of an act in certain proscribed ways, than direct positive obligations.

[26] Indeed, property law displays a marked reluctance to count positive duties as property rights. For example, traditionally the burden of a servitude must "touch and concern" the land for burden to run to subsequent owners. In applying this test, courts have been far less willing to find the touch-and-concern requirement satisfied for servitudes imposing positive duties than for those imposing negative ones. A negative obligation operates as a constraint on the owner, simply transferring control over some aspect of the parcel from the owner to someone else. A positive obligation does something else: the owner's privilege-right to perform the act in question remains, supplemented by a duty to do something with an additional resource – his person.

[27] It won't be possible to perform both contracts, but each promise is at least entitled to full compensation. Though property law doesn't usually work this way, the dual conveyances could result in some form of co-tenancy between the rival recipients, but in that case each would receive what is effectively a fraction of the original owner's rights. For a more detailed discussion of this aspect of property law, see Stern 2017, pp. 1178–84.

[28] Stern 2017, pp. 1203–7.

and it may often be easier to communicate the content of negative rights than positive ones.[29]

3.1.1.3 Thing-based Rights

The right to exclude others implies something to exclude from, both as a matter of ordinary language and in terms of how theories of the role of exclusion in property work. Stated differently, a right to exclude doesn't refer to any and every negative claim-right but only to those that impose duties not to use particular "things." Thus, a right that a business not collude with competitors to fix prices, that an employer not discriminate on the basis of race, or that a highway motorist not drive recklessly are each negative claim-rights, but they aren't "rights to exclude." Understood in terms of exclusion from *something*, the right to exclude stresses the way a property-holder's rights are delineated, in substantial part, with reference to the boundaries of individually conceptualized things, whether tracts of land, physical objects, or more abstract entities like corporations, internet addresses, or symphonies.

Unfortunately, the phrase "right to exclude" is sometimes used to refer to other negative claim-rights connected with property law, even when the scope of those claim-rights isn't defined with any reference to the boundaries of particular things.[30] Such usages, however, eliminate any special connection between the right to exclude and property law – eliminating the distinction between property and, say, employment discrimination law. They are also inconsistent with the point of speaking in terms of the right to "exclude," rather than simply the right to forbid something, which is to emphasize the role of thing-boundaries in articulating the scope of property law duties.[31] Rights to be free from interference in some general sense (including rights of quiet enjoyment protected by the law of nuisance) should not be considered instances of the right to exclude, except insofar as they borrow from the idea of boundary-crossing or unauthorized use of an asset.

Thingness in the law of property is important for several reasons. First, it points us to some of the distinctive problems that property law confronts. Property law can usefully be thought of as extending the sphere of personal dominion to entities beyond body and soul, making those items

[29] See Merrill and Smith 2001b.

[30] Merrill 2000. ("Servitudes, including easements, profits, and real covenants, all include the right to exclude others from interfering with a particular use of land.")

[31] See Merrill and Smith 2007 (arguing that "[t]he right to exclude directs us to very simple signals of boundary crossing, in a nonreciprocal fashion").

of the external world characteristics or properties, so to speak, of various persons.[32] The trouble, however, is that the connection between particular persons and particular slices of the external world is generally nonobvious. Possession, in the nonlegal sense, is one of the more intuitive ways in which such a connection might be drawn. But while property law borrows from the idea of possession and often attaches normative weight to it, property law nevertheless stands in opposition to possession, almost by definition. A thief in possession must give back what he has stolen. The task property law must accomplish, therefore, is to establish title to external things. And this problem of titling isn't easy.[33]

Second, like the negative character of property duties, the thing-based organization of property law helps to implement the principle of nonoverlapping rights essential to the structure of property law.[34] Insofar as the things of property law are ordinarily delineated in nonoverlapping fashion, property rights are built on a distinct, nonoverlapping conceptual foundation. Finally, Henry Smith and others have suggested numerous ways in which thingness helps to reduce the challenges of communicating and receiving information in property law, as by simplifying the general duties imposed on others (e.g., don't touch, not don't be a pest) and by narrowing the scope of information relevant to different legal actors in various paradigms in which resource use is disputed.[35] In all of these ways, the thing-based structure of property law is important and the right to exclude, properly understood, can help us see it more clearly.

3.1.2 *Three Additional Clarifications*

3.1.2.1 Prohibiting Use, Not Entrance

Notwithstanding accounts of property as "the law of things," things alone are never sufficient to describe the scope of a property right; it is necessary to have some conception of the category of actions bearing the proper relationship to the thing to bring them within the scope of the entitlement. It is also necessary to have an understanding of exceptions to a property-holder's thing-rights,[36] but that's another question besides. Before that issue arises, we must first know what we are excepting from – what actions

[32] See Penner 1997, p. 112 (developing a "separability thesis" about the concept of property).
[33] See Arruñada 2011.
[34] See Arruñada 2011, pp. 20, 30–1, and accompanying text; see also Stern 2017, pp. 1177–80.
[35] See generally Smith 2012.
[36] E.g., privilege of necessity, fair use.

prima facie implicate the property-holder's rights. On this score, unfortunately, the right to exclude isn't very straightforward. What people who refer to the right to exclude are really talking about is one person's right to prohibit another's use of a particular resource, not necessarily to "exclude" that person. The usual meaning of the verb "to exclude" is something like to prevent entry or expel, an essentially spatial concept.[37] In ordinary English, "exclude" isn't a synonym for prevent or prohibit. To be sure, when the asset used to structure a property right is itself defined in spatial terms, there may not be much difference between a right to forbid another's use and the right to forbid another's entry. The way we typically "use" space is by entering it; even if we usually intend to do other things once inside besides merely being present, presence is a precondition. It exaggerates only slightly to say that real property law concerns rights to three-dimensional space, and there are other property assets with a strong spatial aspect as well. The most obvious way to use a car, for instance, is to drive it – and that means getting inside. To that extent, a right to exclude is a sensible way to describe the prohibitory aspects of property-holding.

The trouble, however, is that all sorts of other resources to which the same basic structure of rights applies are not so spatial. The owner of a diamond necklace isn't interested in a right to prevent others from stepping foot within the space the necklace occupies. She is interested in others not wearing the necklace, which is what her right in fact guarantees against. Wearing is easily described as a type of use. It isn't easily described as entry. The point is even clearer with rights to intangible assets. If I purchase a share of corporate stock, or an assignable debt, or, for that matter, a knighthood, I am entitled to demand that others not exercise the prerogatives those rights confer, not to stop anyone from going or being anywhere.[38] Likewise, if I acquire a patent, others may not use or

[37] The Random House Dictionary defines "exclude" to mean:

1. to shut or keep out; prevent the entrance of.
2. to shut out from consideration, privilege, etc.: Employees and their relatives were excluded from participation in the contest.
3. to expel and keep out; thrust out; eject: He was excluded from the club for infractions of the rules.

Random House Dictionary Of The English Language (2nd edn., 1987).
The definition given by Merriam-Webster is:

(1a) to prevent or restrict the entrance of; (1b) to bar from participation, consideration, or inclusion.
(2) to expel or bar especially from a place or position previously occupied.

Merriam Webster's Collegiate Dictionary (10th edn., Merriam-Webster, Inc., 1994).

[38] Cf. Honoré 1960, p. 131, who sees no right to exclude others in a chose in action.

sell the patented invention without my consent, but there is no place they are forbidden to enter. Many lawyers have perhaps become accustomed to the suggestion that a person can be "excluded" from a necklace, however unnatural the expression may be in everyday English. But the risk of confusion is great, and if we are trying to explain a very basic feature of the law, we should be clear about what we really mean: the right to forbid the use of a thing.[39] For assets defined in spatial terms, this translates to the right to forbid the other person to enter within the relevant space. For most other types of assets, however, use means things like touching, deploying, or similar forms of active and direct interaction.

3.1.2.2 Assumptions about Systematicity and Scope

The concept of the right to exclude is highly formal, so much so that it sweeps in a number of entitlements not conventionally thought to be property rights. If A makes a contract with B promising not to set foot on Blackacre, B's legal entitlement by its terms would appear to qualify as a "right to exclude" – even if Blackacre is owned by Z and B is a total stranger to the property, with no claim upon it whatsoever. To go a step further, if C obtains a restraining order barring D from setting foot within 300 yards of the public playground around the corner from her house, it is possible her right against D might also be described as a right to exclude.[40] Indeed, in British legal usage, these are referred to as "exclusion orders."[41] In this sense, the right to exclude transcends any view of property as a closed system, in which rights are classified as property because they are understood as components of a larger branch of law that somehow unites and harmonizes them.[42] It's rather like defining an American telephone number as a string of ten digits. A string of ten digits is only a telephone number when it has been assigned to a particular telephone or group of telephones and incorporated within a larger network that connects other numbers and telephones to it; the number is meaningless outside the context of the system within which it operates. As an account of what property is, the right

[39] Parchomovsky and Stein 2009. ("The right to exclude ... empowers the owner to prevent others from using, occupying, or taking her property.")

[40] Cf. Beckett and Herbert 2010.

[41] See *Chambers Concise Dictionary* 402 (2007). Early appearances of the "right to exclude" in U.S. law most commonly referred not to property but to a sovereign's powers over its borders.

[42] The idea of systematicity here is that any individual property right will be part of a larger system in which rights of other people and over other, similar resources are interrelated. This is somewhat different from the idea of property as a system in the sense of having recurring formal patterns or common institutional strategies for dealing with practical problems. See Smith 2015.

to exclude omits the important way in which property entitlements relate to one another within the confines of a larger system. Rights to exclude may be a key part of any property system, but only some rights to exclude in the literal sense qualify as property rights.

A second and perhaps even more important assumption concerns scope. The right to exclude is often referred to in a kind of abstract, disembodied form, with no reference to who is being excluded or the extent of the exclusion. On its face, the notion of a right to exclude doesn't necessitate a general right to exclude all or most people under all or most circumstances. It isn't at all idiosyncratic to say that having a Red Sox ticket confers the right to watch the Red Sox play baseball, without adding that the ticket doesn't confer the right to watch the team any day, any time, any place. A right to exclude a single person or a right to exclude others only in a limited set of circumstances is still a right to exclude.[43] It is therefore important to guard against the temptation to assume a right to exclude entails a broad scope or an unrestricted domain of exclusion.[44] A right to exclude isn't intrinsically broad in terms of either who may be excluded or the extent of their exclusion.[45]

[43] This understanding appears to be consistent with claims about the right to exclude. In his robust celebration of the right to exclude, for instance, Professor Merrill denied that "property requires a certain quantum of exclusion rights," arguing only that the right to exclude is the measure of property. Merrill 1998, p. 753.

[44] In more recent writings, Merrill has suggested that the right to exclude should be understood as a residual right – a kind of background default that kicks in when more specific exceptions have been exhausted. See Merrill 2014; see also Merrill 2012 (remarking that "what is often loosely described as the 'right to exclude' can be characterized with greater precision as twin rights of residual managerial authority and residual accessionary rights"). This refinement seems to suggest a kind of conceptual breadth, since the unprovided-for category is in some sense infinite. But on further reflection, any categorization is infinite in this way, since the category can absorb an infinite number of members, including new forms that were not contemplated at the time the category was devised. In fact, it is possible to articulate the exception in open-ended terms and the residuum quite specifically – i.e., "Alice has the right to exclude, but everyone except Bob is exempt from it" – in which case it is the exception that seems the more elastic, rather than the default. Cf. Kocourek 1920 (considering case in which "A, a land owner, has granted an easement to every person in the state to walk across his land except to B").

[45] More modestly, we should at least be consistent about our assumptions; it does not do to make one set of claims premised on a broad version of the right to exclude (for example, the gatekeeper thesis discussed in Section 3.4) and another premised on a narrow version (for example, the claim that the right to exclude describes all important property forms, including servitudes and easements).

3.1.2.3 Immunities and Remedies

It has been suggested that the right to exclude is intertwined with protection against nonconsensual divestment, or what are called immunities in the Hohfeldian lexicon.[46] And indeed there might seem to be a certain kind of correspondence between the right to exclude and immunities against termination or transfer. A right to exclude prevents someone else from acting upon a particular resource, while an immunity against divestment prevents someone else from acting upon the right. Of course, property entitlements, including the right to exclude, frequently are subject to involuntary divestment, whether through eminent domain, the satisfaction of judgments and debts, or, arguably, the imposition of new regulations. One might reply, however, that that is just another manifestation of the obvious truth that property rights are bounded; liabilities to divesture simply mark the limits of any right to exclude, no different from a restriction on those whom the holder is entitled to exclude.

But that's the problem. For this very reason, the notion that there is an especially tight connection between the right to exclude and immunity from involuntary termination or transfer doesn't hold up. In actual practice, other aspects of property-holding – the right to use property, for instance – can lay equal claim to protection from involuntary divestment, as indeed can immunities against divestment themselves.[47] The point is a simple one: any right is weakened to the extent others can dissolve or transfer it without the right-holder's consent, especially if those others are the very people legally burdened by the right. In this sense, it isn't terribly remarkable to assert that the right to exclude implies some measure of protection against involuntary divestment. That's true of most, and maybe all, legal rights. There's no special conceptual connection between the right to exclude and immunities against divestiture.

This brings us to the subject of remedies. In their famous article, Guido Calabresi and Douglas Melamed distinguished between different forms of "protection" that might attach to a primary legal right.[48] An entitlement protected by what Calabresi and Melamed called a "property rule" can only be transferred from one party to another if the entitlement-holder consents, while an entitlement protected by a "liability rule" can be transferred from one party to another as long as the party receiving the entitlement

[46] See, e.g., Honoré 1960.

[47] This may seem esoteric but immunities that protect immunities are often the fulcrum of questions involving constitutional protection of property.

[48] Calabresi and Melamed 1972.

compensates the holder for its loss at an objectively determined price. The paradigmatic example of property rule protection is an injunction, while the paradigmatic example of liability rule protection is an award of compensatory damages. Unfortunately, Calabresi and Melamed's property rules are often equated with property rights, with the right to exclude serving as the connection between the two.[49] This is ironic, since Calabresi and Melamed themselves were careful to stress that the particular "view of the Cathedral" they depicted concerned the "second order" decision regarding the "manner in which entitlements are protected," and not the nature of the underlying rights.[50] They were not, in other words, seeking to provide a basis for distinguishing between property and other types of legal rights.[51]

At any rate, the right to exclude should be clearly distinguished from "property rules." The Calabresi and Melamed framework is commonly treated as a way of thinking about remedies problems, but in an important sense, that isn't quite right. Calabresi and Melamed were interested in remedies only insofar as, practically speaking, choices about remedies were the functional equivalent of choices about immunities and liabilities – that is, rules about transferring rights. But as we have just seen, immunity from divestment is conceptually distinct from the right to exclude. The right to exclude doesn't itself require immunity from divestment any more than a right to exclude on Monday requires a right to exclude on Tuesday. Even if it's true that awarding only compensatory damages for rights violations is tantamount to giving the violator a kind of private eminent domain power, such a power isn't incompatible with the right to exclude in a way that would differentiate it from any other sort of private right.

The result is no different if instead we think of remedies as remedies – responses to legal wrongs[52] – rather than as de facto transfer rules.

[49] See Burk 2013 (stating that "we typically speak of property rules as conferring on their holders a right to exclude, and liability rules as conferring on their holders a right to be paid"); Flynn et al. 2008; Sterk 2008.

[50] See Calabresi and Melamed 1972, p. 1092. Indeed, their famous and controversial "Rule 4" proposal arose from the difference between rights and remedies, although admittedly their analysis did considerable violence to the standard concept of a previously specified right, for whose violation the legal remedy is a reaction. See Calabresi and Melamed 1972, pp. 1116–7. Still, the very possibility of combining a determination of "no-right" with a "liability rule" arises from the recognition assignment of the primary right operated independently of the remedial rule used to protected it.

[51] It seems they adopted the term "property rule" simply because they believed property law made heavier use of this form of protection than, say, the liability-based regime of (unintentional) personal injury torts.

[52] Or, in a more broadly, responses to legal misordering.

Conceptually speaking, the right to exclude doesn't demand any particular remedial response. For starters, the right to exclude – for example, a duty not to trespass on land – could still exist perfectly well in a world where no one ever broke the law and thus no remedies were needed. In such a world, the right to exclude would simply determine what obeying the law entails. The right to exclude thus consists at least in part of something other than any remedies that the law might supply. And on further reflection, that is all it entails. Corrective justice and deterrence theories offer reasons to support a general principle of compensation for violations of private rights, at least as a minimum standard for relief. The idea is that one who violates a right should "make whole" the person whose rights have been violated.[53] That concept is no more or less compatible with rights to exclude than any other sort of private right, such as a right to performance of a services contract. To be sure, there may be very good practical reasons to couple exclusion rights with either strong or specific remedies.[54] As a conceptual matter, however, the right to exclude doesn't make any remedial demands that would distinguish it from other legal rights.

3.2 Exclusion Stories

I turn now to several wider accounts of the role played by rights to exclude within the law of property. It seems clear that exclusion is a significant part of property law. All known societies have rules about theft, trespass, and related ideas, and, as I shall argue, even rules governing the *sharing* of property, generally entail exclusion rights. Real questions remain, however, about just how important exclusion rights are to the institution of property and about whether their role is generally beneficial, pernicious, or something else altogether. In this part, I will sketch several prominent claims about the effect of exclusion rights, some of which are positive and some of which are negative. One conclusion is that the stronger arguments about the role of the right to exclude, both for and against, conflate the existence of exclusion rights with the scope and distribution of those rights. More modest arguments centered on what might be thought of as administrative considerations, rather than ideal resource use, provide a clearer explanation of what exclusion rights do.

[53] See Laycock 2010, pp. 14–5.

[54] See Smith 2015. Cf. *eBay Inc. v. MercExchange, L.L.C.*, 547 U.S. 388, 394 (2006).

3.2.1 Exclusion and Gatekeepers

One of the most important arguments about the right to exclude is that it sets up a property-holder as the "gatekeeper" for a particular resource and that this gatekeeper role is key to the effectiveness of property as a legal institution. The form of exclusion, on this view, is linked to the functional advantages of property, and more precisely, of private property. On this view, the right to exclude represents a "delegation" of authority to manage a particular thing; rather than having government officials decide how a resource ought to be used, property law endows private parties with discretion to choose among a broad set of possible uses. This is said to offer a number of practical advantages, including the creation of incentives to invest in the cultivation of resources and the reduction of transaction costs that enable voluntary transfers of legal rights to those who value them more highly.[55]

This may well be a good account of the genius of private property, if genius there be. The trouble, though, is that it doesn't have much to do with the existence of exclusion rights, as opposed to the way they are configured. To the extent the right to exclude confers significant discretion to manage a resource, it is because the right to exclude from that resource has been broadly defined, allowing the exclusion of most or all people, with relatively little qualification in scope – not because it has been defined in terms of boundary-crossing. In principle, the managerial aspect of private property-holding wouldn't be significantly undermined if owners were protected only against actual interference, rather than against unauthorized use of any kind, as long as the law recognized an owner's normative priority in determining how a resource is to be used. Not only that, the discretion imagined by the gatekeeper view also requires that others not have their own rights to exclude, which is to say, it requires privilege-rights of use or the *exclusive* right to exclude. Rights to exclude are ubiquitous in property. When an asset is held in common by everyone in a community, each person within the community will have a right to exclude others for the duration of his or her use, to prevent others from taking more than a certain share of the resource, or a combination of the two.[56] There is no shortage of rights to exclude in the tragic commons,[57] and, even more

[55] See Merrill 2014, p. 10; Fennell 2007 ("The point of exclusion from boundaries is to facilitate the effective matching of inputs with outcomes."); Demsetz 1967.

[56] Within the larger rubric of common property, divisions are drawn in a number of different ways. See generally 20 *Am. Jur.2d Cotenancy & Joint Ownership* §§ 40–41; Allen 2014.

[57] Cf. Fennell 2011.

clearly, in the tragic anti-commons.[58] It is the distribution of rights to exclude, and also of privileges to use, that creates the gatekeeper structure.

And while the gatekeeper story speaks to an important dimension of a private property system, there is much about the operation of property that it omits. Some assets, like rivers and lakes, generally aren't owned in anything the classic Blackstonian sense. Equally, there are types of property rights, like security interests and servitudes, that don't fit the managerial model. Though attempts have been made to shoehorn them into a general gatekeeper theory of property,[59] these rights can be thought to entail "managerial authority" only in the trivial sense that any legal right can be said to confer a measure of decision-making power on its holder.[60] Now it may be that these rights shouldn't be thought of as exclusion rights; I have argued as much.[61] But to the extent property is described as a matter of gatekeeping made possible by the right to exclude, the significance of other property forms raises questions about the overall explanatory force of that narrative. A theory of property that, for instance, omits many of the property-based devices central to capital and credit is decidedly limited.

3.2.2 Exclusion and Information Costs

The right to exclude is also defended on grounds having to do with what could broadly be classified as administrability concerns. In one of the more sophisticated treatments of this idea, Henry Smith has posited a dichotomy between "exclusion" and "governance" within property law. Exclusion is an approach, paradigmatically represented by the right to exclude, in which rights are delineated through the use of proxies – so that, for example, boundary-crossing serves as an approximation for interference with a property-owner's use of land, the real object of the law's protection. Rights are costly to specify, communicate, and understand, and an exclusion strategy seeks to reduce those costs by using simpler variables than those that genuinely matter. Smith also suggests that exclusion entails the bunching together of a relatively wide range of complementary resource

58 See Heller 1998.

59 See, e.g., Merrill 1998, p. 748 (arguing that because the holder of an easement of right of way may obtain an injunction to prevent others from blocking the right of way, "[t]he easement holder thus is given a gatekeeper power with respect to the exercise of his or her limited interest--essentially a right of access").

60 Cf. Stern 2013 (arguing that all rights can be thought of as a species of property, even if they are not themselves property rights).

61 See Stern 2017, pp. 1190–1.

attributes, which is to say, he suggests that exclusion entails broad rights. It isn't simply that boundary-crossing substitutes for interference, but that all or most boundary-crossings will be governed by the same right, held by the same right-holder. From the standpoint of information costs, the logic here is fairly straightforward. If the point is to make it easier to delineate rights, all things being equal, fewer and less jagged boundaries will make delineation easier. Smith's exclusion strategy, then, represents a combination of simplified duties and broad rights. In both respects, the effect is to minimize the extent to which the legal system is called upon to specify individual uses and users as it sets about the task of promoting proper resource use.

This account goes considerably farther than the original gatekeeper story in explaining the right to exclude. First, the use of proxy variables to simplify the task of specifying individual rights does provide a plausible account of how rights to exclude might do some good. This is so even if we redescribe the right to exclude not as a matter of boundary-crossing per se but as the right to forbid a given use of a given resource: use can be thought of as a decent, though imperfect, test for interference. Second, unlike the standard gatekeeper story in which exclusion is about optimizing incentives, Smith's information cost account provides a clearer connection between the right to exclude and relatively bigger and lumpier legal entitlements. To be sure, Smith's argument doesn't establish a formal link between broad rights and rights to exclude. But the view he advocates helps illuminate the intuition that the right to exclude ties in with the advantages of broad rights. Both the right to exclude and the robust Blackstonian vision of undiluted authority are offshoots of the same larger effort to create a simplified system to govern resource use.

3.2.3 *Exclusion and Social Obligation*

This discussion would be incomplete without acknowledging the considerable hostility that the right to exclude generates. Exclusion-centered theories of property have been attacked from various quarters, and while the complaints and perspectives are diverse, the general theme is that the right to exclude is excessively atmostic, individualistic, and antisocial.[62] On this view, the right to exclude leads to a world in which coöperation is suppressed and egoïsm is celebrated, a world of Ayn Rands and Ebenezer

[62] See, e.g., Alexander 2009a.

Scrooges.[63] Exclusionist views of property should be suppressed in service of altruism, generosity, sharing, and consideration of larger social needs.

At one very basic level, this argument is at war with itself. A person can hardly share something that doesn't belong to her; there is nothing generous about giving away someone else's things.[64] True generosity requires something to give away. Further, a regime of what Duncan Kennedy and Frank Michelman call "forced sharing" is likely to entail just as many rights to exclude as one without such obligations.[65] If an asset is held in common by everyone in a community and subject to a regime of mandatory sharing, each person has the right to exclude others either for the duration of his or her use or to prevent others from taking more than their rightful share, or both. When one commoner tells another to "let someone else have a turn," it is a right to exclude that is being asserted. The difference between such a system and a system of conventional private property is qualitative, not quantitative. It lies in the allocation, not the existence, of exclusion rights. What C. B. MacPherson called the "right not to be excluded" isn't the opposite of the right to exclude, as is often supposed, but a way of arguing for a different configuration of exclusion rights.[66] Rights to exclude are ubiquitous, and perhaps even inescapable, in property law.

But the social obligation complaint against the right to exclude isn't so easily dismissed. A subtler version of the critique maintains that a conception of property centered on the right to exclude others undermines an ethos of collaboration and a sense of interdependence. Celebrating the owner's "sole and despotic dominion" evokes an idea in which every man *is* an island entire of itself, and describing the situation in terms of the "right to exclude" seems to go out of its way to stress property's negative consequences for others.[67] Regardless of whether the right to exclude implies broad rights as an analytic matter, the rhetoric of exclusion implies a kind of Blackstonian absolutism and promotes an essentially antisocial outlook.

[63] The right to exclude may also be criticized in this vein as inefficient, to the extent it discourages efficient transfers of property rights or grants rights to exclude that do more social harm than good.

[64] One way in which we know, for instance, that American Indians did have property notions, contrary to popular myth, is that Indian tribes had well-developed practices of gift-giving, which would not be possible without some sense of mine and thine.

[65] See Kennedy and Michelman 1980.

[66] MacPherson 1978, p. 201.

[67] Cf. Rose 1996 (arguing that, "taken to an extreme, the in-your-face rhetoric of property rights can undermine actual institutions of property, suggesting that anything goes, and that the property owner need not care in the least for his fellows").

Perhaps. But it isn't obvious that creating broad rights to exclude concentrated in a single set of hands tends toward a culture of hermits and misanthropes. The language of strong property rights could entail a strong dose of conscience and communal obligation. Just as the right of free speech doesn't mean one should express whatever nasty thought springs to mind, the right to exclude doesn't mean one should ignore the welfare of others. The notion of self-ownership, manifest most obviously in widespread antipathy toward human slavery, happily coexists with the idea that we all bound by a variety of nonlegal obligations to serve one another – the world is full of volunteers. It is difficult to say whether weakening the legal commitment to personal autonomy would bring about more or less generosity of spirit, but it is not difficult to conclude that a substantial degree of generosity to others can survive a legal regime in which individuals are treated as autonomous decision-makers.

A Blackstonian exclusion right can itself be seen as a strategy for coöperation. In a close-knit community, particularly one with a hierarchical structure, the need for hard-and-fast rules about control over resources is less urgently perceived. A monastic order might perhaps do away with property altogether, with the head abbot deciding who does what with what. But in a large and complex society, some measure of decentralization is necessary given the sheer volume of decisions that need to be made and communicated. Specialization and complexity make it more difficult to perceive how individual problems relate to the common good – to take the bird's eye view, so to speak. Not only that, to the extent a large society will tend to be more heterogeneous, there is cause for a more pluralistic institutional regime that allows different people to pursue different ends. What counts as the common good is more attenuated in the face of greater diversity because there is, by definition, less that is common. And if all of this is true, coöperation in a larger and more variegated society may well require clearer boundaries, both because they are necessary to bargaining and negotiation and because it is harder to achieve clarity in the first place. The rules governing a close-knit society can be relatively well comprehended despite their complexity. But in a broader world with interactions among strangers separated from one another along every conceivable matrix – physical, economic, philosophical, social, cultural, you-name-it – it is harder to achieve shared expectations without simplifying the rules that are to be expected. In short, if a coöperative regime is one that enables human players to work well together, it is surely to some extent true that division is sometimes an important part of the story.

A boundary-driven conception of property certainly cannot be ruled out a priori.[68]

One other question about sociability and exclusion is also worth considering. Before we deplore the absence of a sense of interdependence, we should ascertain the nature of the reason we want it in the first place. Is it because we care about a right-holder's mental processes or conscience, or is it instead because we care about the results that flow from collaboration? So long as it is the latter – interdependence as a means to an end, rather than an end in itself – it isn't sufficient to show that the Blackstonian vision of property tends to discourage rights-holders from considering larger social needs in order to condemn it as antisocial. Private property can be understood as a coöperative device, a "strategy" for managing social resources. But it's a regime of specialization and decentralization, in which individual actors do not fully perceive the social function they perform, as Adam Smith famously argued. A group of workers in a car factory could assemble a car working as a team, with everyone having a hand in everything, or they could be divided into specialized functions and operate independently of one another. The latter is less coöperative in the sense that there is less interaction between any given worker and the rest of the production team, but not in the sense that it fails to promote a single common goal of the group. And if the specialization model makes it possible to achieve that common goal more successfully – perhaps simply because the assembly crew would otherwise be at one another's throats – it would seem to facilitate collaboration and the pursuit of collective goods, however unwittingly. In short, if it is actions, rather than consciences, with which we are interested, the social obligation case against Blackstonian-style exclusion is less straightforward than it is often taken to be.

3.3 The Essence of Property

I turn finally to arguments about the centrality of the right to exclude, and especially to the claim forcefully made by Thomas Merrill that the right to exclude is the "sine qua non" of the institution of property. These arguments, I hope to show, do not stand up to scrutiny. While rights to exclude

[68] Other more sociological arguments can be made for Blackstonian, or classically liberal, systems of private right as systems of social integration. Private rights, including property, may encourage attitudes of tolerance. They may enable coöperation between those of sharply divergent outlook and opinion. Cf. Oman 2017; Rose 1992. And, to the extent they tend toward greater aggregate social wealth, they may diminish the likelihood of war and unrest.

are an important element of private, common, and public property, they are only that – an element. Property law is better understood in terms of control or dominion than exclusion.

3.3.1 Exclusion Imperialism

In his influential essay on the right to exclude, Merrill argues that the right to exclude is, quite simply, the measure of property: "To the extent one has the right to exclude, then one has property; conversely, to the extent one does not have exclusion rights, one does not have property."[69] In his view, although other rights like the right to use a resource and to transfer rights in it to others are important, only the right to exclude can be considered "essential" to property. The right to exclude does play a large role in property law, and for this reason, his celebration of exclusion has a certain plausibility. The arguments offered to support its unique primacy, however, do not hold up and to some extent contradict each other.

The principal argument Merrill makes for the centrality of the right to exclude is that, he claims, other rights associated with property like the right to use a resource can be logically derived from the right to exclude but not vice versa.[70] In his telling, the right to exclude generates a right to use because the right-holder can selectively choose not to exclude others and thereby determine how a resource is used. He argues, however, that the right to exclude cannot similarly be derived from the right to use, since we can readily imagine being allowed to use property – that is, having privilege-rights of use – without having the right to prevent use by others.[71]

This is a neat argument but it rests on a false comparison.[72] Merrill's formal derivation of the right to use from the right to exclude implicitly defines

[69] Merrill 1998, p. 753.

[70] A similar claim is made by Simon Douglas and Ben McFarlane. They argue that because a nonowner of a resource owes no duties to refrain from using it to anyone other than the owner, the owner's privilege-right to use the resource is analytically no different than the privilege-rights of anybody else and therefore have nothing to do with having a property right in the resource. See Douglas and McFarlane 2013, pp. 223–6. But that difference – a privilege that means no duties are owed to anyone but the owner and a privilege that means no duties are owed to anyone, full-stop – is obviously critical. It's cold comfort not to be liable for trespass to A when one is liable for trespass to B. See also Section 3.5.1.

[71] See Merrill 1998, p. 744.

[72] Even if Merrill were correct that the right to exclude is the source material from which other property rights are constructed, the suggestion that this establishes the "primacy" of the right to exclude is problematic. Other theorists of property assert the primacy of the right to use property in the sense that it supplies the purpose for having the right to exclude. Both camps might well agree that the right to exclude is the means to secure the right to use,

the right to use only in terms of allowing *others* to use an asset in ways acceptable to the property-holder. For purposes of this argument, he leaves out any right of the property-holder to do anything herself. It is, after all, a bit strange and probably inaccurate to speak of the property-holder having the right to exclude herself, which she waives when she farms her land or reads her book or spends her money. But notice that when Merrill explains why the right to exclude cannot be derived from the right to use, he imagines the right to use *only* in terms of use of the property by the property-holder herself, leaving out use by others. That, however, is the one right he couldn't account for in his use-comes-from-exclusion narrative. If Merrill defined the right to use more broadly to encompass the right to determine how others use a given resource – the way he defines the right to use when he concludes that it can be derived from the right to exclude – it would be obvious that the right to exclude can be derived from the right to use in just the same way Merrill derives the right to use from the right to exclude.

Merrill argues the right to transfer can be deduced from the right to exclude because a transfer is simply a form of self-exclusion. The present owner of a resource can decline to exclude the transferee but choose to exclude everyone else, including herself. This argument gets as far as it does because Merrill has already assumed that the right to exclude includes the right not to exclude, which is to say, the power to waive the right. But if we think of that power as something separate that is combined with the right to exclude, the derivation argument dies aborning. It's not hard to imagine a situation in which the right to exclude doesn't result in its holder being able to "include" a transferee. It is certainly conceivable that property law could establish a form of co-ownership in which each co-owner had an independent right to exclude outsiders. In such an arrangement, a co-owner wouldn't be able to transfer his own rights in the property simply by declining to exercise his right to exclude.[73]

In addition, it is hard to see how the right to exclude itself implies that its exercises should be irrevocable such that the transferor could not

its ultimate end. One can say that ends derive from means because the ends would not be achieved without the means. One can equally say that means derive from ends because the means would not be undertaken but for a desire to bring about the ends that result from them. Primacy, then, isn't a useful term here because it is argumentative. There are multiple senses in which the term might be used, and those senses essentially track the ultimate conclusion to be reached. By contrast, Penner's account of exclusion as the "formal essence" of property, to be distinguished from the normative interest it serves, is preferable because it is neutral on the question whether ends or means, substance or form, is primary.

[73] While this is not the default arrangement in co-tenancy situations, it can be established by agreement, and in any event, it is certainly possible as a conceptual matter.

suddenly decide to start excluding the transferee. A right to exclude at Time 1 stands in opposition to a right to exclude at Time 2, and the concept of the right to exclude cannot tell us which of the two takes precedence over the other. A theory of property that can account for transfers only to the extent they are revocable clearly misses something essential. Nor is it apparent how the transferee of property himself acquires the power to transfer it to others. One may say that the original transferor has actually decided not to exclude whomever the transferee decides to include and to exclude whomever the transferee decides to exclude, but this is more than a little bit elaborate and doesn't seem to capture the nature of the power to transfer as an attribute of property-holding equal in stature, rather than subordinate, to the right to determine present uses. It's certainly very difficult to see how the power to *acquire* property – for example, the power to appropriate unowned things and make them one's own – can be derived from the right to exclude, since there can be no rights to exclude without the power to acquire them in the first place. The power to acquire is in many ways the mirror image of the power to alienate, and it seems much more straightforward to think of the power to acquire and the power to alienate as bearing essentially the same relationship to the right to exclude. They establish its beginning and end; neither one is a byproduct of it.

Merrill also argues for the essential status of the right to exclude on what he calls historical grounds, by which he means that "the right to exclude is the first right to emerge in primitive property rights systems."[74] At the outset, we might question the premise of the argument. A tadpole is certainly no more the essence of a frog than, well, a frog. Many human creations were established or significantly developed for military purposes – airplanes, the Internet, the US interstate highway system – but while those military functions continue, we wouldn't consider them the essence of any of those projects.

At any rate, the lessons Merrill draws from the historical record are questionable. The earliest form of property in land, he tells us, was likely the usufruct, and the hallmark of the usufruct is the right to exclude others. Members of nomadic tribes planted crops in parcels farmed exclusively by a particular tribe member, but the tribe member's rights were

[74] See Merrill 1998, p. 745.

limited, lasting only so long as the land was being used for farming. Tribe members had no general rights against trespassing.

The "usufruct" is a term from Roman law, and the situation imagined in Merrill's essay isn't a usufruct in the classical sense, which referred to rights to use and obtain the fruits from property owned by someone else – something like a profit – rather than a sort of enclosure of formerly common land.[75] I note this not to be technical or pedantic but to call attention to other ways of thinking about the situation. Merrill assumes the key feature of the usufructuary arrangement is the right to exclude others, but if what the usufruct does is to give access to resources within someone else's control, the right to use – the right to commit what would otherwise be trespass or theft – is at least as salient as any right of exclusion.

What the rights Merrill discusses effectuate thus depends on our assumptions about the background state of affairs before its institution: is it a regime of open access or a regime of general exclusion? And in primitive conditions, it isn't obvious that the significance of property norms lies primarily in the right to exclude others as opposed to a right not to be excluded. A usufruct might well constrain the chieftain or warlord who could otherwise have claimed everything for himself, and in this sense, the use aspect of the right could be far more significant than any right to exclude. It's worth remembering that the system of fee tenancy undergirding Anglo-American land law emerged of what were originally essentially licenses to use lands belonging to manorial lords – and ultimately the crown – rather than a situation in which all was held in common.[76] Fee ownership, in other words, was less about requiring others to stay out than about giving the fee-holder a right to enter and use. I suggested earlier that rights to exclude may be the *conceptual* starting point for a property system, but in doing so I cautioned that this should not be taken to mean that privilege-rights to use resources are outside a property system where one operates. The establishment of property transforms the character of the preexisting natural liberty to use things by bringing them within the property system. If that is correct, property rights entitling individuals to use propertized resources come into being at least as early as property rights entitling individuals to prevent use by others.

[75] See Institutes 2.4.pr. ("Ususfructusestiusalienis rebus utendifruendisalvarerum substantia.") ("Usufruct is the right to the use and fruits of another person's things so long as the substance of the things is preserved.") See also Institutes 2.4.1.

[76] See Dukeminier et al. 2010, pp. 209–10, 215–8.

3.3.2 *Control, Not Exclusion, as Property's Central Idea*

Arguments about the centrality of the right to exclude have a kind of superficial plausibility because other attributes of property-holding are indeed related to that right. Claims that these other attributes can be derived from the right to exclude draw upon resemblances between these elements in order to claim that exclusion is the parent concept. But the reality, I will argue, is that exclusion is a sibling, not a parent. The similarities that bring together exclusion, use, and alienation all derive from another, larger idea, not reflected in any of these more specific jural elements. The idea is an old one. It is that of dominion, or more colloquially, control. Property is formally analogous to a kind of jurisdiction, a position of normatively-binding decision-making over a defined subject-matter.[77]

The basis for this conclusion is very simple. The right to prohibit various uses of a thing is an aspect of the concept of being able to control its use. So is the right to use it. Those ideas are subsumed within the idea of control, and frankly it seems there is little else to be said by way of affirmative argument. But the point can be advanced somewhat further, I think, by focusing on some of the deficiencies of an exclusion theory of property, in which the right to exclude is viewed as the lynchpin of how property works.

First, framing property in terms of the right to exclude is not only confusing but it tends to provoke unnecessary hostility. It is confusing because exclusion in many cases is a very poor description of what a property-holder's prohibitory right entails.[78] It provokes hostility because it suggests that the essence of property lies in saying "no" to people, rather than in making yes-or-no decisions.[79]

Second, a view of property centered on the right to exclude has trouble accounting for property rights other than present ownership. It is hard to find any right to exclude in a mortgage, for instance. While Merrill argues that a mortgage represents a kind of contingent or future right to exclude, that often isn't really true; a mortgagee may have a right to sale but not to ownership. In any event, it isn't the content of the future rights that gives them their proprietary quality, but rather the priority of the mortgage over other claims to the mortgaged property. It's difficult to see how the right to exclude has much to do with an affirmative easement or servitude,

[77] Unlike most political jurisdiction, however, this power can be exercised in a more clearly self-interested fashion. Cf. Ripstein 2017.

[78] See Sections 3.1.1.1 and 3.1.2.1.

[79] Cf. Section 3.2.3.

whether in the form of a privilege-right enabling the holder of the dominant tenement to do something he would otherwise be prohibited from doing or a claim-right requiring the holder of the servient tenement to do something she otherwise would not have to, such as pay money.[80] In the case of a right-of-way, the law may provide rights against interfering with its exercise, but the right to exclude is about boundary-crossing, not interference in some generic, free-floating sense,[81] and it isn't essential to such privileges that there even be protection against interference anyway.[82] Doctrinally, moreover, the difference between an easement and a license is generally treated as a matter of revocability and termination (including by transfer – i.e., "running with the land"). A right to exclude is still a right to exclude, however, even if it doesn't survive transfer.[83]

Third, at a more general level, framing property in terms of the right to exclude tends to denigrate the status of other formal components of property rights, most obviously the right to use a resource. Takings doctrine in US constitutional law, for instance, purports to treat any diminishment of the right to exclude as an automatic taking, while reserving this treatment for only the most extreme curtailments of a property-holder's use-rights.[84] These doctrinal pronouncements cannot be squared with reality, however. To offer just one glaring example, public accommodations laws rather significantly reduce an owner's right to exclude but are not treated as takings.[85] Even so, a vast discrepancy remains between constitutional constraints on exclusion restrictions, on the one hand, and use restrictions, on the other. No justification for this gap has been offered, other than assertions of the "treasured" status of the right to exclude.

Fourth, the exclusion perspective omits other institutional features of property law, such as systematicity and priority of claims against others. Property law supposes a system of mutually exclusive entitlements; it

80 But see Merrill 1998, p. 744.

81 It is a little strange to describe one person's right that the owner-occupier of a given piece of land not interfere with that person's access right or not engage in certain uses of the property as a right to exclude.

82 See, e.g., *Matera Investors, Inc.* v. *Sunset Lake Fishing and Hunting Club*, 696 F. Supp.1510 (M.D. Ga. 1988); *Mikesh* v. *Peters*, 284 N.W.2d 215, 216–19 (Iowa 1979); *Gearns* v. *Baker*, L.R. 10 Ch. 355, 357 (Ch.App. 1875).

83 At some point, of course, revocability may undermine the suggestion that there's any right there in the first place. It does not do so automatically, however. An at-will employee, for instance, may not have any legal basis to challenge a dismissal, but unless and until an actual dismissal occurs, there is a very real legal relationship at play.

84 Compare *Loretto* v. *Teleprompter Manhattan CATV Corp.*, 458 U.S. 419 (1982) with *Tahoe-Sierra Preservation Council, Inc.* v. *Tahoe Regional Planning Agency*, 535 U.S. 302 (2002).

85 See Heart of *Atlanta Motel, Inc.* v. *United States*, 379 U.S. 241, 258 (1964); *Pruneyard Shopping Center* v. *Robins*, 447 U.S. 74 (1980). See also *United States* v. *Causby*, 328 U.S. 256 (1946).

divides the world into distinct, nonoverlapping things and allocates rights in each individual thing so as to avoid giving different people separate, incompatible ownerships (or other legal rights) of the same resource.[86] This view of property understands each right in a given thing to be part of a complete whole, and each whole to be part of a larger system of rights over things generally. It stresses a view of property as a system of rights that relate to one another. A perspective centered on the right to exclude, by contrast, tends to regard property simply as a collection of entitlements with certain formal features. One result noted earlier is that the right to exclude struggles to distinguish between rights generated by property law and rights arising from some other body of legal rules, so long as they can be characterized as rights to prohibit using something. Another is that the right to exclude simply overlooks the role of priority and titling within property, making it hard to understand the property dimensions of complex systems ranging from water law to security interests to ownership of intangible choses in action. The concept of priority is a critical part of property law – arguably, indeed, a conceptual lynchpin – but the right to exclude doesn't speak to priority.

Finally, and perhaps most importantly, the exclusion perspective leads to misunderstanding because the idea of the right to exclude itself rests on an artificial dichotomy between use, on the one hand, and exclusion, on the other. It is generally a point of agreement among advocates of an exclusion-centered view of property that property – and, critically, the right to exclude – exists to serve interests in the use of resources, and the problem with the use/exclusion distinction comes out most clearly in considering this idea. Suppose, for example, George owns a vacant lot, which he has no intention of using for anything now or in the foreseeable future. And suppose a neo-Nazi group wants to hold a rally on George's lot. George is vehemently opposed to the neo-Nazi group and would like to do all he reasonably can to prevent their rally from taking place. In particular, he wants to deny them the use of his lot. George has no interest in *using* his lot himself or in letting anyone else use it. The only thing he wants is for the neo-Nazis not to use it. As the owner of the lot, George does indeed have the right to exclude the group from using the lot, but that right isn't grounded in his interest in use. George has an interest in exclusion itself. If property rights are indeed defined and justified as a means to help individuals

[86] See generally Stern 2017.

realize their purposes with respect to particular resources, then the purpose at issue is quite simply a purpose to exclude.[87]

The difference between use and exclusion depends on an artificial narrowing of the concept of use such that deciding what happens to a thing somehow fails to encompass deciding what does not happen to it. Since every state necessarily precludes its opposite, a clear distinction between deciding how a thing should be used and deciding how it should not be used is highly unstable. What is the difference between an interest I might have in exclusion "for its own sake" and an interest in exclusion because, like Greta Garbo, I want to be alone?[88] The idea that property is grounded in an interest in use is attractive and consistent with some very basic cases, but its promise is ultimately false as a way of understanding property more generally. It is plausible to speak of an interest in operating a clinic for alcoholics that is distinct from a derivative interest in excluding someone else from setting up a bar on the premises. But it is not possible to speak of an interest in making money from the sale of a good that is separate from and antecedent to an interest in excluding others. The interest is, quite simply, an interest in excluding those who are unwilling to pay a stated price and in not excluding those who are willing to pay it. Exclusion is intrinsic to the interest.

The problems I have outlined here arise out of the bifurcation of the right to determine the acceptable uses of a resource into privilege-rights to use and claim-rights to exclude. While the distinction between the two can sometimes be useful, it gives a skewed view of property law when taken as a general statement of what property is all about or how it works. By contrast, the idea of control unites these two ideas in a unified conceptual

[87] Cf. Smith 2009. ("No one except a fetishist would believe that exclusion is a positive good.")

[88] Penner attempts to grapple with this question, suggesting that "use" should be understood in a broader sense to refer to "a disposition one can make of something that is purposeful and can be interfered with by others." See Penner 1997, p. 70. Use therefore need not be a state of constant activity; I am using the clothes in my closet, the money in my bank account, or the land that I've left in a natural state for the sake of wildlife. But, he says, "[n]o one has any interest in merely excluding others from things, for any reason and no reason at all." Penner 1997 What does it meant to exclude someone "for no reason"? Does simply desiring to exclude the person or being happier if the person is excluded count as a reason? What about flexing one's muscles and feeling powerful? What about simply preferring a respite from labor, development, and toil, even by others? Cf. Melville. ("I would prefer not to.") Penner wishes to distinguish between an interest in determining the disposition of a thing and the denial of access to the thing by others, but the question is why denial of access isn't a disposition. For Penner, the answer appears to be that denial of access ceases to be a disposition when it isn't supported by the right kind of reasons. In the end, therefore, it seems to be a simple normative or moral judgment that drives the distinction, not an analytical one.

whole and provides a more durable and a more accurate picture of the conceptual heart of property law.

3.4 Conclusion

The title of this chapter contains a deliberate ambiguity. In part, the intention has been to summarize and evaluate current thinking about why the right to exclude matters – that is, in what ways, good and bad, the right to exclude should be thought of as important to the law of property. In doing so, however, this chapter has also sought to show how different assumptions about what the right to exclude means affect those conclusions. Unless and until we are clear and consistent in defining the right to exclude, we will be unable to reach clear judgments about its place within the larger institution of property. The right to exclude is more precisely understood as a matter of rights to prohibit use of a resource by others, a proposition with several important formal elements that tell us a good deal about what property is and what it isn't. The right to exclude is easily misunderstood and manipulated, and it is critical to keep a clear focus on what its constituent elements are – including the significance of boundaries in defining the content of duties property imposes on others and the essential point that the right to exclude need not be broad in scope or relatively unqualified.

In teasing out these formal features, we have briefly considered some arguments about the normative attractiveness of the right to exclude. The right to exclude can plausibly be explained as a response to high information costs and the need to simplify legal structures beyond what might be ideal in the absence of administrative or institutional considerations. When it comes both to praise and criticism of the right to exclude, important strands of argument tend to confuse the form of exclusion with the breadth of property rights. We have also considered the claim that the right to exclude is the essence of property. Though the arguments advanced in support of this position are flawed, they have considerable force because the phenomenon rights to exclude are important to property and closely related to other critical elements. Ultimately, however, property is a matter of control over individual resources, and separating exclusion from the larger concept of control out of which it derives distorts our understanding of property.

4

Using Things, Defining Property

CHRISTOPHER M. NEWMAN

Property is not just exclusion, and exclusion is not an end in itself.[1] Property protects a particular sort of interest that people have in being spared the interference of others in their attempts to make a life for themselves. It transforms the indefinite, impossible-to-obey maxim "don't interfere with other people's life plans" into a set of bounded principles that people can actually follow. It does this by identifying places where people's preferred ends are likely to collide, specifying ways to allocate priorities among those ends, and providing rules that define and limit the obligations we all take on to avoid interfering with those ends to which priority has been assigned. Loci of likely conflict are "things." The actions that a given individual wishes to take with respect to such a locus are "uses." The status of priority given to one person's desired uses is an "interest."[2] Property is born

Besides the editors and contributors to this volume (in particular James Penner), I would like to thank Eric Claeys and Henry Smith for helpful comments.

1 While they differ in various respects both from each other and from me, there have by now been numerous formulations of the core idea that exclusion is not the end of property but an instrument toward the end of vindicating an interest in use. See, e.g., Claeys 2009 (defining property as a "right to determine exclusively how a thing may be used"); Katz 2008 (arguing that the "central concern" of the structure of property ownership "is not the exclusion of all non-owners from the owned thing but, rather, the preservation of the owner's position as the exclusive agenda setter for the owned thing"); Mossoff 2003 ("It is not exclusion that is fundamental in understanding property; the fountainhead of property is found in possession, i.e., the use of something, and it is this fact that serves as the primary element in the concept property."); Penner 1996 (defining the right to property as "the right to determine the use or disposition of an alienable thing in so far as that can be achieved or aided by others excluding themselves from it"); Alchian 1965. ("By a system of property rights I mean a method of assigning to particular individuals the 'authority' to select, for specific goods, any use from a nonprohibited class of uses.")

2 By "interest" in this context I mean a justifiable claim to regard the use of something as a component of one's well being in a manner that others should respect. Thus I view the existence of some interest as a prerequisite for the recognition of a right, along the lines of Raz's discussion of the relation between the two. See Raz 1986, pp. 165–83. As the text indicates, the respect called for might take various forms and be reflected in various combinations of positive jural relations that could then be termed "interests" in the legal sense. Arguments as to precisely what renders a claim of interest justified are beyond the scope of this paper. My

when someone is recognized as having an interest in using a thing that others are obliged to take into account in some fashion.

We tend to fixate on one salient way of taking such an interest into account – categorical self-exclusion from the thing in question. But not all interests in use are comprehensive enough to require such drastic measures. Not all uses of the same thing ineluctably collide, and not all would-be users have persuasive justifications for laying claim to priority in all possible uses of a given thing. Some property interests confer priority for only a narrow set of uses, and all that is required to respect them is tailored noninterference with those uses rather than wholesale exclusion from the thing. There is only one form of recognition that all use-interests necessarily require of us: renunciation of standing to prescribe what the interest-holder does within his sphere of priority. To put it in Hohfeldian terms, privilege is as fundamental as right.[3] It is true that, absent any right of noninterference, my ability to exercise a use-privilege will often be vulnerable to hindrances from others. Nevertheless, the use-privilege relieves me of the most immediate barrier to purposeful action: It means I need not preemptively hinder myself.

I shall develop the above contentions concerning the nature of property by engaging with three lines of thought that cut against them. The first two appear in Simon Douglas and Ben McFarlane's paper, "Defining Property Rights."[4] They begin by using Hohfeldian analysis to reach the conclusion that the idea of a use-privilege is inadequate to define anything distinctive about the nature of property law, leaving the right to exclude others from a physical thing as the only distinctive entitlement that property confers on owners. Second, they use various examples from case law to argue that property doctrine does not in fact protect any interest in the use of property, but only an interest in excluding others from it, so that "the structure of property law can be understood without examining the positive uses that A may make of A's thing."[5]

Both strands of Douglas and McFarlane's argument assume the concept of "thing" to be stable and merely seek to establish that exclusion from things, rather than use of them, is the organizing principle of property law. A distinct though closely related question is whether the notion of

key claim is that interests ground privileges as well as rights, and that indeed it is the nature of the privilege that determines the scope of the right.

[3] For definitions of the Hohfeldian terms "privilege" and "right," see Hohfeld 1913–14.

[4] Douglas and McFarlane 2013.

[5] Douglas and McFarlane 2013, p. 223.

"thing" in property should be expanded as far as I have just done above. James Penner argued in "The Idea of Property in Law," for example, that intellectual property should not be conceived of as a property right in an intangible thing, but merely as a monopoly over defined classes of activity.[6] Christopher Essert has recently gone further, suggesting that things be dropped from the concept of property altogether, so that all property rights are conceived of as unmediated exclusive rights to control activity.[7] I shall attempt to steer between these positions. I argue, on one hand, that the concept of "thing" within the context of property is coherently broader than that of "physical object." On the other, I argue that the identification of some discrete "thing" as an object of property provides a necessary focal point for the concepts of use and interest that are both functionally and normatively essential to property as a human institution.

4.1 A Use-Centric Account of the Structure of Property

We are used to thinking of property as a right to exclude and use-privileges as incidental by-products of that right. I want to sketch a different approach, one that treats use-privileges as prior and then asks what sorts of rights might be justified in their support. I shall define property as a legal interest that people have in the use of a thing. Any property interest will at minimum identify a thing and some class of activities with respect to it that the owner has a privilege to engage in. Borrowing from Essert, I shall denote this class of activities "ϕ."[8] The scope of ϕ may be fairly narrow as compared to the universe of possible actions that might be taken with respect to the thing, as in a privilege to traverse a given forest, to gather fruit from its trees, or to draw off a certain amount of water from a river flow. We usually call these narrower claims "usufructory," and such claims generally pertain to things (land, rivers) that are potentially susceptible of numerous non-conflicting uses, such that to engage in my privileged use need not displace most others.

On the other hand, the scope of ϕ may be very broad, consisting of every possible action having the thing as object. Such claims are "possessory," in that they assert a privilege, either to engage in activities that by their nature practically displace all other uses, or else to select and engage in

[6] Penner 1997, p. 118.
[7] Essert 2014.
[8] See Essert 2014, p. 579.

any conceivable usufructuary activity at will from moment to moment, regardless of whether it displaces or conflicts with any uses others may wish to make. I have referred to this sort of privilege – the kind associated with outright ownership of a chattel or fee simple ownership of land – as a "sovereign use-privilege."[9] This privilege is part of what enables the possessory owner to act as, in Larissa Katz's phrase, "supreme agenda setter" for the owned thing,[10] and it negates, not only the duty to refrain from using the owned thing, but also the duty to use it in any particular way, or at all. To fully and effectively set the agenda of course, one will need not merely a possessory use-privilege, but an accompanying right as well. The sovereign use-privilege alone entitles one to disregard others' attempts at use, but not to require that they desist. Whether usufructuary or possessory, a privilege to use a thing is an "ownership" interest if it is protected by robust immunity from unilateral divestment by others.[11]

Conceptual discussion of property tends to focus on ownership of possessory claims accompanied by robust rights to exclude as the paradigm, with usufructuary claims treated as anomalous exceptions, or carve outs, to the possessory holdings of others.[12] In fact, the two sorts of interests are pervasively interpenetrative, and there is no reason why usufructuary holdings may not precede and exist independently of, as well as be superseding to, the later-arising possessory claims pertaining to the same thing. It seems to me that much could be gained from conceiving of them more coequally. While there are good reasons for possession and exclusion to be the predominant strategy for resolving use conflicts in many (and perhaps most) contexts, there are also many problems that are better solved through usufructuary regimes, and it is unfortunate that these are sometimes misconceived as alternatives to "property," rather than different forms of it. Either approach involves the same basic questions: Under what circumstances does a person acquire an interest in use of a thing that others should justly take into account? How broad is the scope of that interest and how much burden does it justify placing on others? What set of institutions and norms permits people to recognize, comply with, and enforce just claims?

[9] See Newman 2017.

[10] Katz 2008, p. 292. Of course, to effectively set the agenda for a thing one needs rights as well as privileges.

[11] See Newman.

[12] This can be discerned to some extent in some of the various definitions quoted in footnote 1.

4.2 The Analytical Argument against Use-Privileges as Defining Attributes of Property

While it is not the main thrust of their piece, Douglas and McFarlane offer an analytical argument as to why an owner's interest in use cannot be seen as the distinctive feature of property. The argument proceeds as follows: If A is sole owner of a car, she has a use-privilege vis-à-vis B, which means that she owes no duty to B to refrain from using the car.[13] A has the same use-privilege vis-à-vis C, D, and every other person in the world. Douglas and McFarlane note, however, that X too owes no duty to B to refrain from using A's car, and that this privilege of X's also holds good against C, D, and every other person in the world except for A. They further state that "[i]n its content, X's liberty against B is identical to A's liberty against B."[14] It follows that this privilege cannot be what renders A's relationship to the car distinct. What makes A's relationship to the car distinct – the only thing that makes it distinct – is A's "right to exclude," which is to say, the fact that everyone else owes A the duty of refraining from use of the car. No-one other than A has a claim-right forbidding use of the car, and while everyone else is equally bound by the corresponding duty, they owe that duty to A and A alone.

I wish to contest the analytical claim that A's and X's respective privileges against B are "identical in content." As a first step, we need to specify what sorts of information count as part of the "content" in question. One way of making this claim would be to limit the relevant "content" of each privilege to nothing more than the extension "absence of duty [owed to some person] to refrain from using A's car." Hohfeld himself can seemingly be enlisted in support of this approach. At one point he asks us to consider the case in which A is owner of Blackacre, and has also entered into a contract with B in which B promises never to enter Whiteacre, which is owned by X. Hohfeld asserts that A's right that B not enter Blackacre and A's right that B not enter Whiteacre are, "intrinsically considered, of the same general character," in that each can be described as imposing a duty on B to exclude himself from some piece of land.[15]

[13] Douglas and McFarlane 2013, pp. 220–1. They use the term "liberty." I stick with Hohfeld's term "privilege," in part for reasons mentioned below.

[14] Douglas and McFarlane 2013, p. 221.

[15] Hohfeld 1916–17 (emphasis in original). Douglas and McFarlane's claim that the two privileges they compare are "identical in content" sounds even stronger than Hohfeld's claim that his two duties are "of the same general character." The difference could be simply that Hohfeld's two duties pertain to different pieces of land, or it could be that Hohfeld is actually making a weaker claim.

James Penner has criticized Hohfeld for this, on the ground that one cannot understand a right or duty without describing its place "within a pre-existing normative framework[.]"[16] The concern is that by ignoring the distinction between property and contract one loses sight of the practical reasons for complying with a duty.[17] A closely related objection is that, while this level of granularity is useful for describing the operative content of one's duty as applied in a given context, it does not capture the level on which people actually apprehend and make sense of their duties. If adhered to, this granular level of description results in a cognitively unwieldy list of discrete duties (e.g., "do not enter Whiteacre; do not enter Blackacre; do not use this car; do not use that car ...") whose logical interrelations are obscure, and which constantly wink into and out of existence along with changes in contingent investitive facts about the world.[18] In practice, we do not walk around with open-ended laundry lists of discrete rights and duties in our heads, but with descriptions of those relations couched at a higher level of abstraction – ones that both indicate a relation's place in the normative framework and permit us to derive the practical implications of that relation in a given concrete context. In choosing how to define the content of a Hohfeldian relation, it is thus necessary to decide which level of abstraction best serves the purposes of the analysis, and Hohfeld can be criticized for a tendency to insist that anything not captured at the lowest level of analytic specification is superfluous and misleading.[19]

While Douglas and McFarlane do not directly address this question as to the proper level of abstraction at which to define a Hohfeldian right or duty, their argument does not appear to hinge on adherence to the lowest level, at which A's and X's privileges are identical purely because their content consists of "I owe [someone] no duty to refrain from use of this car." Indeed, to take this position would undermine their argument. If this were the "identical content" of A's and X's privileges that renders the use-privilege inadequate as a defining feature of property, one could cite Hohfeld's example of a contract-based right-to-exclude as similarly rendering nondistinctive the property owner's own such right. Instead, Douglas and McFarlane provide an account of the two privileges that treats them as contextual applications of a single principle identified at a higher level of normative abstraction. In their view, A's privilege of ignoring B's use-preferences with

[16] Penner 1996.
[17] Penner 1996.
[18] For a lengthier discussion of this problem with Hohfeld, see Newman 2018.
[19] Newman 2018.

regard to the car is merely an instance of a broader privilege shared by A, X, C, D, and everyone else. As they put it, "A's liberties in relation to a particular thing derive simply from the general proposition (prior to and broader than property law) that any action of A is permitted if not wrongful."[20]

I think this conception of Hohfeldian privilege is mistaken. In this account, privilege is implicitly seen as the undifferentiated background space not currently occupied by duties, a residual state of affairs with no affirmative normative force or inertia. Duties are imagined as objects, while privilege is just space, and any expanse of space (whether A's or X's, and whatever objects one describes it in reference to) is equivalent to any other. But privilege as Hohfeld defined it was not the absence of a duty, but the opposite – the negation – of one: "'The privilege of entering is the negation of a duty to stay off."[21] Logically speaking, duty and privilege are each the negation of the other, and it would be equally valid to imagine duty as the undifferentiated background default space, with privileges being affirmative objects sometimes used to displace or negate it.[22] One could, in other words, point to a general proposition (also prior to and broader than property law) to the effect that "any action of A is enjoined if not privileged."

It would be better, however, to treat neither duty nor privilege as a default background space, but rather to treat both duties and privileges as objects subject to principled definition whose boundaries demarcate both their own limits and those of their opposites. While it is often convenient to define the static limits of a privilege by saying, as do Douglas and McFarlane, that it does not include "wrongful" acts (as in, "you have freedom of speech, except for defamation"), the dialectic can run the other way – sometimes we delimit a category of action identified as "wrongful" by excluding from it types of activity that we regard as privileged (as in, "you must not defame someone, unless you are providing truthful information to someone with a valid interest in it"). Either way we are describing the same boundary line, but our choice of definitional strategy in a given case may depend on which approach to it offers more intuitive normative clarity. Instead of extrapolating the precise point at which the outer limits of some principle of "wrongfulness" finally peter out, it may be easier to identify areas where any residuum of wrongfulness is clearly outweighed by the countervailing interest in some type of autonomous activity.

20 Douglas and McFarlane 2013, p. 223.

21 Hohfeld 1913–14, p. 32.

22 This, indeed, is how state licensing regimes function – by prohibiting entire classes of activity as a default matter unless the actor has obtained permission to engage in them.

A privilege, then, is not merely the absence of a duty, but an interest having coequal affirmative force and existential inertia. The extent to which, and circumstances in which, either privilege or duty may make dynamic inroads into the other depend upon the relevant configuration of liabilities and immunities, which in turn define the powers and disabilities of legal actors to alter existing relations. The immunities that accompany various privileges may be more or less robust; privileges associated with constitutionally recognized liberty interests (such as freedom of speech), tend to be protected by robust ones that repel or limit most attempts to replace the privilege with a duty.

How, then, to define the content of a privilege? Douglas and McFarlane reconcile Hohfeldian analysis with the thing-centric nature of property by emphasizing that even though Hohfeld calls for focus on right/duty relations between persons as opposed to any "right to a thing," this does not preclude the possibility that "the content of those rights may be defined by reference to a thing."[23] The same is true of privileges. Indeed, I would claim that in practice both duties and privileges are always defined by reference to things. Duties and privileges each define an actor's legal status with regard to some action. As a practical matter, any action necessarily involves things as both subjects and objects, and these things are the necessary (if sometimes implicit) markers we use to distinguish one action from another. An action is always done with something (at minimum, the actor's person), and it is usually done to something as well.

To speak of a privilege merely in terms of "negation of duty" is insufficiently precise. Just as one cannot adequately describe a duty without providing some definition that allows us to determine the scope of the actions it enjoins, one cannot adequately describe a privilege without providing some definition that allows us to determine which conceivable injunctions it negates. As Douglas and McFarlane point out, being an owner of a property interest does not mean A has a privilege to engage in any use of that property falling within ϕ regardless of its consequences to others.[24] There are many actions that constitute uses of A's property that she has a duty to B not to engage in, such as using her car to run B over. Clearly then, the content of A's use-privilege cannot be defined simply as "the negation of any duty to refrain from any conceivable use of the car," nor can we define the content of B's correlative no-right as "the negation of any claim-right that would forbid A to use her car in particular ways."

[23] Douglas and McFarlane 2013, p. 222.
[24] Douglas and McFarlane 2013, p. 221.

The proper answer, I suggest, is that A's use-privilege consists specifically of the negation of any duty to comply with the discretionary preferences of other people as to how the car shall or shall not be used. B's corresponding no-right is the no-right to impose his discretionary use-preferences with regard to the car on A.[25] A's duty not to run B over does not contradict her sovereign use-privilege over her car, because the principle animating that duty is not defined in terms of prohibited uses of her car. It is, rather, a duty not to cause harm to B's person, and while one of the applications of this duty is to forbid A from running B over with her car, the applicability of the duty does not turn in any way on the identity or ownership of the particular object that might be used to cause such harm.

In prior work, I have argued that there are two formal criteria that help to distinguish between these two types of claims – namely, ones that implement a right to set the discretionary use agenda for something, and ones that implement a right whose defining principle is the protection of some interest independent of that thing. As applied in a concrete context, either type of right might result in a claim to forbid A to take some particular action using her property, but only those falling in the first category actually derogate from her sovereign use-privilege. The distinction I am trying to draw thus requires us to keep in mind the earlier discussion concerning the different levels of abstraction – intensional and extensional – at which the content of a jural relation can be identified. The motivation for the attempt to formalize the distinction is that parties on either side are likely to want to blur it – property owners will seek to portray any limitations on their activities as violation of their property rights, and would-be usurpers of discretionary control over others' property will seek to portray themselves as vindicating interests in something else. My formal criteria are stated as follows:

A rights claim which, as applied in a given context, purports to forbid an owner to take (or to refrain from) action X with respect to her owned object Y is consistent with the owner's sovereign use-privilege (i.e., does not derogate from her ownership of Y) if both:

- the identifying characteristics of object Y are irrelevant to the question whether the asserted right is violated and
- the claimant is required to show that action X (or its omission) constitutes interference with the claimant's own preexisting interest in some other recognized protected interest Z.

[25] One might use Katz's felicitous expression and abbreviate each of these to, respectively, a privilege to ignore other's attempts to set the agenda for the thing, and a no-right to do so.

On the other hand, a claim forbidding (or requiring) an owner to take action X with respect to her owned object Y does conflict with the sovereign use-privilege if both:

- the identifying characteristics of object Y form part of the statement of the claimed right and
- the claimant is not required to show actual interference with his own preexisting interest in anything other than Y.[26]

When A forbids others to use her car, in order to establish her claim-right she is required to identify the car and the facts showing that she is its owner, but is not required to identify any harm to any interest other than her desire to control its use. Conversely, her use-privilege as owner means she can ignore with impunity any claim that she has a duty to take (or refrain from taking) given actions involving the car, unless that duty can be defined and justified by reference to something other than the claimant's bare interest in the car's use.

I would argue that the general baseline freedom of action to which Douglas and McFarlane refer should be described as a similar yet analytically distinct sovereign use-privilege that applies to our own persons (I shall refer to this as "personal liberty"). It follows the same paradigm spelled out above, with one's person occupying the position of "owned object Y." Thus if B purports to order A to use her car to drive him to the ice cream parlor, his order lacks force because B labors under two distinct no-rights, either of which is sufficient to negate it: a no-right to impose discretionary preferences on A's use of her person, and a distinct no-right to impose them on A's use of her car. It is true that the class of conceivable claims ruled out by the latter no-right form a subset of the claims ruled out by the former, because as a practical matter one cannot use an object without also using one's person. It is nevertheless both analytically and practically meaningful to distinguish between the two. This is readily understood when it comes to duties: Suppose that I contract with P never to enter any building dedicated to gambling without his permission. When it comes to the casino that P happens to own, I am under two distinct duties, each of which has as one of its contextual applications that I should not enter the building without his permission. This overlap does not collapse the two duties into one or render them "identical in content," though they do provide me with identical as-applied guidance when I contemplate whether or not to enter P's casino.

[26] Newman 2017.

The analytical distinction between personal liberty and the property owner's sovereign use-privilege is evident when one considers the extent to which the two privileges are respectively vested with immunity. Consider two different laws, each of which has the effect of imposing a duty on a landowner with regard to use of her land. Law 1 is a general criminal prohibition of the act of coal mining. Under the above test, such a law conflicts with personal liberty: it applies directly to one's person (thus requiring a showing that the person is subject to jurisdiction) and forbids activity not defined by any interference with some other preexisting vested interest. It does not, however, conflict with the landowner's sovereign use-privilege over her land, because its applicability does not turn on the use of any identified property and thus does not impose anyone's discretionary use preferences on any specified thing. That the law conflicts with personal liberty does not make it invalid, because personal liberty is not absolutely immune but subject to liabilities defined by the constitutional norms governing such lawmaking. In the US regime, such a law might be subject to due process scrutiny, but assuming it to be validly enacted no landowner – even those whose land contained active, previously legal coal mines – would have any legal claim to be compensated for the costs imposed on her by the law. Law 2, on the other hand, is a local land-use regulation that singles out parcels of land in a specific area and bans coal mining thereon. Such a law, even though validly enacted, might – if it were found to destroy all economically viable use of a given parcel – be regarded as a regulatory taking triggering a right to compensation.[27] In other words, the content of the set of immunities/liabilities that circumscribe the state's power to expropriate use-privileges may well differ depending on whether the taken privilege is one pertaining to person or property.

While not a strictly analytical point, I would argue that the distinction between personal liberty and property-based use-privilege has intuitive normative purchase as well. People understand the sovereign use-privilege as a key element of what it means to own something, expressible in the phrase "If it's mine, I can do what I want with it," as well as the corollary, "If I can't do what I want with it, it's not really mine."[28] Neither of these expressions is merely an application of the broader principle "don't tell me what to do." Introspection reveals that there are situations in which, even though either personal liberty or one's status as property owner might

[27] See *Lucas* v. *South Carolina Coastal Council*, 505 U.S. 1003 (1992).

[28] Cf. Douglas and McFarlane 2013, p. 227: "there is not much point in owning something that you are not permitted to use."

equally be invoked to resist a purported command, the latter is the more psychologically salient. If someone peremptorily orders you to stop using or to hand over a chattel that you own, the first instinctive objection may often be "This is mine" rather than the equally relevant, "Don't order me around." And even when you owe someone a duty of performance giving them some basis to "order you around", that right is often qualified by your privilege as owner to decide which of your owned things you will and will not use in the fulfillment of this personal duty.

I thus contend that it is erroneous to characterize the privilege/no-right relation subsisting between A and B with regard to A's car as identical to that subsisting between X and B. A has an in rem privilege with regard to her car, which places her in an identical privilege/no-right relation with everyone else.[29] Her specific privilege against B is one instance of this in rem privilege, which from A's perspective would be described by the maxim "I don't have to comply with anyone else's discretionary preferences concerning use of my property." For B's part, he possesses a specific no-right against A with regard to her car, which is an instance of an in rem no-right whose maxim would be "I can't prescribe how other people use their property." A is the only person who stands in this relation as privilege-holder against everyone else with respect to the car, and this position is unique in exactly the same sense as her position as holder of the right to exclude.

What of X and B? It is true that X too has a specific privilege against B regarding use of A's car, but it is not an instance of the same in rem privilege A has. X has no in rem use-privilege with regard to A's car, for A has a right to impose on him her use-preferences concerning it. There is more than one in rem relation from which we could derive as an instance X's specific privilege against B, but none of them is identical to A's sovereign use-privilege as owner of the car. As I have pointed out above, the most salient of these is the in rem privilege whose maxim is "I don't have to comply with anyone else's discretionary preferences concerning my personal actions." This in rem relation is not focused on the car or its ownership at all, but use of A's car is nevertheless among the class of actions for which it may furnish relevant specific privileges against certain persons.

One can also, however, derive X's specific privilege against B from another in rem relation, one whose structure does focus on the car and its ownership. In addition to B's no-right to prescribe the personal actions of others, one might describe B as having an in rem no-right to prescribe

[29] See Newman.

uses, not merely to owners of their own property, but to others generally of things that B does not own. One might argue that the true principled basis for B's inability to prescribe uses of A's car, whether to A or to X, is not that A owns it, but merely that B does not own it. On this account, both X and A possess a corresponding in rem privilege whose maxim is "I don't have to comply with the discretionary preferences of others concerning use of things they do not own." So described, the content of A's privilege is indeed identical to that of X's, and treats A's ownership of the car as irrelevant. I do not dispute the existence of such an in rem privilege; in fact I think it (as well as the correlative no-right) embodies a useful normative principle to which people have frequent recourse: "If it's not mine, it's not my place to tell people how to use it." The key point, hopefully clear by now, is that this in rem privilege is still analytically and normatively distinct from A's affirmative use-privilege as owner of her car. That a specific relation of identical content may be derived as an instance of two different in rem relations does not mean that those two in rem relations are themselves identical in content, just as the intensions "morning star" and "evening star" are not identical in content even though they both have Venus as their extension.[30]

Again, one can perceive the analytical distinction between the two privileges more clearly by considering the respective configurations of immunities and liabilities that accompany them in a dynamic setting. A's sovereign use-privilege against B with regard to her own car is robustly vested; generally speaking, A may not be deprived of this privilege without her consent. B, whether acting alone or in concert with others, has no private legal means of taking the privilege from her (i.e., of acquiring a claim right against A to impose discretionary preferences on her use of the car), and should the state purport to confer such a right on B without A's consent, it would likely trigger constitutional protections against deprivation of property. X's use privilege against B concerning A's car, however, is not vested. A can delegate her authority over her car to B at any time (e.g., by bailing it to him), at which point X's privilege against B will disappear without any need for X's consent to this.[31] Similarly, if the state were to purport to vest B with authority to dictate the permissible uses of A's car, while A would likely have standing to object to and perhaps be compensated for this, X would not.

[30] See Smith 2013.

[31] A's power to effect such changes in jural relations, by the way, is yet another defining aspect of property that is missed when one treats the right to exclude as its only distinctive feature.

4.3 Protection of the Interest in Use as an Organizing Principle of Property Doctrine

Having concluded that in order to describe the distinctive nature of property law one must look solely at the nature of the duties it imposes, Douglas & McFarlane argue that the only such duty is that correlated to the "right to exclude." This right, they contend, is not defined by any interest of the property owner in use, but rather consists solely of a duty not to deliberately or carelessly interfere with A's physical thing.[32] To be clear, I do not understand Douglas and McFarlane to deny that property rights do in fact serve to protect an underlying interest in the use of resources. Rather, their contention is that while such protection may be a desired indirect result of property law, the structure of the duty directly imposed by property law is neither coextensive with nor defined by reference to the owner's interest in use. I want to argue the opposite, that the "right to exclude" is best explained as a strategy for protecting an interest in possessory use, and that the structure of property rights generally is animated by recognition of both a right to noninterference and the need to cabin that right in ways that render it cognitively manageable and normatively proportionate to the burdens it imposes on dutyholders.

At the outset, I wish to clarify an aspect of Douglas & McFarlane's usage that is sometimes imprecise. They distinguish, correctly, between a privilege (what they call a "liberty") to use something, and a claim-right to prevent someone else from interfering with one's use. They sometimes refer, however, to interference with actual use as a deprivation of liberty.[33] If the term "liberty" is a stand-in for the Hohfeldian "privilege" (as it was throughout the earlier analytical argument), then we need to distinguish between depriving someone of a privilege in the jural sense and interfering with their exercise of it as a practical matter. Strictly speaking, the only way to deprive someone of a use-privilege in the Hohfeldian sense is to impose on them some duty that negates it. Thus an injunction forbidding A to use her car deprives her of a use-privilege. An action that has the consequence of rendering it physically impossible for her to make some use of her car (such as somehow interdicting all possible supplies of gasoline) does not deprive her of a use-privilege in the Hohfeldian sense. This may be an area in which the common connotations of the term "liberty" result

[32] Douglas and McFarlane 2013, p. 226.

[33] See e.g., Douglas and McFarlane 2013, p. 228: "it is possible to deprive an owner of his liberty to use his thing without breaching a duty not to physically interfere with it."

in obfuscation, for we do refer to some practical impediments to action as deprivations of liberty. If I lock you in a jail cell, I have assuredly deprived you of liberty as most people would understand the term. I have not, however, deprived you of any Hohfeldian privilege so long as you are under no duty to remain there. Strictly speaking, then, it is erroneous to describe a claim-right as "protecting a privilege." What protects a privilege – the only thing that can be said to protect *any* jural status quo in the Hohfeldian universe – is an *immunity*. What a claim-right against interference serves to protect is rather one's practical ability to exercise one's privilege.

Accordingly, Douglas and McFarlane frame their inquiry as one into whether case law supports the existence of any "duty not to impair the owner's ability to use." The thrust of their argument on this score is as follows: All of the torts through which property rights are enforced – conversion, trespass, negligence, nuisance – require physical interference via boundary crossing, and thus exclude from the realm of culpability myriad activities that have the effect of interfering with an owner's ability to use her property in accordance with her preferences.[34] Furthermore, in liminal cases where courts are called upon to determine whether a person's protected interest in something "counts" as a property right, the existence *vel non* of a right to exclude appears to be the predominant touchstone.[35] I do not dispute that property torts are limited to acts defined in part by reference to boundaries. But those acts are not necessarily defined by boundary *crossings*. Moreover, there is an important difference between saying "property doctrine is concerned only with policing boundaries" and saying "property doctrine is concerned with interference in use, but implements this concern by making use of boundaries." I will argue that the latter is a more accurate and useful description of the doctrine.

Just as it is evident that the ability to exercise a use-privilege is extremely precarious without some sort of right against interference, it is evident that the scope of any such right – and its correlative duty – needs to be carefully calibrated. For people to be both able and willing to comply with such a duty, the actions that it requires one to forego must be readily identifiable and the opportunity costs of compliance must be plausibly outweighed by the benefits gained through the universal compliance of others. The former criterion implies that most types of interference we are expected to avoid will have to be defined in fairly clear categorical terms that can be applied with fairly low levels of information. The latter implies that the

[34] Douglas and McFarlane 2013, pp. 226–32.

[35] Douglas and McFarlane 2013, pp. 233–7.

duties so defined must leave dutyholders with ample zones of privilege in which to make their own uses of their own resources. Given these constraints, it is unsurprising that property doctrine does not seek to impose a broad duty to refrain from any action that may have the effect of impeding the success of someone's desired use of her property. To comply with such a duty would require one to have knowledge of everyone else's ends and to foresee an open-ended set of possible causal links between one's own actions and the eventual disruption of those ends. Douglas & McFarlane are correct, then, that property law does not impose anything so broad as a "duty not to impair the owner's ability to use."

But nor does property law limit itself to policing "rights to exclude." Or rather, one might say that not all rights to exclude are keyed simply to boundary crossings. It's worth pausing to clarify this point. Ultimately, any right to exclude pertains to a class of activities ϕ that dutyholders are forbidden to engage in.[36] When we speak of a right to exclude others "from a thing" – and when the "thing" in question is a tangible object – what we usually mean is a right to exclude others from a class of activities ϕ whose key defining characteristic is that they involve physical interaction with the boundaries of that thing. If the thing is land, this means boundary crossing. If it is a chattel, it means some form of tangible contact. It is also possible to define ϕ by reference to actions having as their object an intangible "thing," such as the list of exclusive rights given to copyright owners. And as I will describe in the next paragraph, it is also possible to define ϕ in terms that make use of the boundaries of a tangible thing, but do not require boundary crossing. In order to avoid confusion, I shall henceforth use the term "right to exclude" to mean only a right that forbids dutyholders to engage in a class of activities defined solely in terms of crossing or touching the boundaries of a given thing. In other words, a right against trespass.

Above I described two different classes of use-privileges – "usufructuary" privileges pertaining to relatively narrow classes of activity that leave uses of the thing available to others, and "possessory" privileges pertaining to classes of activity that effectively or potentially monopolize all use of the thing in question. A usufructuary owner's ability to engage in privileged activity ϕ with regard to thing X is protected by a *right of noninterference with* ϕ, not a right to exclude others from X. As Douglas & McFarlane point out,[37] this right of noninterference is narrower than a "duty not to

[36] This is Essert's key point, which I discuss below.
[37] Douglas and McFarlane 2013, p. 236.

impair the owner's ability to ϕ" – for the reasons described above, it does not forbid *all* activities that render ϕ more difficult, but only those that do so by means of occupying or altering X itself. Thus my right of way across Blackacre is not infringed by interdicting my supply of fuel, but it is by placing obstacles within Blackacre that would prevent passage. To decide whether an action occupies or alters X requires reference to the boundaries of X, and so those boundaries play a crucial role in circumscribing the set of actions that violate my right. Nevertheless, "boundary crossing" is neither necessary nor sufficient to constitute such violation. My right of way does not categorically forbid anyone else to set foot in Blackacre, or even to occupy the specific path I use to traverse it. Because of this, a person may go from complying with my right to violating it without crossing any boundary, simply by remaining within the boundary but altering his activity to something obstructive.

The sovereign use-privilege of an owner of land in fee simple (or of title to a chattel) entitles her to choose from an open-ended set of possible uses – including that of purposefully leaving the thing untouched – and to switch between them from moment to moment. In order to protect her ability to exercise this privilege using solely a right of noninterference, the set of forbidden activities would have to change from moment to moment to mirror her chosen uses. This would make compliance and enforcement impractically dependent on prediction (or reconstruction) of the owner's intended uses, and result in the owner's freedom of use being impeded by the need to constantly announce her intentions and eject parties whose previously non-interfering activities have now become so. As Henry Smith has argued at length, the right to exclude vastly lowers the information costs of both dutyholders and enforcers, while affording owners the crucial space they need to investigate and cultivate potential uses free of opportunistic usurpation.[38] The right to exclude is thus explainable entirely as a practically necessary device for protecting a certain type of interest in use.

Moreover, the right to exclude does not exhaust the relevance of the owner's interest in use to defining the duties of others. The trespass rule effectively forbids all actions that might impede use by means of physically occupying the thing, but it is also possible to impede use without occupation, by altering attributes of the thing that affect its usability. This is what we mean by nuisance. Douglas & McFarlane portray actionable nuisance as continuous with trespass in that it too is said to be defined by boundary

[38] See Smith 2004.

crossing, albeit of a less substantial nature.[39] I would argue that it is better to conceive of nuisance as defined by alteration of attributes of the thing that damage its suitability for "use and enjoyment" without physically displacing the owner from occupation. The duty to refrain from nuisance is less precisely delineated than the duty to refrain from trespass, but it is still far from encompassing all activities that may have the consequence of "impairing the owner's ability to use." This narrowing is achieved primarily by means of two limitations on the scope of the duty that keep it within manageable and tolerable bounds.

First, already noted, is that nuisance is limited to actions that alter attributes of the thing itself. As with the right of noninterference discussed above, this criterion makes use of the boundaries of the thing to narrow the set of potential causal chains stemming from my actions that I must consider, but not via focus on "crossings" per se. What do I mean by "altering attributes of the thing itself," when the "thing" in question is land? In cases of nuisance we are usually not concerned with land qua dirt, but with land qua location that can be occupied so as to provide the situs of activities. For land to provide "use and enjoyment" in this sense, the conditions "on the land" – which really means, "in the habitable space within the land's boundaries" – must be such as to permit human beings to occupy the space comfortably enough to engage in their desired activities. If I open a pig farm next to your homestead, the gravamen of your nuisance claim is not that microscopic particles are crossing the boundary, but that olfactory conditions within the boundary have become intolerable to human repose. Suppose I own a right of way that entitles me to traverse Blackacre, and every time I do so I operate a deafening air horn. I will be guilty of nuisance even though no unauthorized boundary crossing has occurred. What has occurred, rather, is alteration of the conditions within the boundary, from ones in which you can hear yourself think to ones in which you cannot. If I own no such right of way but operate my horn from just outside your property line, the nature of the claim against me is not changed in any meaningful respect by the irrelevant fact that now the offending vibration of air molecules must cross a boundary line to reach the ears of an occupant. Similarly, the key issue in a claim of aesthetic or moral nuisance is not whether photons are crossing your property line, but whether the visibility or proximity of certain things or activities alters the conditions of life inside that line in ways that the law is prepared to treat as actionably harmful.

[39] Douglas and McFarlane 2013, pp. 230–2.

The right to be free of nuisance is also limited by a second principle that makes it much narrower than one defined simply by boundary crossing. It would be intolerably broad to enjoin all actions perceptibly altering conditions within Blackacre. Nuisance law therefore employs a "significant harm" test that expressly requires the claimant to point to some form of "use and enjoyment" of the land that is actually impeded by the alteration.[40] Moreover, the significant harm test is governed by objective norms that limit the forms of "use and enjoyment" an owner can justifiably claim to protect in a given locale.[41]

Thus, the idiosyncratic homeowner who would like his neighbors to leave him in absolute silence and freedom from wafting odor will not win a nuisance suit simply by establishing the existence of sensorial boundary crossings. Rather, the court will do exactly what Douglas and McFarlane claim property law does not do, namely "examine the positive uses" that both he and his neighbors may be reasonably expected to make of their respective holdings, in order to determine whether one should be suppressed to protect another. They concede that this sort of "reference to the use of the land" is necessary when enforcing an easement,[42] but do not acknowledge that it plays a central role in nuisance as well. In structure, the fee simple owner's right to be free of nuisance is the same as the usufructuary owner's right of noninterference. Just as a right of way is a usufructuary right to traverse land, the right against nuisance is a usufructuary right to use and enjoy land in ways regarded as presumptively reasonable in the given locality. Each is protected by a right that is tailored to forbid only actions that interfere with the use-interest by means of altering conditions on the land itself.

The nuisance inquiry is far more qualitative and fine-grained than application of a simple boundary rule, and thus far more costly. That property law nevertheless requires it shows exclusion to be an approximative strategy for protecting use, one to be supplemented or superseded in contexts where it is not suited to the purpose. A regime that enjoined only possessory boundary crossings (trespasses) would leave the interest in use and enjoyment of property unprotected from nonpossessory interference,

[40] See *Restatement (Second) of Torts* § 821D (1977) (defining nuisance as "a nontrespassory invasion of another's interest in the private use and enjoyment of land"), § 821F (stating that liability for nuisance exists "only to those to whom it causes significant harm").

[41] See *Restatement (Second) of Torts* § 821F (stating that harm must be "of a kind that would be suffered by a normal person in the community or by property in normal condition and used for a normal purpose").

[42] Douglas and McFarlane 2013, p. 236.

while one that enjoined all perceptible boundary crossings would severely undermine that same interest by limiting it to the few categories of use having no discernible spillover effects on neighbors. The doctrines of trespass and nuisance work in concert to determine what sorts of interference with use one can reasonably expect property law to address, exploiting the advantages of boundaries and exclusion where useful but resorting to evaluation of competing uses where necessary.

Even if one accepts the above arguments with regard to tangible property, one might object that other recognized forms of property, such as intellectual property, consist solely of defined exclusive rights that cannot be construed as protection against interference with use of the owned thing. Here the "thing" in question is abstract and intangible – a work of authorship or invention – and the activities with respect to it that are enjoined by the author's exclusive rights do not threaten the owner's own practical ability to engage in the same activities. My copying, distribution, or public performance of an author's work[43] do not of their own force prevent the author from using and enjoying the same work. Because an intellectual work is nonrival, the author's use privileges with regard to it are in no need of protection from practical obstruction.

Here too however, the seemingly bright-line exclusive right turns out to be based on and qualified by doctrines that focus on the owner's interest in use. In the case of copyright, for example, while an author's ability to enjoy the expression embodied in the work (by reading, watching, or listening to it) is in no need of protection, her ability to use the expressive value of the work as a basis for exchange is vulnerable to actions making that value preemptively accessible to others. The exclusive rights granted to a copyright owner are designed to give her control over the primary activities through which such access-granting takes place.[44] While these rights define categories of activity that can be likened to boundary crossing (in that they consist of actions having the work or a copy of it as direct object), they do not rule out all types of interaction with the protected work that can be so described. Thus, while copyright excludes public acts of distribution (and the reproduction necessary to such distribution), performance and display, it does not give owners any control over acts through which consumers enjoy the contents of the work in private, even though such acts "cross" the work's "boundaries" to exactly the same extent.

[43] See 17 U.S.C. § 106 (enumerating exclusive rights of copyright owner).

[44] See 17 U.S.C. § 106 (copying, preparation of derivative works, distribution, performance, display).

In short, the copyright owner does not have a "right to exclude" others from the work as such. Rather, she has a usufructuary right protecting from interference her ability to engage in economic exploitation of the work.[45] Instead of prohibiting all unauthorized interactions with the work, copyright law focuses on the owner's relevant use-interest in controlling access for purposes of exchange, and defines as infringing only categories of activity that threaten significant and direct interference with it. Again, these categories do not include all activities that might "impair the ability" to exploit the work, but only ones that do so through competing uses of the work itself. Even with regard to these nominally bright-line, trespass-like categories, copyright doctrine employs additional doctrines, such as fair use and first sale, that exempt nominally infringing actions where a finer-grained look shows that they do not in fact interfere with the owner's recognized interests in use.[46]

4.4 The Role of Things in the Concept of Property

I have just described intellectual property as an instance of the general paradigm of identifying an "interest" in "use" of a "thing," and determining what scope of protection for that interest is appropriate. It is undeniable, however, that once we depart from actual physical objects, the meanings of "use" and "thing" begin to look very different. One might object that such use of these terms is merely a strained metaphor that obscures rather than aids rigorous analysis. Indeed, James Penner made such a claim with regard to intellectual property in The Idea of Property In Law, where he characterized as "idiotic fiction" the idea that "intellectual property constitutes property in ideas (patents) or expressions (copyright)," asserting

[45] Eric Claeys has previously spelled out the usufructuary structure of intellectual property in much greater depth. See Claeys 2014. Patent law, while facing some different practical issues owing to the differences between inventions and works of authorship, has a closely analogous structure to copyright when viewed at this level of abstraction. Trademark is somewhat different. As Adam Mossoff has pointed out, in trademark the true object of ownership is the business's goodwill, and the mark is the means by which the value of this goodwill is exploited by triggering the expectations customers have as a result of it. See Mossoff 2017. I would analogize the exclusive right to use a mark in commerce to an easement appurtenant to the business's goodwill. Like a servient tenement, the encumbered word, phrase, or symbol is still available for others to use, limited only by a duty of non-interference in the trademark owner's ability to use the mark as a focal point for commercial goodwill. The requirement of "likelihood of confusion" shows this to be a nuisance rule, not a trespass rule.

[46] See Newman, 2018, pp. 92–3.

that it really is "a certain class of rights to monopolies."[47] Penner was aware that one might make the same move with regard to tangible things: "Why, then, do we not say that the landowner has a monopoly on various uses defined in reference to the land, of course, but no direct property right in the land itself?"[48] While Penner rejected this move (giving reasons that I shall criticize anon), Christopher Essert recently took it up with a vengeance, arguing that the concept of property can and should dispense with a focus on things altogether.[49] Essert's thesis is that we should conceive of property rights as providing owners with control over categories of activities (denoted ϕ), such that "A has a property right when A has the (transferable) right, good against the world, that others not ϕ without her permission."[50]

Before stating my qualms about Essert's approach, I will attempt to offer an account of the meanings of "use" and "thing" for purposes of property theory that I hope will be resistant to the criticism that they are mere vague metaphors or "idiotic fictions." I would define a "thing" for this purpose as a discrete and intelligible nexus of human activity with respect to which actions by different persons are likely to come into conflict. The most obvious examples of this are the paradigmatic ones of physical objects that one cannot occupy, manipulate, or consume without directly preempting an opportunity for someone else to do the same. Note however that while "land" tends to be lumped in with these, it is itself already a step up the chain of abstraction from such "things" as acorns and cars. While continents and islands may fit naturally within the intuitive physical notion of "thing," the various parcels of land into which we divide them up for purposes of property law do not have natural boundaries. Such boundaries as we assign are abstract constructs no less notional than those defining a "work of authorship," as anyone can tell you who has actually attempted to locate in real space the lines so prettily drawn on a land office plat.[51] The various procedures through which the scope of such boundaries is first

[47] Penner 1997, p. 118. Note that while it would presumably make no difference to Penner's stated position, I would say that the correct objects of ownership in patent and copyright are, respectively, "inventions" and "works of authorship," each of which is a narrower concept than the one referenced in the quote.

[48] Penner 1997, p. 120.

[49] Essert 2014.

[50] Essert 2014, p. 579.

[51] And that's only conceiving of the "land" in two dimensions. Once one adds in the *ad coelum* rule, any notion that a parcel of real estate is a "thing" in the usual physical sense of the term fails scrutiny.

assigned (whether via principles of legitimate unilateral first possession or through some a priori legislative/administrative line drawing) are all informed in significant part by the question of the uses to which it is anticipated the land will be put and the amount of space needed to carry them out without hindrance – i.e., by the problem of use-conflict.

Physical "things" then, are those with respect to which actions by different persons are likely to come into physical conflict. But that is not the only kind of conflict. The idea of conflict presupposes the idea of purpose, and actions are said to conflict any time they are "at cross-purposes" with each other, so that one (or possibly both) hinders realization of the purpose of the other. If two actions have this relation to each other, it will be possible to identify some "thing" with respect to which they seek to make incompatible use. By "use" of a thing, I mean action that either seeks to derive some benefit from that thing or consumes possibilities for others to do so.[52] Thus in my copyright example above, a work of authorship is a thing even though it does not correspond to any single identifiable physical object – many such objects may be copies of the work, but none is the work itself. Nevertheless, the work is a discrete and intelligible thing: while liminal problems certainly arise,[53] there is no difficulty in understanding what discrete object of apperception is signified by the name "War and Peace." Conflict does not occur (and thus the work is said to be "nonrival") to the extent that the only human purposes under consideration are those of enjoying (via one of the extant copies) the expression contained in the work. If however one person wishes to use the work's value as a medium of exchange, that purpose will very likely conflict with actions of others making the contents of the work easily accessible.

Just because someone's purpose with respect to a thing creates the potential for conflict is not, of course, sufficient reason for recognizing a property interest. Just as clearly, my definition includes a great many "things" that ought not to be treated as objects of property – the affections of a desired mate, for example.[54] This is as it should be; not all things should be owned. But all ownership involves things as I have defined them,

[52] See Newman 2011.

[53] As they do with physical things. See Newman 2011, pp. 268–88 (discussing Roman and common-law doctrines of *specificatio* and *accessio*).

[54] Not that such things have never been so treated, as implied by the tort of alienation of affection. Of course, to validly appropriate the affections of one's desired mate so as to acquire rights of noninterference therein, one had first to reduce them to (constructive if not actual) possession via the rule of capture known as marriage.

and the qualities included in my definition of "thing" are prerequisites for something being conceivable as an object of property rights.

Penner described intellectual property rights thus:

> They are rights directly to a practice of exclusion, as directly as are property rights in chattels or land, correlating to duties in rem by which all subjects of the legal system have a negative duty not to do something. The duty is not one to refrain from interfering with material objects, but to refrain from working an invention or copying an original work or from representing one's business or its products by a certain name or symbol.[55]

With this description I have no quarrel whatsoever; it strikes me as perfectly accurate. What I disagree with is the accompanying statement that intellectual property rights are "abstract legal rights, with no direct connection to anything, tangible or intangible."[56] Are not inventions, works, names, and symbols intangible things? Do they not stand in the same conceptual relation to their respective duties of noninterference as do chattels and land? Penner's answer is no, because there is a difference in the characterization of the landowner's and IP owner's respective use-rights. The landowner's use-rights are, he says, "essentially indefinable, comprising every possible use of land." Whereas the IP owner has exclusive rights only to specific enumerated uses that form a small subset of the limitless number of ways in which ideas or inventions may be used. This response, I think, reflects the perspective I sought to supplant in Section 4.1 – that only interests characterized by exclusive possession qualify as "property."

In Sections 4.1 and 4.3 I have offered arguments for regarding usufructuary interests as full-fledged instances of "property," and shown how intellectual property rights – despite obvious salient differences – follow the same logic and structure as usufructuary interests in tangible resources. I've also tried to point out that while the use-*privileges* of a possessory owner are "essentially indefinable, comprising every possible use," the accompanying *rights* are not. There are many beneficial interactions with land (i.e., uses) that are beyond the reach of either trespass or nuisance law, many of which fall into precisely the same categories of use that Penner cites when speaking of the limitless number of ways in which ideas can be used. Land, too, can be the object of aesthetic appreciation (both sensory and non), contemplation, and study. Penner admits that "[p]assers-by may gain value from looking at one's garden," but that is far from the only sort of pleasurable or useful information they may obtain without trespass, and they may also use

[55] Penner 1997, p. 119.
[56] Penner 1997, p. 119.

its atmosphere as the carrier of sights, sounds and smells, and its ground as one of vibrations, that the owner might heartily prefer to exclude.[57]

Essert's argument hinges on the example of what he calls the "Ideal License," which amounts to what most people would call – though he does not – a privately owned monopoly on the provision of taxi services.[58] Essert constructs his "license" to share most of the features of core property rights, and argues that its lack of any focal thing should not disqualify it as property, because the functions purportedly served by things in the concept of property can adequately be addressed in other ways.[59] I have little difficulty accepting Essert's "Ideal License" conceptually as a kind of property right (albeit a normatively unjustified one on the merits), but I would argue that it too is focused on a sort of abstract "thing" – the occupation of providing taxi services. Essert's "Ideal License" is intelligible as a property right because the occupation of providing taxi services is a discrete and intelligible nexus of human activity with respect to which we can readily posit human interests potentially in conflict. People who wish to engage in this occupation need privileges at least, and may need some rights of noninterference. Whether or not I believe those interests to legitimately justify an exclusive right as broad as the Ideal License (I don't, at least not without making some counterfactual assumptions about the world), the right is structured in such a way as to permit one to recognize the conceivability of such a purpose.

I take Essert's point to be that if one is willing to stretch the notion of "thing" this far afield from discrete physical objects, one should admit that "thing" really means nothing more than "classifying concept that can be defined with sufficient clarity to serve as a means of distinguishing actions that count as ϕ from those that do not." If thing-centric accounts of property embody (as I think they do) certain normative premises about the kinds of purposes property is supposed to serve, Essert can be seen as making what amounts to a positivist move. He leaves space to evaluate any given species of property based on how functional and normatively justified it is, but wants us to relegate those questions to a different realm from

[57] Penner elsewhere makes a similar point himself. Penner 1997, p. 72: "I can take pleasure in your body simply by seeing it, or in your conversation simply by listening. I can similarly appreciate the beauty of your garden sculpture as a passer-by. I can even have an interest (the exact nature of which is interesting) in your not destroying the Poussin which hangs in your hall, even though I may never actually have the chance to see it. There must, therefore, be defined limits to property rights, that is to the owner's exclusive rights to the things he owns."

[58] Essert 2014, p. 573.

[59] Essert 2014, p. 574.

the conceptual one of whether a particular entitlement should be termed a "property" interest.[60] As signaled above, I too am willing to recognize certain entitlements as exhibiting the conceptual attributes of property regardless of whether I consider them to be normatively justified examples of it. Nevertheless, I find myself objecting to Essert's proposed definition along the same lines as the usual natural lawyer's critique of positivist accounts of law: it abstracts away from crucial factors that make the institution the concept refers to (and hence the concept) distinctive and worth having.[61]

At minimum, I would contend that in order to be functional and normatively justifiable, any property right along Essert's lines will have to define ϕ by reference to some discrete and intelligible nexus of human activity that satisfies the following criteria:

1. It permits us to provide a coherent account as to some purpose for which an interest in the specified type of activity would be assigned to a given individual.
2. The interest must be one that could serve the same purpose in the hands of a transferee.

The first criterion is functionally necessary because without it there will be no animating principle to guide liminal determinations as to which concrete activities should be construed to fall within the exclusion and which should not. Essert argues that the difficulty of deciding what constitutes "driving a taxi" is no greater than that of deciding what constitutes actionable interference with land.[62] I would agree, but only provided that we know what the underlying purpose of the exclusive right in taxi driving is with at least as much specification as we know what it means to have an interest in the use and enjoyment of land. Absent that, a free-floating exclusion from "driving a taxi" would provide no nonarbitrary rationale for deciding whether the exclusion covers such things as: driving in exchange for nonmonetary benefits, operating a rickshaw, or picking up people who do not call or hail but use an app like Uber.[63]

[60] Essert 2014, p. 593.

[61] To be clear, the scholars like Henry Smith and Thomas Merrill to whom Essert is responding do not frame themselves as doing anything called "natural law," nor does Essert frame himself as a positivist. I, however, am resisting what Essert sees as a clarifying conceptual move in part on the ground that what it filters out has normative import essential to the concept.

[62] Essert 2014, p. 582.

[63] The point that exclusion in isolation from an interest in use fails to provide coherent guidance has been made before. See Mossoff 2011; Claeys 2009.

It is practically impossible to define ϕ by providing an ex ante enumeration of every specific physical motion that would violate the exclusive right. It is conceptually possible to define some bright-line rule that could be applied to determine whether a given action violates the right, but as a practical matter no such bright-line rule would be tolerable if applied without exception, and no actually existing institution of property works in that way. As I discussed in Section 4.2, even the most seemingly clear and obvious form of such a rule – the exclusion of perceptible incursion across spatial boundaries – has never been and could not be applied consistently without leading to results that no human society would accept. There are good reasons (many of which have been explained by Henry Smith) as to why a fair amount of exclusive overbreadth is worthwhile, but one cannot even make that judgment without having some notion as to the purpose(s) we are trying to achieve by recognizing the exclusive interest in the first place. In sum, even from a purely functional perspective we never actually grant a right to exclude unmoored from any notion as to the purpose underlying the grant, and such a purpose always involves some thing.

This first criterion is also normatively necessary, for without some posited purpose that can be evaluated there will be no basis for anyone to regard the duties imposed by the property right as justifiable. For present purposes it doesn't matter whether the purpose offered sounds in natural law ("an individual has a justified moral claim to be free from interference in activity ϕ") or utilitarianism ("general welfare will be improved by assigning to some individual a right to control activity ϕ"). Either way, there will have to be some account as to the nature of the relationship between the individual and the thing in light of which the posited purpose makes sense.

The second criterion is necessary because otherwise the transferability condition built into Essert's definition will conflict with the first, so that upon transfer the right will cease to offer coherent answers to the functional and normative questions just mentioned. Indeed, by including the transferability condition in his definition, Essert implicitly imports the sorts of contingent normative considerations that the rejection of thing-centricity seems intended to eliminate. Whether an exclusive right is regarded as transferable in practice is tightly bound up with the nature of the relationship between the thing and its owner, and whether that relationship is susceptible of transfer without normative consequences.[64]

[64] See Penner's discussion of the "separability thesis" at Penner 1997, pp. 105–27.

If thing-centricity is to be jettisoned as a defining feature of property, why exactly is transferability being retained?

If anything, my own impulse toward overarching conceptual minimalism would cut the other way, in favor of treating as "property" any set of jural relations that reflect the interest a person has in a thing, and leaving contingent the question whether any particular such relations are or should be transferable. This would make the right to bodily integrity a sort of property right, which strikes me as conceptually justifiable because it uses the contours of a defined thing to provide specific content to what would otherwise be a vague duty of noninterference. The argument against this approach is that even though the two rights are similarly structured, there is something normatively different about the relationship I have with my body and the one I have with my car.[65] I accept this argument because I understand property to be a normative concept.

Similarly, I readily accept the observation that property can be classified as one subset of mechanisms through which rights falling within Essert's defined class can arise. It may well be that, as Essert suggests, focusing on that class as an object of analysis will yield helpful insights that will also apply to property, to the extent that property is in the business of assigning exclusive rights. I resist the suggestion that it is helpful to apply the label "property" to everything in this class however, because it abstracts away from the factors that make property's normative content intelligible. Additionally, as I have argued throughout, property isn't only in the business of assigning exclusive rights.

Imagine that some eccentric sovereign chooses to create a new species of entitlement and assign it to some individual. We shall call this new entitlement "boojum." The person who possesses boojum has the transferable right, good against the world, to exclude other people from engaging in a class of activities ϕ defined as the sum of the following:

1. Operating a motor vehicle at any speed in excess of 42 miles per hour.
2. Engaging in social interaction of any sort with James Penner.
3. Wearing plaid.
4. Whistling Dixie while walking past a graveyard.

I think it would be very difficult to identify any intelligible "thing" to which all the activities contained in ϕ can be related. This absence leaves us at a loss to explain why these particular activities have been grouped together as part of a single proprietary interest, what human purpose the interest

[65] See Penner 1997, pp. 105–27.

serves, why the interest is transferable, or how liminal cases concerning the application of ϕ should be resolved. The absence is of no concern to Essert, who, I take it, must accept this interest as satisfying his conceptual definition of a "property right." He might well agree that it would be a strange and probably unjustified sort of property right to recognize, but would maintain that conceptually it is a property right all the same – just as one can criticize a particular positive law as strange and unjustified, but still recognize it as a law. I am inclined to say that what Penner mistakenly claimed of intellectual property is actually true of boojum: it can *only* be labeled a monopoly, an unmediated exclusion of others from some class of activities as such. It is to property as a chassis without wheels or engine is to a taxicab: some of the characteristic structure is present, but not enough to take you anywhere you want to go, which is after all the key point.

Now imagine something identical to Essert's Ideal License, except that it is granted for the sole purpose of regulation. We shall call it the Ideal Commission, and assume it to be the brainchild of a Kantian theorist of public administration who believes that the way to good government is to ensure that anyone with regulatory power may use it only in accordance with duty denuded of any form of self-interest. Thus whoever owns the Ideal Commission has a transferable *in rem* right to exclude others from providing taxi services, but is also strictly forbidden to engage in or make use of taxi services himself, or to derive any benefit, monetary or nonmonetary, from permitting others to do so. The exclusive rights of the Commissioner are intended to be used solely to ensure the integrity of those who enter into the occupation, and the Commission's transferability exists solely in order to permit the Commissioner to hand off this responsibility to someone worthy when he or she no longer feels able to fulfill it. It is therefore also forbidden to derive any personal benefit in connection with the transfer of the right. In this scenario, the Ideal Commissioner, while owning a transferable right to exclude with respect to the occupation of taxi service, has been denied any interest in use or enjoyment of that occupation.[66] He has rights, but no privileges. I think it would be strange to call the Ideal Commission a property right rather than a curious form of public office. The key distinction here being that while one is not supposed to profit from one's public office, one *is* supposed to benefit in some way from one's property. I would argue that this aspect of property – that it

[66] For this to truly work, we would have to go further and posit that the Commissioner is barred from even having knowledge as to the actual state of the taxi industry, lest he derive satisfaction therefrom.

serves to render the object of property rights more beneficial to the owner than it would otherwise be – is also at least as fundamental as the condition of transferability that Essert includes in his conceptual definition.

Essert invites us to imagine angels exercising property rights to control each others' recreational activities, without any underlying problem of use-conflict to solve.[67] I am put in mind of Milton's angels, who engage in a form of congress that involves total and mutual interpenetration throughout their beings, with no concern stemming from physical limitations, emotional entanglements, or the moral consequences of reproduction.[68] Whatever they're doing, I think it would be misleading to treat it as the defining example of what human beings call sex.

[67] Essert 2014, pp. 590–1.

[68] See John Milton, Paradise Lost, VIII.622–9.

5

Is Original Acquisition Problematic?

NICHOLAS SAGE

One principle of political morality that should command wide-ranging support is this: at least *prima facie*, each person should respect each other's choices. Something like this principle should presumably have a place in any political theory that can broadly be called liberal. Including not only orthodox liberal accounts but also various strands of libertarianism, as well as the 'republican' and Kantian theories that have enjoyed a resurgence in recent years.

The principle of respect for choice provides the basis for a remarkably straightforward justification of property rights arising from acts of original acquisition. In essence: an original acquisition of property is a person's exercise of choice over an unowned object; once this occurs, each other person must refrain from interfering with the object so as to respect the first person's choice.

Yet very few theorists of property embrace this straightforward account of original acquisition. Liberal theorists who might well endorse the principle of respect for choice, were it put to them, and even theorists who explicitly endorse such a principle, tend to pursue quite different justificatory strategies.

For example, the libertarian philosopher Bas van der Vossen has recently sought to justify original acquisition by postulating a certain natural right. It is not necessarily the kind of right 'with which we are familiar in our everyday lives.'[1] According to van der Vossen, each person has a natural 'conditional claim-right,' to impose an obligation on other persons to respect his ownership of an object. (Correlatively, each person has a natural conditional duty, to respect such obligations imposed on her by others.) The right is 'conditional' because the right-holder must do something to activate it: perform a conventional act of acquisition. He thereby

My thanks to the editors and contributors to this volume, the other participants at the Singapore workshop, and Chris Essert and Ketan Ramakrishnan.

[1] Vossen 2015, p. 72.

'manipulates certain non-normative facts about the world, facts that 'trigger' his natural conditional right.'[2]

Another example is the Kantian political theory that Arthur Ripstein explicitly bases on the principle that each person should respect each other's choice.[3] When Ripstein comes to justify original acquisition, he does not invoke the principle of respect for choice in a straightforward way. Instead, following Kant, he appeals to another principle, the 'postulate of public right.' This is a moral requirement that persons who cannot avoid conflict – such as conflict over claims to objects – enter a 'civil condition' containing public legal institutions. Those institutions must include a legislature. The legislature must make laws that reflect the '*a priori* united will' of all persons. Such laws, according to Ripstein, must legitimize the creation of property rights by original acquisition.

This kind of theorizing about original acquisition gives rise to a puzzle. Why would liberal theorists not embrace a straightforward choice-based account? This is the puzzle I address in the present paper.

One reason for rejecting an approach along the lines of the choice-based account is familiar. Such an account presupposes that some objects may be unowned – such that no person has any normative claim over them. In other words, the account presupposes the possibility of a truly *original* acquisition. Whereas if one presupposes, for example, some form of common ownership of all things, the choice-based account has no ground on which to operate. Indeed, as Pufendorf long ago recognized, 'upon supposition that all Men had originally an equal power over Things,' no straightforward justification of original acquisition seems possible.[4] Yet, many contemporary liberal theorists accept that at least some objects, at some points in time, may be unowned. In any event, this issue has been discussed extensively and I will not pursue it.

I identify two other obstacles that block liberal theorists' adoption of the choice-based account. These obstacles arise due to assumptions that theorists make about the nature of, on the one hand, acts of original acquisition, and on the one other, extant property rights. They arise, that is, because of assumptions about what original acquisition and property *are*.

I proceed to doubt the validity of these assumptions about the character of acts of acquisition and property rights. I also show how the choice-based

[2] Vossen 2015, p. 73.

[3] Ripstein 2009.

[4] Pufendorf 1729 [1672], IV.IV.5.

account, by adopting different assumptions, provides a plausible alternative understanding of property's original acquisition.

My aim here is mainly diagnostic: to identify what stands in the way of the choice-based account for theorists of a certain stripe. I will not otherwise try to make the account seem appealing. However, it should emerge that it has the following merits. It explains the original acquisition of property in a straightforward way. The views it presupposes about the nature of original acquisition and property are not implausible. The only moral principle it invokes, respect for choice, is intuitively attractive – at least, attractive *prima facie* or *pro tanto*. I do not suggest this is the only principle of political morality, that respect for choice would be valuable in a world without other goods, or that property claims arising from acts of acquisition should be absolute.

While I will mention many contemporary property theorists and a few historical figures, my aims are not exegetical – especially with regard to the historical figures. Relatedly I should note that, because the obstacles to the choice-based account I discuss are closely connected, separating them is somewhat artificial. Hence in discussing theorists' work I will often single out one aspect of a compound argument. I believe this brings out the relevant issues more clearly.

I

One obstacle that blocks the choice-based account of original acquisition is the drawing of a certain sort of distinction between acts of acquisition and extant property rights. In this part I will (a) identify the distinction, (b) show why it precludes a straightforward account of original acquisition, (c) cast doubt on its validity, and (d) show how the choice-based account avoids it.

A

Let us begin with a famous historical formulation of a problem, which seems to confront anyone seeking to justify the original acquisition of property. As Pufendorf puts it, the problem is that 'we cannot apprehend how a *bare Corporal Act*, such as Seizure is,' could create a property right.[5]

To bring out this aspect of Pufendorf's thought, consider a concrete example of an act of acquisition. The classic example in the literature is a

[5] Pufendorf 1729 [1672], IV.IV.5 (emphasis added).

person seizing a small, hitherto unowned object, such as an acorn, an apple, or a shell. Alternatively, the person might perform a slightly more elaborate act with respect to the object, such as eating the acorn or the apple. Or she might interact with a certain space, such as by occupying a plot of empty land, or sowing crops upon it. Pufendorf's thought is that this kind of act is merely the movement of a person's body, into contact with another, nonhuman body. It is a 'bare' (or in another translation, 'mere') corporal act.[6] Which prompts the question: why should such an act give rise to the special kind of legal or moral claim represented by a property right?

A similar thought appears in many other historical discussions of the justification of property – including discussions not directed solely at the problem of original acquisition. Consider, for example, Kant's distinction between 'empirical' and 'noumenal' possession.[7] 'Empirical' possession occurs where a person is in spatio-temporal contact with an object, as where she grasps an apple. 'Noumenal' possession is a claim by a person over an object that is not dependent on spatio-temporal contact between them. Such as a continuing claim someone might assert over an apple she has momentarily put down. Kant draws this contrast to point out what exactly a property theorist must seek to justify: not empirical, but noumenal possession.

Variations on the same thought appear in the work of many contemporary property theorists in the broadly liberal tradition. For example, Allan Gibbard begins a famous paper by distinguishing a merely *physical* act or change from the creation of a *moral* right or constraint.[8] Like Kant, Gibbard uses this distinction to identify what a theorist of property must seek to explain. Gibbard assumes that a merely physical act concerning an unowned object is generally legitimate.[9] This seems sensible, because people unobjectionably perform such acts all the time – they grasp and eat fruit, crush leaves underfoot, and so on – and it would be strange if they had to go to any lengths to justify that behaviour to others. Indeed, though he is not explicit about it, Gibbard seems to accept that in at least some circumstances it is wrong for other persons to interfere with physical acts of this kind.[10] However, Gibbard emphasizes that the merely physical act

[6] Pufendorf 1934 [1672], IV.IV.5.
[7] Kant 1996 [1798]. Of course Kant also discusses original acquisition.
[8] Gibbard 1979.
[9] Gibbard 1979.
[10] Gibbard 1979 (since he talks of a 'right' to use things physically).

is not what a theorist of property must address. She must explain the creation of a moral constraint, i.e., property.

Other contemporary theorists evince the same intellectual tendency in different ways. For example, they describe an original acquirer's act, such as seizing an object or occupying a space, as merely 'discretionary' or 'contingent.'[11] Or they characterize it is as a sort of 'fact' or event.[12] Theorists are also inclined to set out formulae in which the act of acquisition appears as an algebraic variable: 'an action or set of actions *a*, such that anyone who performs *a* with respect to some resource *ipso facto* becomes owner of that resource.'[13] By contrast, theorists invariably describe a property right in terms that presuppose a very different normative status. A property right is never 'mere,' or 'arbitrary,' or just a 'fact.' It is of course a 'right,' or a form of 'ownership.' It is either a legal claim or a 'moral constraint.'[14] Or, in perhaps the most abstract terminology: property is a 'normative situation.'[15]

Before reflecting on the nature of the distinction that, with any luck, is coming into focus, let us note a few other, somewhat different, versions that often appear. First, theorists often distinguish a person's right to her *body* from her *nonbodily* property rights, in the following context. The theorist acknowledges that a certain basic act – such as grasping or eating an apple – is generally legitimate and wrong for others to disrupt. But the theorist explains this by invoking a person's body, rather than her property rights. Presumably, each person has a right to her body, and so if she connects her body to an object, such as an apple, then another person's interference with the object, say by knocking the apple away, will be like an assault or battery. Thus, we can explain why such an interference is wrong, without invoking property rights. Property is put at issue only where someone asserts a claim over an object unconnected to her body. In this vein, Jeremy Waldron argues:

> Our duty not to knock the food out of the hand of someone who is eating it is derivative from the general duty not to assault. But such duties fall far short of duties to respect property rights. ... [T]hese duties would at most protect de facto physical possession. They would not be sufficient to establish ownership entitlements.[16]

[11] Waldron 1988, pp. 3, 112, 116–7, 266ff; Ripstein 2009, p. 24.
[12] Epstein 1979, p. 1240.
[13] Waldron 1988, p. 263. See also Thomson 1990, p. 324.
[14] E.g., Gibbard 1979, p. 78.
[15] Ripstein 2009, p. 24.
[16] Waldron 1988, p. 270. See also Kant 1996, 6:247–8, 251.

Another approach contrasts the *use* of an object with its *formal ownership*. Thomas Scanlon asks us to imagine a bucolic scene, disrupted:

> Imagine that a family is living in the wilderness when a group of strangers comes along and drives them off part of their land and takes their crops. This strikes us as a clear wrong. ... But it is open to question whether what we feel to be violated in such cases is really a ... right to property. ... For [such] cases strike us as clear wrongs only if we suppose ... that what is taken is of use to the person who loses it.... A system of property rights goes beyond this primitive right by specifying formal criteria of ownership.[17]

For Scanlon it is easy to see why one should not take an object someone else is using. It is less easy to see why one should refrain from taking an object that is not of use to the person from whom it is taken. The latter situation must be explained to account for property rights.

Scanlon also draws another, related distinction. He suggests certain basic acts with respect to objects might be protected as a matter of *natural* right, whereas property is *conventional*, posited, or social.[18] A basic act such as sowing crops could occur in a state of nature, and even there it would be wrong for others to disrupt. By contrast, full-blooded property rights are surely created by legal or social institutions and could not exist in a state of nature.

Finally, another related view holds that an act of acquisition is *simple*, while a property right is *complex*. Hence Judith Jarvis Thomson points out that it is not easy to see how any action an acquirer might perform on an object could, in itself, establish property.[19] According to Thomson, property is a complex cluster of Hohfeldian rights, liberties, and powers. How could somebody's mere act with respect to an object produce that complex deontic cluster?

In sum, theorists of property are inclined to distinguish two different situations, each involving a connection between a person and an object. On the one hand, the theorist calls attention to some *basic act* a person might perform with respect to an object – the kind of act that might constitute an original acquisition. For example, a person grasps an apple, or sows some crops in a field. Or, she performs some other act that appears to have a relatively primitive – *physical* or *empirical*, *bodily*, *usufructory*, *natural*, or *simple* – character. The theorist then distinguishes a second situation, which involves a *property right*. In this situation there is a more refined or

[17] Scanlon 1982, pp. 124–5.

[18] Scanlon 1982, pp. 124–5. See also Kant 1996 [1798], 6:255–8, 264–5.

[19] Thomson 1990, p. 324.

sophisticated connection between a person and an object. For example, the person who had been grasping an apple, or sowing some crops, stops doing so, but continues to assert a normative claim. Or, a person maintains some other connection to an object of an apparently *moral* or *noumenal, nonbodily, formal, conventional*, or *complex* character.

B

We have identified one obstacle to a straightforward account of the original acquisition of property: distinguishing the character of basic act with respect to an object – the kind of act that might constitute an acquisition – from that of a property right. Any such distinction precludes a straightforward approach along the lines of the choice-based account.

To see this, consider the rather extreme view on which a basic act with respect to an object, such as taking hold of an apple, is a mere arbitrary fact or event, whereas a property right is a normative condition. On this view, it is obviously an open question why the occurrence of the fact gives rise to the right. Richard Epstein makes this point, somewhat hyperbolically, when he observes that the mere fact of someone being the first to take possession of an object cannot explain the creation of property:

> The fundamental objection against ... theories of first possession ... is that ... it is simply not possible to move from a non-ethical premise to an ethical conclusion without there being a logical gap in the argument. Put in the context of the first possession rule ... [there is] an unbridgeable logical gap between the *fact* of possession and the *right* to possession.[20]

It is misleading of Epstein to say the gap is 'unbridgeable.' However, there is an explanatory or justificatory 'gap' between a mere fact or event, on the one hand, and a normative condition on the other. A property theorist seeking to account for the original acquisition of property must erect some sort of theoretical structure to bridge the gap: she must adduce a further argument that shows why a mere fact brings a right into being.

Hence, for example, we saw van der Vossen postulating a somewhat unfamiliar 'natural conditional claim-right' – to impose obligations on others – which an acquirer 'triggers' by performing an act of acquisition. Van der Vossen characterizes an act of acquisition as the 'manipulat[ion] of certain non-normative facts about the world.' He is therefore obliged to explain how such an act could bring about the normative condition of property. To do so, he postulates a special natural right.

[20] Epstein 1979, p. 1240.

The difficulty we have identified does not, however, arise only on the extreme view that a basic act with respect to an object lacks any normative import whatsoever. It also arises on more moderate views, which implicitly or explicitly acknowledge that the act has some normative significance, but nevertheless distinguish it from a property right. If the act and a property right have a distinct character or significance, nothing we say about one of them – that it exists, that it is justified, etc. – itself tells us anything about the other.

Thus, the difficulty we have identified arises if one takes it to be significant that an act of acquisition is *physical* or *empirical*, *bodily*, *usufructory*, *natural*, or *simple*, whereas a property right is by contrast *moral* or *noumenal*, *nonbodily*, *formal*, *conventional*, or *complex*. On all these views there is a gap between the act and the right, and an open question why performing the act brings the right into being. A theorist seeking to justify the original acquisition of property must erect a relatively elaborate theoretical structure to bridge the gap.

C

I will now raise some doubts (no more) about the tendency to distinguish the character of a basic act with respect to an object, such as an act of acquisition, from a property right. I will make three points.

First, in developing a moral theory of property, the ultimate aim of discussing basic acts and property rights is presumably to address whatever normative significance they have. Yet, the characterizations of the basic act that theorists propose do not directly relate to its normative significance. Thus, it is questionable whether those characterizations are appropriate in the context of a moral theory.

As we have seen, most theorists tend to accept – in my view rightly – that even a very basic act such as grasping an apple has a certain normative significance: it is *prima facie* legitimate and moreover wrong for others to disrupt. If you hold an apple, other things being equal I should not take it or knock it away. At the same time, many theorists seek to characterize this kind of act as, for example, a mere *fact* or *event*, or as *physical* or *empirical*. But of course merely factual, physical or empirical goings-on have no normative significance whatsoever. So it is unclear why one would adopt those characterizations of the basic act, in the context of a moral theory. Why not focus instead on whatever aspect of the act makes it normatively significant?

Perhaps less obviously, other characterizations of the basic act raise similar concerns. Consider the view that associates an act such as holding an apple with a person's entitlement to her *body*. At the outset an important clarification is needed here. Someone who interferes with the apple you hold may also interfere with your hand or arm. But whatever wrong occurs in this situation could also occur were you not holding anything. So we must exclude that situation in order to consider the normative significance of our basic act, holding an apple. We should imagine that someone plucks an apple off of another person's outstretched palm. (Or consider an example of Ripstein's: someone comes with a straw and sips the soup out of another's bowl.[21]) Now, can a person's entitlement to her body account for the wrongfulness of plucking an apple from her outstretched palm? Not if the entitlement to the body ends at the edge of the body.[22] So on this view, at least, associating the basic act with a person's body is merely a distraction.

Similarly, characterizing a basic act as *usufructory* is problematic. Because the act seems to have a certain normative significance regardless of whether any use is involved. When I hold an apple, at least *prima facie* you should not interfere even if the apple is inedible and I have no other use for it. Some normative significance accompanies mere possession. Likewise the characterization of the basic act as *natural* – as opposed to conventional – does not, without more, account for its normative status. Nor does the characterization of the act as *simple*. Simplicity and complexity are not normatively relevant in themselves.[23] In sum, all of the proposed characterizations of the basic act seem rather dubious if one is interested in its normative significance.

Second, a theorist who adopts any of these characterizations of the basic act can of course address the issue I have just raised. All she must do is supply some further argument or principle, which explains why a non-normative phenomenon, such as a physical movement, has normative significance – why it is wrong for others to disrupt. However, I suggest that by doing so, the theorist will only tend to confirm that her initial

[21] Ripstein 2009, p. 94.

[22] But compare Wheeler 1980. While my overall argument has affinities with Wheeler's, one crucial difference is that I claim choice or purposiveness is normatively significant, whereas he assumes one's body has such significance, leading him to make notoriously tendentious claims about the scope of a person's body.

[23] Note that similar issues will arise if we consider the other side of the coin, so to speak. At least some of the characterizations of property rights that theorists propose do not directly relate to property's normative significance. For example, characterizations of a property right as formal, conventional, or complex. Hence it is questionable why one would emphasize those aspects of property when developing a moral theory.

characterization of the basic act is misleading, at least in the context of a moral theory.

For example, we could explain why a *physical* act such as holding an apple is normatively significant – why it is wrong for others to disrupt – by adducing some further argument or principle. Perhaps, for instance, there is a moral principle that each person should be free to consume beneficial things.[24] Having done this, however, it seems misleading to characterize the basic act as *physical* when developing a moral theory of property. Instead, we should characterize the act as an exercise of the freedom to consume things. And so in discussing the original acquisition of property we should presumably ask, not why a merely physical act creates a property right, but why an exercise of the freedom to consume things does so.

Likewise, we could address the difficulty I raised for the *bodily* characterization of a basic act, by, say, postulating a moral principle that each person is entitled to control objects with her body. That would explain why it is wrong to pluck an apple from another's outstretched palm. However, adducing this principle only confirms that it is misleading to characterize a basic act, such as grasping an apple, as *bodily*. The act is morally significant because it is an exercise of a right to control. And so, in developing a moral theory of property, we should presumably ask about the connection between *that* kind of act and a property right.

Similarly, we could conceivably alter the *usufructory* account to explain the significance of mere possession, but having done so, I suggest, we ought to amend our characterization of the basic act accordingly, and discard the usufructory characterization as misleading. To salvage the *natural* view we could develop a more substantial conception of the natural – perhaps connecting the basic act to an aspect of human nature. But then, we should presumably adopt that characterization when developing a theory of property. We should ask, for example, why a certain sort of manifestation of human nature establishes a property right.

Third, if we amend our characterization of the basic act in the way I have suggested, to reflect its normative significance, the theorist's proposed distinction between the act and a property right will break down. For example, if we recharacterize the supposedly *factual*, *physical*, or *empirical* act of grasping an apple as an exercise of a freedom to consume beneficial things, then it clearly has a *normative*, *moral*, or *noumenal* aspect. Accordingly, we have lost our initial basis for distinguishing a basic act from a property right. Likewise, if we recharacterize the supposedly *bodily* act of holding

[24] Cf. Gibbard 1979, p. 78.

an apple as an exercise of a right to control, the act turns out to have a significant *non-bodily* aspect. Again, if we amend the usufructory characterization to account for the normative significance of mere possession, it would seem that a basic act must have some important non-usufructory, i.e., *formal*, aspect. Finally, if we view the act as some sort of manifestation of human nature, it seems likely that that conception of human nature may also feature in an explanation of the normative significance of property. In which case, we will no longer be able to distinguish property by characterizing it as purely *conventional*.

The various distinctions between a basic act and a property right seem to face a recurring set of difficulties. The distinctions either fasten on normatively irrelevant aspects of the phenomena in question, or else break down. While I certainly have not supplied any knock-down arguments here, a plausible conclusion is that we should try to avoid drawing a distinction between the act and the right in the first place.

D

On the choice-based account of the original acquisition of property, there is no normatively significant distinction between a basic act with respect to an object, such as an act of acquisition, and a property right. The act and the right are normatively unified – they are *the same* normative phenomenon – because each exhibits a person's choice.

On this view, there is no open question about why an act of acquisition ought to create a property right. There is no gap between the act and the right that must be bridged, and so no need to erect a theoretical structure to do the bridging. An act of acquisition creates a property right just because, in essence, it *is* a property right, making its first appearance on the scene.

To argue for this view I will address, first, the character of an act of acquisition, second, the character of an extant property right, to show we can understand each as exhibiting a person's choice.[25]

Contemporary theorists, as we have seen, are often remarkably agnostic about the character of original acquisition – about exactly what one must do to establish a property right over an unowned object. This is reflected in their use of algebraic formulae: 'an action or set of actions *a*, such that anyone who performs *a* ....'[26] A better view is that an act of original acquisition,

[25] My argument here largely follows Benson 2002.
[26] Waldron 1988. See also Vossen 2009.

whatever else it may also be, always has a certain character: it is a person's exercise of choice over an object.

At least throughout much of the world, the understanding of original acquisition as an exercise of choice appears in the law of property. Indeed, many students of the common law learn this in the first hour of their Property course, which begins with the Supreme Court of New York's decision in *Pierson* v. *Post*.[27] (Apologies to the lawyers for a brief recapitulation.) In 1802, in wintry Long Island, Lodowick Post was pursuing a fox with hounds when he was interrupted by a 'saucy intruder,' Jesse Pierson.[28] Pierson appeared in sight of Post, killed the fox Post was pursuing, and carried it off. The question was whether Post, by his initial pursuit, had acquired 'a right to, or property in, the fox,' so that Pierson's subsequent intrusion amounted to trespass.[29] The court and the parties accepted as uncontroversial that, in both the common and civil law, a property right in a wild animal is created by 'first possession.' The dispute concerned what amounted to 'possession' in the case at hand. The court held that Post's mere pursuit of the fox was insufficient. To establish a property right in a wild animal one must actually capture it, either by 'manucaption,' by mortal wounding, or by securing it with a net, snare or other means so as to render its escape impossible.[30] According to the court, this kind of act creates a property right,

> since, thereby, the pursuer manifests an unequivocal intention of appropriating the animal to his individual use, has deprived him of his natural liberty, and brought him within his certain control.[31]

[27] *Pierson* v. *Post*, 3 Cai 175 (1805). *Young* v. *Hichens* (1844) 6 QB 606 is the English equivalent.

[28] *Pierson* v. *Post* 1805, p. 181.

[29] *Pierson* v. *Post* 1805, p. 177.

[30] *Pierson* v. *Post* 1805, pp. 178–9.

[31] *Pierson* v. *Post* 1805, p. 178.One could focus on the first part of this quotation – the 'manifestation of an unequivocal intention' – and conclude that taking possession creates property because it is a sign of the acquirer's intent. See Rose 1985. But that would not fully explain *Pierson*. A mere manifestation of intent is insufficient. Indeed, by pursuing the fox, Post manifested his intent in a manner barely less equivocal than if he had manhandled the animal. Moreover, he might have ridden through Long Island shouting his intention to the rooftops, published it repeatedly in every available medium, carved it on a monument of stone; still, no property right would arise on that basis alone. See also *Brumagim* v. *Bradshaw*, 29 Cal 24 (1870) ('A mere intention to occupy ... however openly proclaimed, is not possession.'). Hence the second part of the quoted reasoning must be crucial: the acquirer must deprive the object of its 'natural liberty' thereby bringing it 'within his certain control.' See also *Brumagim* v. *Bradshaw* 1870, p. 44 ('subjection to the will'); *Young* v. *Hichens* 1844, p. 611 ('actual power').Taking possession creates property, not merely because of what it signifies, but because of what it is, a taking of control.

The rule of original acquisition by first possession does not apply only to foxes or other wild animals. It is a strikingly pervasive feature of law and morality more generally. Courts have applied it to everything from the occupation of land to the use of radio frequencies, and it appears in the instinctive resolution of acquisition disputes by children ('finders, keepers') and adults ('first come, first served') alike.[32]

Another way to put the rule of original acquisition by first possession is to say that an acquisition occurs when a person subjects an unowned object to her choice. 'Choice,' here, is an agent's purposive determination. (We might alternatively say, her 'action' or 'control.' Though any word I use here may potentially mislead.) This conception of choice is rooted in the philosophical tradition,[33] but it is admittedly narrower than contemporary usage of the word, and so some clarifications are in order. All I can do here is roughly sketch the contours of a certain conception of choice, and suggest it might be something – not the only thing – worthy of notice by a liberal theory of political morality.

Choice should be distinguished from *wish*. A desire to achieve something in the future, such as to get hold of an object one does not yet have, is merely a wish. You can wish for just about anything – for the moon. (So it is unlikely a political system could grant everyone's wishes.) *Pierson* v. *Post* helpfully illustrates the distinction between choice and wish. When Lodowick Post initially pursued the fox across the beach, he wished to catch it. Whereas the 'saucy intruder' Jesse Pierson subjected the fox to his choice by capturing it.

Of course, one could dispute the precise conclusion of a case such as *Pierson*. Does one really subject a wild animal to one's choice only by manucaption, mortal wounding, or securing it with a net, snare or other means so as to render escape impossible? Perhaps it should suffice if one chases the animal into a cul-de-sac from which escape is highly unlikely. Property students are taught *Pierson* in part so they can debate such issues. My point is only that one can, in principle, distinguish choices and wishes with respect to objects, and through an exercise of judgement apply such a distinction in a case such as *Pierson*.

Choice is also distinct from *use* or usufruct. When Jesse Pierson caught and held the fox, i.e., took *possession* of it, he subjected the animal to his choice or purposive determination. That sufficed for a property right. It was irrelevant whether Pierson planned to put the fox to any further use.

32 Lueck 2003.

33 Ripstein 2009, pp. 14, 40; Kant 1996, 6:213; Aristotle 1999, 1111a25.

(Whether he had further as-yet unrealized ends or wishes – to skin the fox, in order to sell the skin, in order to buy some whiskey, etc.[34]) It would be wrong for Post to interfere with Pierson's purposive determination of the object, regardless of whether doing so also disrupted any further use. For example, it would be wrong merely to stroke the fox without Pierson's permission.

Choice is also distinct from *labour* or effort. A choice may involve no significant labour, as when you catch an apple that falls into your hand, or occupy land by standing on it.[35] Conversely, you may labour on an object without subjecting it your choice. Post, for example, laboured on the fox by chasing it, though he failed to catch it.

Finally, the term 'choice' is less than ideal because it connotes self-conscious or intellectual decision-making. The purposive determination envisaged here need not be like that. Compare the way a normally functioning person may act, for example moving or positioning her limbs, even when not self-consciously directing herself towards doing so.

It is relatively easy to assert that an act of acquisition amounts to a person's exercise of choice over an object. What about an extant property right? A fully developed argument here would require engagement with the enormous literature on the nature of property ownership, which I will not undertake. Instead I will assume it is not implausible to think that a property right embodies the owner's choice over an object, and consider likely objections. Some we have already encountered.

One objection I suspect underlies the tendency to distinguish basic acts, such as grasping apples, from property rights. The objection is that a person who actually touches an object maybe purposively directing it, but a person who is not touching the object cannot be. However, this objection is based upon a misconceived form of empiricism. It equates a person's choice or purposive determination with a particular physical or empirical episode involving a spatio-temporal connection. In truth, that I put down my apple does not mean the object ceases to be subject to my choice. I may continue to choose its position and condition even if I do not touch it – even if I turn my back or walk away. This is an illustration of the general point that some characterizations of human conduct do not merely denote empirical episodes in space or time.[36] For example, to say that someone

[34] Ripstein 2013. Partly for this reason I do not characterize property as a 'means.' Contrast Ripstein 2009, pp. 66–8.

[35] Epstein 1979, pp. 1225–6.

[36] Ryle 2002, especially ch. V. Indeed, some characterizations cannot denote particular spatial or temporal episodes: it cannot correctly be said of someone that 'he is now engaged in

'speaks French' is not necessarily to claim he is at this moment emitting certain sounds, but to claim he is ordinarily able to do so. Hence we may say someone speaks French even if he is asleep. Likewise, to say that an object is subject to a person's choice is not necessarily to say she is currently touching or moving it, but that she is ordinarily able to do so.

If we can understand an object to be subject to someone's choice even when she puts it down, or steps away, we can understand any property right as exhibiting the owner's choice. Your objects of property are subject to your purposive determination even if you happen to be asleep, or even if you fly off to another part of the world and do not return for years. (Though of course, at some point you may be taken to have abandoned them.) I suggest your 'property' is the set of objects subject to your choice in this way.[37]

Another objection would be that the choice-based account fails to recognize the *conventional* aspect of property. A legal property right is the creature of detailed positive law, which defines the scope of the right in a way not necessitated by the abstract idea of a person's choice. The law tells us how far a right over real estate extends below and above ground level, whether it covers water flowing through the land, what volume of noise made by a neighbour will constitute undue interference, and so on.

The conventionality objection has been addressed by others. Gerald Gaus and Loren Lomasky point out that property law is not obviously more conventional or positive than any other area of law such as, say, freedom of speech or copyright. Yet we would not on the basis of their conventionality alone deny that freedom of speech or copyright law may reflect a liberal concern for human agency.[38] I make a similar claim on behalf of the choice-based account of property. The account is consistent with property being to a large extent conventional. The account need only deny any normatively significant distinction between the natural or brute choices someone could make in a state of nature, and the choices someone makes in the real world of social institutions and conventions.

A final, related objection would point to property's *complexity*. In the tradition of Hohfeld and Honoré (and Thomson), a property right is

possessing a bicycle.' Ryle 2002, p. 116. Ryle is sometimes thought of as a sort of empiricist (or 'behaviorist'), whatever the truth of that, 'choice' as I am presenting it is a normative idea.

[37] Of course in any legal system the recognition of some property rights may be overly enthusiastic, allowing people to assert claims over objects that are not, or no longer, subject to their choice.

[38] Gaus and Lomasky 1990.

a multifarious bundle or cluster of deontic relations with respect to an object, the precise composition of the bundle varying from case to case. How could this be explained by so simplistic a conception of property as the choice-based account?

Again, others have addressed the complexity objection. James Penner has famously argued that the complexity of property may be overstated.[39] Property of course appears incredibly complex if we lack a coherent organizing idea to unify its various incidents. However, the appearance of complexity might dissipate if we could bring such an idea into focus. Moreover, Peter Benson has suggested that the idea of a person's purposive control of an object can explain at least the main incidents of legal property rights – possession, use, and alienation – and that property's other significant incidents reduce to those three.[40]

II

Returning to the theoretical literature on the original acquisition of property we would find we are not yet done in clearing the way for a straightforward, choice-based account. Another crucial obstacle remains. It involves a view about what I will call the 'form' of property rights and acts of acquisition. Again I will (a) identify the view, (b) show why it precludes a straightforward account of original acquisition, (c) cast doubt on its validity, and (d) show how the choice-based account avoids it.

A

We can begin again with Pufendorf. His statement of the challenge confronting a theorist who seeks to justify original acquisition, with which the previous part began, continues: 'we cannot apprehend how a bare Corporal Act, such as Seizure is, *should be able to prejudice the Right and Power of others*.'[41] One way to elaborate this aspect of Pufendorf's thought is as follows. An act of acquisition is just one person's action. The acquirer decides, say, to seize an object. It is difficult to see how such an action could have a normative effect *upon other persons*, by creating a property right.

At least on one reading, Kant articulates a similar idea. He claims, 'When ... I will that something external is to be mine, I thereby declare that

[39] Penner 1996.

[40] Benson 2002.

[41] Pufendorf 1729 [1672] (emphasis added).

everyone else is under an obligation to refrain from using that object.'[42] But for Kant it is difficult to see how one person could, through her merely 'unilateral will,' impose obligations on other persons.[43]

Variations on the same thought often appear in the work of contemporary property theorists. Earlier we saw Gibbard distinguish a merely physical act with respect to an object from the creation of a moral right. In drawing this distinction, Gibbard notes that the creation of a moral right is particularly problematic because it means the acquirer is able

> to bring [another person] under new moral constraints: to make it cease to be morally permissible for him to do certain things ... or to make it morally permissible to coerce him in certain ways.[44]

The same intellectual tendency is evident in discussions about property not directed at the particular problem of original acquisition. In particular, theorists in the tradition of Hohfeld often make the following point about the nature of property. Naïvely, one might suppose that a property right is just a person's claim over an object. We might say: her unilateral claim over the object. This view has some folk and traditional legal usage on its side – in everyday life one's 'property' is, roughly, the stuff one has, or the assets one controls. However, Hohfeld and his followers reject this naïve view. They contend that a property right must be *correlative* in form.

According to Hohfeld a property right is 'correlative' in the sense that it always corresponds to a duty, on the part of another particular person, with respect to the right's subject-matter.[45] A 'duty' 'is that which one ought or ought not to do.'[46] So for example, Hohfeld characterizes a property right concerning land as follows: 'if X has a right against Y that he shall stay off the former's land, the correlative (and equivalent) is that Y is under a duty toward X to stay off the place.'[47]

Hohfeld maintains that a property right must be correlative in part because he believes all rights are relational: they involve a relation between a person and another person.[48] If one assumes a property right is relational,

42 Kant 1996 [1798], 6:256. See also Kant 1996 [1798], 6:260–1.

43 Kant 1996 [1798], 6:256.

44 Gibbard 1979, p. 78.

45 Hohfeld 1919. For Hohfeld, talk of 'a' property right is too simplistic, but we can ignore this for present purposes.

46 Hohfeld 1913–14.

47 Hohfeld 1913–14.

48 Hohfeld 1913–14, p. 75. An apparently troubling implication of the naïve view is that someone could have a property right even if he were alone in the world – Adam, before Eve arrived, for example, or Crusoe before Friday. E.g., Pufendorf 1729 [1672], IV.IV.3; Kant 1996 [1798], 6:260–1.

it cannot, as the naïve view suggests, amount merely to a person's unilateral claim over an object. Instead, it seems, the right must correlate with a duty on the part of another person.

The correlative conception of a property right has been so influential that by the early twentieth century Hans Kelsen, for example, could express incredulity that the naïve view 'continues to be maintained' – 'despite the repeated objection that the legal power of a person over a thing consists in nothing else than a specific relationship to other subjects, namely, in their duty to refrain from interfering.'[49] The correlative view continues to be affirmed by property theorists today.[50]

B

The correlative conception of a property right is another obstacle to a straightforward account of original acquisition. If the right is correlative in form, then an original acquirer of property obtains a claim on another person. Which prompts the question: how can an acquirer, by performing an act of acquisition, entitle herself to such a claim?[51] A property theorist who seeks to justify original acquisition will have to advance some relatively elaborate argument in order to answer that question.

Indeed, original acquisition now seems especially difficult to justify if one endorses the moral principle that each person should respect each other's choice. Because an original acquisition of property itself appears to violate the principle of respect for choice. By acquiring a claim on the duty-bearer, the right-holder determines what the duty-bearer ought or ought not to do, and to that extent determines the duty-bearer's actions or choices. To use the terminology that 'republican' and Kantian political theorists tend to favour: the right-holder *dominates* the duty-bearer. The duty-bearer is rendered *dependent* upon the right-holder.

Hence for example we saw Ripstein seek to justify original acquisition by appealing to a 'civil condition' of public legal institutions. Ripstein accepts that original acquisition is problematic because one person unilaterally establishes a claim on another. To fix the problem, he argues that laws passed by properly functioning public institutions in some sense

[49] Kelsen 1934.

[50] E.g., Essert 2014.

[51] See further Vossen 2015, p. 66. By contrast, someone who does not assume the correlative view may regard original acquisition as obviously unproblematic. See Feser 2005.

reflect the '*a priori* united will' of all persons, and so can legitimize acts of acquisition that would otherwise be objectionable.

C

I will now raise some doubts about the view that a property right is 'correlative' in form whereas an act of acquisition is merely 'unilateral.' There is reason to suspect that the act and the right must have the same form – and that that form that is *neither* correlative nor purely unilateral.

My argument rests on an assumption we have already encountered: that even a basic act with respect to an object, such as grasping an apple, has a certain normative significance. The act is *prima facie* legitimate and wrong for others to disrupt. Furthermore, I will assume here that it is at least *prima facie* wrong for someone to interfere with another person's *property right*. To this extent, then, a basic act and a property right apparently have a similar normative significance.

In light of those assumptions, we have reason to doubt, first of all, that a basic act with respect to an object is properly characterized as merely 'unilateral' – as just a person's claim over an object. The act has certain normative implications for other persons, entailing that their disruption or interference is wrongful, and in this respect the act is similar to a property right. Given its normative implications for other persons, a *property right* must, as Hohfeldian theorists insist, be understood in relational terms. It cannot be understood as just an individual's unilateral claim over an object. If that is true of property, it is presumably true also of our basic act. To understand the normative significance of a basic act such as grasping an apple, it would seem, we must view it in relational terms.

Second, however, there is reason to doubt that the shared relational form of acts of acquisition and property rights could be the 'correlative' one that Hohfeld identifies. Because if a basic act, such as grasping an apple, involves the actor making a correlative claim on other persons' actions, this calls into question the legitimacy of all such acts. Whenever someone grasps or eats a piece of fruit, tramples leaves underfoot, and so on, we would have to say that she makes claims on other persons. Those persons could therefore object to her moral imposition. Indeed, on this view, a basic act such as grasping an apple is *prima facie* illegitimate. Consequently, we have reason to look for some other understanding of the basic act – and, by extension, since they seem to share the same normative form – of a property right.

Of course, a theorist seeking to defend the correlative view could adduce some further argument, designed to explain why a basic act is legitimate despite its apparently troubling normative implications for other persons.[52] Even if such argument succeeds, however, we should be tempted to investigate whether there is a more straightforward approach. It seems strange that we should have to go to any lengths to justify basic acts such as holding apples and walking through leaves. Surely, one might suppose, there must be some alternative understanding of a basic act on which it does not raise any problem of justification in the first place.

In conclusion, I suggest we should be sceptical of the tendency to characterize acts of acquisition as purely unilateral, and property rights as correlative. It seems that both the act and the right have the same form – which must be relational but *not* correlative.

D

On the choice-based account, a basic act with respect to an object and a property right have the same form. However, that form is captured neither by a naïve 'unilateral' nor by the Hohfeldian 'correlative' view. To show this, I will present an alternative view of the form of a property right. Subsequently, it should be easy to see that the same view can extend to a basic act such as an act of acquisition.

We are looking for an alternative understanding of a property right, which depicts it as relational but which is not the Hohfeldian correlative view. What alternative form of relationality could a property right exhibit? Recall why the correlative view is problematic. The problem, couched in 'republican' or Kantian terms, is that on this view the right-holder dominates the duty-bearer; the duty-bearer is dependent on the right-holder. Now, if we can conceive of a relation of domination or dependence in this context, we may alternatively be able to imagine a relation of *independence*.

In a relation of dependence, one person's choices are determined by another. By contrast, in a relation of independence, one person's choices are impervious to determination or disruption by another. Note that, while independence is a relation, it presupposes some content that is defined nonrelationally.[53] In order to uphold a person's

[52] See Vossen 2015, pp. 69–71. See also Breakey 2009.

[53] At least, each relation of independence presupposes some content defined without reference to that particular relation. The content may be defined by another relation.

choice as independent – impervious to disruption by another person – we must able to define what that choice is, prior to the alleged disruption.

Which brings us to the choice-based account of property. On this account, as we have seen, a property right exhibits the right-holder's choice over an object – an apple, a fox, land, etc. In this way, the content of the right is defined non-relationally, by reference to the right-holder's unilateral choice. However, that is not the end of the story. A property right is not *purely* unilateral; it also involves a relation. Specifically, a relation of independence, in which the right-holder's choice is impervious to determination or disruption by another person. On the choice-based account, this relational aspect is supplied by a principle of political morality that should by now be familiar: the principle that each person must respect each other's choice.

In sum: the choice-based account understands 'a property right' to be: a person's choice over an object, combined with a moral principle mandating the independence of each person's choice. I suggest this conception can also easily extend to a basic act with respect to an object, such as grasping an apple. The significance of this act too is that it exhibits a person's choice, which others must respect.

We now have the materials in place for a remarkably straightforward justification of property's original acquisition. An original acquisition of property is a person's exercise of choice over an unowned object; once this occurs, each other person must refrain from interfering with the object so as to respect the first person's choice.

Finally let me briefly consider one likely objection to this view about the form of acts of acquisition and property rights. One might argue that if an acquirer chooses, say, to grasp an apple, with full knowledge of the moral principle of respect for choice, she *effectively* chooses to determine other persons' choices, by capitalizing on the moral principle. However, I suggest that, if a property right truly involves a relation of independence (rather than dependence) then the person who grasps an apple cannot determine another's choice – even if she knows of and seeks to capitalize on our moral principle. Because it is a precondition for the operation of that principle that *another person* has performed, or is about to perform, a certain action – an actual or threatened interference. So all the acquirer can choose – even if she is fully aware of the normative consequences of her acquisition – is that her own choice be resistant to disruption by the action of another, if and when that person makes his own choice to interfere.

In the vast literature on original acquisition in the liberal tradition, it is rare to find a straightforward, choice-based account along the lines I have outlined.[54] Certainly, most contemporary liberal theorists pursue relatively elaborate justificatory routes – involving Kantian postulates, natural conditional claim-rights, and other such devices. If those theorists reconsider the character of acts of acquisition and property rights they may be able to embrace a more straightforward approach.

[54] Two major contemporary exceptions are Benson 2002, and Penner 2013. The major historical exception is Hegel 1991 [1821], § 50. Although he is often interpreted otherwise. See e.g., Waldron 1988, ch. 10.

6

Appropriating Lockean Appropriation on Behalf of Equality

MICHAEL OTSUKA

In what follows, I consider the extent to which John Locke's account of property can be interpreted – or something revisionary that remains recognizably Lockean can be reconstructed from his writings – in a manner that provides a sound justification for an egalitarian distribution of resources in contemporary societies. In particular, I examine Locke's account, in Chapter 5 ('Of Property') of his *Second Treatise of Government*, of the conditions under which one can come privately to own land in a state of nature – where 'land' encompasses land in the narrow sense, spatial regions above and below it, and the natural resources therein. I shall argue that the Lockean 'enough and as good' proviso grounds egalitarian as opposed to libertarian or sufficientarian claims over worldly resources. These egalitarian claims apply to contemporary post-industrial money-based service economies as well as to primitive agrarian barter economies. But the full 'luck egalitarian' complement of equality of opportunity for welfare cannot be derived from a Lockean approach that focuses on our egalitarian claims to unowned bits of the world.

6.1 The Lockean Proviso

According to the Lockean proviso, one can acquire unowned land (and its fruits) provided that, after one has done so, there is 'enough, and as good, left in common for others' (II.27).[1] As I shall interpret the proviso, its justification traces to the following more general underlying normative principle: one is entitled to acquire worldly resources so long as one's acquisition does not give rise to a legitimate complaint on the part of anybody else.

Besides the editors and contributors to this volume, I thank Peter Vallentyne, Alex Voorhoeve, and two anonymous readers for their comments.

[1] This notation refers to §27 in the second of Locke's *Two Treatise of Government* (Locke 1998 [1690]). Throughout this chapter all such references will be to the numbered sections of the *Second Treatise*.

This general principle has been embraced by opponents as well as proponents of egalitarianism. Robert Nozick, for example, famously appeals to the proviso in his defense of the inequalities of laissez-faire capitalism. Nevertheless, his understanding of the proviso is of a piece with the general principle articulated above, since Nozick writes that 'Locke's proviso that there be "enough and as good left in common for others" ... is meant to ensure that the situation of others is not worsened'.[2] The implicit assumption here is that if one doesn't worsen the situation of others, none will have a legitimate complaint.

Nozick embraces a version of the proviso according to which you may acquire previously unowned land (and its fruits) if and only if you make nobody else worse off than she would have been in a state of nature in which no land is privately held but each is free to gather and consume food and water from the land and make use of it. Nozick argues that a capitalist society without a welfare state could emerge from the state of nature without violating this proviso. He advances the view that the lot of each person would be improved by the fruits of capitalism. The improvements would be great enough that no one will be made worse off than he or she would have been if he or she had remained in a state of nature.[3] Surely some in a capitalist society without public or state welfare provisions will starve in the absence of charity. But Nozick must maintain that they are not worse off than they would have been in a state of nature and therefore that they would also have starved (again, in the absence of charity) in a state of nature.[4]

Nozick's version of the proviso is unsound for the following reason.[5] My acquiring unowned land might eliminate other people's opportunities to improve their situation in the future even though it makes people no worse off than they would have been if they had remained in a state of nature. Under Nozick's proviso, one can pre-empt others from making any acquisitions of their own that would improve their situations over that in which they live no better than a meagre hand-to-mouth existence of hunters and gatherers on non-private land. This acquisition is objectionable both because it condemns others to such a miserable existence and because it is manifestly unfair that a first grabber be allowed to monopolize all opportunities to improve one's lot through acquisition.

[2] Nozick 1974, p. 175.

[3] See Nozick 1974, p. 177.

[4] See Cohen 1995, pp. 85–6.

[5] Here I follow Cohen 1995, ch. 3, in a manner that draws on Otsuka 2003, pp. 22–4.

A natural solution to these problems with Nozick's version of the proviso is its replacement with an *egalitarian* version, according to which one's enclosure of land must be such that everyone else retains the opportunity to enclose an equally good plot of land. In other words, 'enough, and as good' should be interpreted to mean 'enough so that everyone else can acquire an equally good share of unowned worldly resources'.[6] Such a reading is suggested by Locke's assertion that 'He that had as good left for his improvement, as was already taken up, needed not complain' (II.34).[7]

Considerations that tell in favour of an egalitarian version of the proviso offer grounds not only for rejection of Nozickian laissez-faire capitalism. They also provide grounds for rejection of more redistributive approaches to justice in holdings which call for the provision of a sufficient level of goods, rather than for the realization of equality above and beyond such sufficiency. To take the most well-known defender of such an approach, Harry Frankfurt has argued that, when everyone has enough, further differences in their wealth and income are not a matter of moral concern. He writes, for example, that we 'tend to be quite unmoved, after all, by inequalities between the well-to-do and the rich; our awareness that the former are substantially worse off than the latter does not disturb us morally at all'.[8] In mounting his case against equality, however, Frankfurt equivocates between two senses of 'enough'. At times, what he means by 'enough' is roughly 'so much that that one doesn't really care whether one has any more'.[9] I agree with Frankfurt that if the differences are ones that people don't really care about, then they are not morally problematic. But here the target of his critique is a straw man, since no sensible egalitarian would mount any serious objection to such differences. At other points, Frankfurt's case against egalitarianism involves an appeal to an understanding of 'enough' which is along the different lines of 'enough to meet one's needs'.[10] Even, however, when 'needs' are expansively construed, so long as people care about more than the meeting of such needs, a Lockean thought experiment involving acquisition in a state of nature can be

[6] I formulated such an egalitarian proviso in Otsuka 2003, p. 24. Here, however, I replace the term 'advantageous' with 'good'.

[7] Karl Widerquist suggests such a reading, by drawing attention to the phrase 'as was already taken up'. See Widerquist 2010, p. 12.

[8] Frankfurt 1987, p. 32.

[9] See, e.g., Frankfurt 1987, sec. VII and the top of p. 33.

[10] See, e.g., Frankfurt 1987, p. 32, from the middle of p. 33 to the top of p. 34, and the top half of p. 37. I am indebted to Jerry Cohen for drawing my attention to the manner in which Frankfurt's case against equality rests on an equivocation.

deployed in order to defeat an account of distributive justice that is limited to the satisfaction of needs.

Imagine that you and I are identical twins who inhabit a two-person state of nature. Each of us would acquire a sufficient amount to meet his needs, generously construed, if he enclosed one tenth of the commons. Suppose that I then proceed to enclose nine tenths of the commons. If you affirm a sufficiency-based account of distributive justice, and the accompanying claim that inequalities above the level of sufficiency are not morally problematic, you would lack grounds to complain of any injustice, since, by hypothesis, I have left you a sufficient amount. Nevertheless, you have a complaint of injustice: namely, that I have not left enough and as good for you to appropriate because I have not restricted myself to a share no greater than half of the commons. Such reflection on Lockean justice in acquisition in a state of nature reveals that we have an egalitarian claim to worldly resources that extends beyond the realm of sufficiency, assuming that this realm is understood as covering needs without also encompassing everything that one has reason to care about. In this light, recall Frankfurt's contrast between the well-to-do and the rich. Assume that they are both situated within this realm and that the explanation of the greater riches of the latter is solely traceable to the fact that they have taken it upon themselves to unilaterally appropriate a much greater portion of the commons. I submit that we would and should now react with moral disapprobation rather than indifference.

A related counterexample can be pressed against John Simmons's reading of the Lockean proviso. According to Simmons, one's appropriation leaves enough and as good for another just in case one leaves that person with 'the opportunity of *a living* – a condition of nondependence, in which one is free to better oneself, govern one's own existence, and enjoy the goods God provided for all'.[11] Simmons notes that this requirement does not necessarily mandate the leaving of equal shares for others. Rather, it is sufficient to leave others with nothing greater than 'access to an independent livelihood'.[12] Once again, as in the case of Frankfurtian sufficiency, so long as there are things that people care about beyond independence, Simmons' version of the proviso permits the monopolization, through appropriation, of access to these things. That, however, would involve the appropriation of an unfairly unequally large share of the earth. We need to move beyond a standard of nondependence to one of equality.

[11] Simmons 1992, p. 293.

[12] Simmons 1992, p. 294.

The following question now arises: how strong a standard of equality does the Lockean account support?

I would resist a weakly egalitarian reading of 'equally good shares' according to which there is such equality just in case shares are such that none would prefer to trade her plot of land with anybody else's.[13] In other words, I would resist a reading where such equal goodness involves the satisfaction of an envy test.[14] To explain my resistance, I ask you to imagine that you and another person are the only two shipwreck survivors on a desert island whose land is of uniformly high quality throughout. The two of you seek to divide the island between yourselves, in accordance with an egalitarian version of the Lockean proviso. Suppose, however, that you are twice as large as the other person and therefore require twice as many calories to survive. If you divide the island equally, then your harvest from the land you farm will never be quite enough to satisfy your appetite. The other person, by contrast, will always have enough to feast. Here I think your smaller colleague will leave you with enough and as good land in an egalitarian sense only if he leaves *twice as much* land for you to acquire. Only then will each of you be left with enough and as good to better yourself to the same degree as the other person. One's coming to acquire previously unowned resources under these terms leaves nobody else at a disadvantage (or, in Locke's words, is 'no prejudice to any others'), where being left at a disadvantage is understood as being left with less than an equally good share of resources (or, in Locke's words, being left with less than 'enough and as good').

To generalize from the above discussion, on my preferred more strongly egalitarian version of the proviso, shares are equally good insofar as they make it possible for each to better herself to the same degree as anyone else, where betterness is specified as the attainment of the same level of welfare as anybody else.[15] Acquisition on such terms would not give rise

[13] Hillel Steiner (Steiner 1987) once embraced such a reading. That article does not reflect Steiner's later (Steiner 1994) view, which is more strongly egalitarian.

[14] Such a test figures prominently in Dworkin's theory of 'equality of resources' – though he applies this test to bundles of natural resources and 'personal resources', where the latter involve physical and mental capacities. See Dworkin 1996, pp. 45–8. In the main text above, however, the envy test is applied more narrowly just to natural resources.

[15] See Otsuka 2003, p. 27. The phrase 'to the same degree' can be interpreted either as 'by the same increment of increase in welfare' or 'to the same absolute level of welfare'. See my discussion in Otsuka 2003, pp. 28–9. A 'same increment' reading can be more plausibly derived from a Lockean focus on claims over land than a 'same absolute level' reading. For the latter, one needs to appeal to different considerations, such as those of luck egalitarian unfairness to which I appeal in the book. I also maintain, however, that the two readings

to a legitimate complaint on the part of anybody else. Any more weakly egalitarian versions of the proviso, such as one that satisfies the envy test, would, like Nozick's or Simmons's non-egalitarian provisos discussed above, unfairly allow some to acquire greater advantage (in terms of well-being) than others from their acquisition of unowned land and other worldly resources. People who are less able to convert resources into welfare would not be compensated for this disability, whereas they would be so compensated on my version.

Under my version of the proviso, unlike Nozick's, we would not see the rise, as we would under laissez-faire capitalism, of a class of largely propertyless workers whose fates are not much better than they would have been in a state of nature, nor would we see the rise of a small class of capitalists with full property rights over enormous expanses of land or other natural resources. Rather, land and other resources would be much more widely dispersed to the equal advantage of all, where such equality would also extend beyond the level that merely reaches Frankfurt's threshold of sufficiency or secures Simmons's condition of nondependency.

Moreover, this equal advantage would be preserved across generations, given that, on my egalitarian reading, the 'enough and as good' proviso applies intergenerationally: the members of each generation are required to ensure that, at their deaths, resources that are at least as valuable as those that they have acquired lapse back into a state of non-ownership. Since, moreover, individuals possess only lifetime leaseholds on worldly resources, they have nothing more than lifetime leaseholds on whatever worldly resources they improve. Any worldly object they improve through their labour lapses into a state of non-ownership upon their death and hence is not bequeathable.[16]

6.2 Money

In the previous section, I have defended an egalitarian interpretation of the Lockean proviso. I have also maintained that, so interpreted, it has substantial implications regarding the distribution and transfer of resources in contemporary societies. One might challenge the notion that a proviso regarding the enclosure of land in a state of nature could have implications

converge, given the sound assumption that we would all be equally badly off, because dead, in the absence of any resources.

[16] For a discussion of the intergenerational implications of an egalitarian version of the proviso, see Otsuka 2003, ch. 1, sec. V.

for advanced industrial societies some distance removed from such circumstances. Such a challenge might be buttressed by the claim that Locke denied that the 'enough and as good' proviso reached as far as a societies that had advanced, via the introduction of money, beyond simple barter economies. In this section, I shall consider and reject this latter claim.

Locke says that 'since gold and silver, being little useful to the life of man in proportion to food, raiment, and carriage, has its value only from the consent of men, whereof labour yet makes, in great part, the measure, it is plain, that men have agreed to a disproportionate and unequal possession of the earth' (II.50). What are his grounds for maintaining that consent to treat gold and silver as money implies an agreement to 'disproportionate and unequal possession'? Is such agreement meant to encompass a suspension of the proviso's 'enough and as good' restriction on enclosure? I would resist such an interpretation of Locke according to which consent to money implies consent to the suspension of the proviso. There is, instead, a plausible reading according to which the proviso retains its force, yet inequality in possession is justified by virtue of the fact that a non-spoilage condition that Locke also places on the acquisition of property no longer imposes such pressing, and equalizing, constraints on accumulation.[17]

Locke offers the following articulation of and rationale for such a non-spoilage condition:

> The same law of nature, that ... give[s] us property, does also bound that property too. God has given us all things richly ... [t]o enjoy. As much as any one can make use of to any advantage of life before it spoils, so much he may by his labour fix a property in: whatever is beyond this, is more than his share, and belongs to others. Nothing was made by God for man to spoil or destroy. (II.31)

Locke also maintains that money gives rise to opportunities for large and unequal accumulations because it overcomes the problem of spoilage of what one produces or exchanges via barter.[18] On this reading, the more industrious and talented will be able to become far wealthier than others

[17] For a contrasting account of Locke's understanding of the bearing of consent to the value of money on inequality, see Penner 2018.

[18] Locke maintains that money can arise 'out of the bounds of society' by means of consent to confer value on gold and silver as mediums of exchange. In maintaining that it can arise in a state of nature, Locke's account of the origins and nature of money is out of line with a chartalist account. According to chartalism, money is essentially an IOU that is either created or authorized by the state, as the only acceptable way of discharging one's tax liabilities, whose payment is coerced via threat of punishment. Some chartalists have argued that, once the manner in which money is bound up with state coercion is recognized, Locke's justification of inequality is undermined (see Bell, Henry, and Wray 2004).

through the increased opportunities that money provides for the accumulation of wealth as the result of production and trade.

I would also maintain that Locke's reference to agreement to a 'disproportionate and unequal possession of the earth' needn't imply the lapsing, or otherwise imply the absence, of a specifically *egalitarian* version of the Lockean proviso. According to Locke, prior to the introduction of money, the demand for land was limited, and nobody had reason to enclose an especially large tract of land. This is for the reason that, in the absence of money, the goods that one could produce from the land were largely perishable (e.g., crops). Hence one could not accumulate much via production or barter with other landowners without violating the spoilage constraint. No non-wasteful purpose would be served by enclosing a very large plot of land. To make this point, Locke asks us to suppose

> an island, separate from all possible commerce with the rest of the world, wherein there were but an hundred families, but there were sheep, horses and cows, with other useful animals, wholsome fruits, and land enough for corn for a hundred thousand times as many, but nothing in the island, either because of its commonness, or perishableness, fit to supply the place of money. (II.48)

He then asks:

> what reason could any one have there to enlarge his possessions beyond the use of his family, and a plentiful supply to its consumption, either in what their own industry produced, or they could barter for like perishable, useful commodities, with others? Where there is not some thing, both lasting and scarce, and so valuable to be hoarded up, there men will not be apt to enlarge their possessions of land, were it never so rich, never so free for them to take: for I ask, what would a man value ten thousand, or an hundred thousand acres of excellent land, ready cultivated, and well stocked too with cattle, in the middle of the inland parts of America, where he had no hopes of commerce with other parts of the world, to draw money to him by the sale of the product? It would not be worth the enclosing, and we should see him give up again to the wild common of nature, whatever was

I would maintain, contrary to these chartalists, that, even if it is only via imposition of taxes that money arises, Locke's argument for inequality goes through with equal force (however great), given that money provides a means of accumulation without spoilage. Note that, even if money arises via a mafia-style protection racket rather than the state, it might still provide a means of accumulation that is justified by the fact that one can now do so without spoilage. One might object that the genesis of such accumulation is unjust, given that it occurs via unjustly imposed money. But if those who accumulate are themselves all *victims* of the protection racket, I don't see how their accumulation would be rendered illegitimate by the fact that they have been unjustly victimized.

> more than would supply the conveniencies of life to be had there for him and his family. (II.48)

An implication of this passage is that where, by contrast, there *is* 'some thing, both lasting and scarce, and so valuable to be hoarded up,' in that case some will be 'apt to enlarge their possessions of land'. As a result, 'disproportionate and unequal possession of the earth' (II.50) might arise, with the introduction of money, in a manner that does not violate the spoilage constraint.

To maintain that such inequality might arise is not necessarily, however, to reject an egalitarian proviso on appropriation. Inequality in land is consistent with such a proviso, so long as the inequality of appropriation arises in circumstances in which a sufficient amount of land remains unowned. To illustrate this point, we can replace the island in Locke's example with a sparsely populated continent of farmers who now possess money. These circumstances will give rise to valuable opportunities, for those who have greater desire to accumulate wealth through productive labour, to appropriate more land than others choose to appropriate. Such unequal appropriation would be consistent with an egalitarian version of the proviso – i.e., would leave others with the opportunity to appropriate an equally good share – so long as there remains sufficient unowned land for others to appropriate. In this case, 'possessions in different proportions' might be fully explained by 'different degrees of industry' (II.48) rather than by any failure to leave enough and as good. Here unequal plots of land would not imply encroachment on anyone else's opportunities to enclose.

Locke maintained that, on account of the resulting 'increase of people and stock', the introduction of money would typically give rise to scarcity 'amongst that part of mankind that have consented to the use of money'. Among these people there would no longer be 'more [land] than the people who dwell on it do, or can make use of' (II.45). In such conditions of scarcity in which all land is appropriated, and none is left unclaimed, universal satisfaction of the proviso implies that each actually appropriates an equally good share of land. Even if we accept the strongly welfare egalitarian interpretation of equal shares that I defended in the previous section, the opportunities to accumulate to which money gives rise may nevertheless yield significant inequalities in levels of wealth at the end of the day. These inequalities will, however, be consistent with what has come to be known as 'luck egalitarianism'. This is because they will be purely a matter of differently chosen 'degrees of industry' among individuals whose plots of land provide them with equal opportunities to better themselves. These differences will not be a matter of factors beyond their control.

6.3 Luck Egalitarianism and the Diminished Role of Labour

Locke appears to regard labour as a necessary condition of coming to have a title to any bit of the world. He writes, for example, that 'God gave the world ... to the use of the industrious and rational, (and labour was to be his title to it;) not to the fancy or covetousness of the quarrelsome and contentious' (II.34).

We should, however, acknowledge that labouring is not the only way to stake a claim to worldly resources. For, if it were, then

> incapacitated individuals who are incapable of mixing any of their labour with worldly resources would be unfairly deprived of any method of acquiring resources which might nevertheless be useful to them. They ought to be entitled to stake a claim simply by publicly proclaiming the boundaries of the worldly resources over which they claim rights of ownership.[19]

I acknowledged that

> [p]erhaps the mere staking of a claim that does not leave others at a disadvantage would not be sufficient to generate a property right. One might need to add that the resources in question must be of some use to the claim-staker, where 'use' is read broadly to include the benefit one could derive from trading them for something else or from investing them.[20]

In defense of such a broad construal of 'use', I draw your attention to II.46, where Locke describes exchange as a form of use – or at least of keeping resources, e.g., plums, useful.[21] It follows that those who are disabled from producing can nevertheless still make use of resources by buying and selling them.

Moreover, Locke's contrast in the passage from II.34 quoted above – between, on the one hand, the claims of the 'industrious and rational' and, on the other hand, the 'fancy or covetousness of the quarrelsome and contentious' – lends itself to a luck egalitarian reading that is sensitive to the

[19] Otsuka 2003, p. 22 n. 29.

[20] Otsuka 2003, p. 22 n. 29.

[21] Locke writes: 'If he gave away a part to anybody else, so that it perished not uselessly in his possession, these he also made use of. And if he also bartered away plums, that would have rotted in a week, for nuts that would last good for his eating a whole year, he did no injury; he wasted not the common stock; destroyed no part of the portion of goods that belonged to others, so long as nothing perished uselessly in his hands. Again, if he would give his nuts for a piece of metal, pleased with its colour; or exchange his sheep for shells, or wool for a sparkling pebble or a diamond, and keep those by him all his life he invaded not the right of others, he might heap up as much of these durable things as he pleased; the exceeding of the bounds of his just property not lying in the largeness of his possession, but the perishing of anything uselessly in it' (II.46).

presence versus the absence of responsible choice. My preferred welfare egalitarian version of the proviso broadens Locke's explicit focus on labour into a wider luck egalitarian sensitivity to the choices of responsible agents, which is perhaps implicit in the passage from II.34. An implication of my approach is that disabled people should have opportunities to appropriate by means of the staking of extensive claims that are useful for the purpose of generating income from the rental and sale of natural resources. The staking of such claims via public proclamation can give rise to property rights, the upshot of which is that others must obtain their permission before they may make use of what has been claimed. The

> disabled could justify their equality of opportunity for welfare not on the grounds of a positive right to demand that unwilling others come to their assistance by sharing the hard-earned fruits of their labour, but rather on the grounds that they have a right to a share of worldly resources that enables them to secure the same level of advantage as anybody else. They would not, therefore, need to respond to any charges of parasitism or free riding, since their case for equality of opportunity for welfare would rest on nothing more than the staking of a claim to a fair share of worldly resources to which nobody else has a prior or stronger moral claim.[22]

6.4 To What Extent Does a Lockean Approach *Justify* Equality?

In this section, I consider the following question: to what extent can equality of opportunity for welfare be derived from our equal Lockean claims to natural resources?

Here I shall begin with an explanation of why the full luck egalitarian complement of equality of opportunity for welfare cannot be derived from a Lockean approach that focuses on our egalitarian claims to unowned bits of the world. Such claims stand in the way only of those inequalities that are sensitive to our holdings in natural resources and will therefore fail to establish such equality of opportunity insofar as levels of welfare are insensitive to such holdings. Where there is such insensitivity, a defense of such welfare egalitarianism will have to be grounded in considerations that are completely external to a Lockean approach, such as the cosmic unfairness of some being less well off than others through no choice or fault of theirs. We need therefore to reach beyond Locke, and appeal to normative considerations that have nothing in particular to do with our claims to natural resources, in order to justify the full complement of equality of opportunity for welfare.

[22] Otsuka 2003, p. 35.

Lockean egalitarian claims over the world do not, for example, justify the redistribution of eyes and other body parts. A pure form of luck egalitarianism would, by contrast, discern an injustice when some are sighted and others blind even when the only way to equalize their fates is by transplanting an eye from each of the sighted to each of the blind.[23] In previous work, I have argued that a robust form of self-ownership is compatible with a comprehensive form of equality of opportunity for welfare.[24] In defending this form of egalitarianism, I appealed to the familiar luck egalitarian claim that it is unfair when some are less well off than others through no fault or choice of theirs. I still maintain that such equality of opportunity for welfare is *compatible with* robust self-ownership. Here I am advancing the different claim that this full complement of equality of opportunity for welfare cannot be *derived from* a Lockean approach which is grounded in equal claims to natural resources.[25]

I should also note that a Lockean-proviso-based argument grounded in equal claims to the world does not involve any commitment to a *telic* form of egalitarianism. For it condemns only those *acquisitions* of worldly resources that do not leave enough and as good for others in a strongly egalitarian sense. This would, in Parfit's terminology, be a deontic version of egalitarianism.[26] It provides, moreover, a third way between, on the one hand, a ubiquitous form of telic luck egalitarianism that applies even to Parfitian divided worlds, natural injustices, and the distribution of body parts, and, on the other hand, reciprocity-based egalitarian requirements that arise only when people enter into social cooperation. On the contrasting Lockean deontic account of egalitarian justice, the act of acquisition triggers requirements of egalitarian justice even if such an act does not give rise to or involve any cooperation with others.

A Lockean approach which focuses on the force of people's claims to unowned land provides justification for an egalitarian interpretation of the proviso on which the measure of the equality of shares is sensitive to people's ability to transform land (and other natural resources) into welfare.[27] There is also a justification, from within this approach, for the strength of claims to land to be attuned to opportunity rather than outcome (i.e., to be

[23] See Cohen 1995, p. 70, and cf. Nozick 1974, p. 206.

[24] See Otsuka 2003, ch. 1, sec. IV.

[25] See Otsuka 2003, pp. 28–9, where I note that the egalitarian version of the proviso that I there defend is not grounded in such equal claims.

[26] See Parfit 1991.

[27] Recall my earlier discussion of the two unequally sized individuals with different nutritional requirements.

responsibility sensitive).[28] Moreover, there is a justification for ruling out, as breach of 'enough and as good', the disruption of equality as the result of the choices of individuals to *transfer* natural resources (either unimproved or improved) to others.[29] More generally, there is a strong Lockean case for egalitarianism insofar as differences in people's opportunity for welfare are a function of their ownership of land (and other natural resources).[30]

Of course, being alive rather than dead is a necessary condition for being able to enjoy any opportunity for welfare. Moreover, given that we would all be dead if we had no access to natural resources, one can always induce an inequality in opportunity for welfare between two people by depriving one, but not the other, of what he needs to survive. But, among those who have enough resources to sustain themselves, there are various sources of welfare that are insensitive to our holdings in natural resources.

It would be a stretch, moreover, to maintain that a Lockean approach provides a justification for the equalization of benefits derived from services (either exchanges or transfers), where inequalities in such benefits are not themselves in any way explained by differences in people's shares of natural resources. A focus on claims to land that are justified by the Lockean proviso will not therefore justify equality of opportunity for welfare in all cases. Consider the following case:

> **Economic Partnership:** Beta and Gamma form an economic partnership from which they exclude Alpha. The partnership itself and the rewards which they receive do not involve resources, since the partnership consists of nothing more than the trading of services. For example, they provide one another with physiotherapy and acupressure in order to alleviate various ailments, or they offer one another tutorials on their differing areas of expertise.[31]

Let us assume that differences in one's ability to generate welfare from the provision of such services are completely independent of one's resource holdings.[32] If there is a case for equality here, it will not be grounded in Lockean claims to land (and other natural resources). Any case for equality

[28] See my discussion in the last section ('Luck egalitarianism and the diminished role of labour').

[29] For a discussion of such cases, see Otsuka 2006, pp. 101–3.

[30] See n. 15 above, which is also relevant to the question, now under discussion, that I raise at the outset of this section.

[31] Here I am quoting from Otsuka 2006, pp. 103–4.

[32] This is a simplifying assumption, given that, as I noted above, lack of food, air, water, and the like will make a difference. As I note later, one's location – one's geographic proximity to others – can also make a difference.

would have to be justified entirely on other grounds, such as a commitment to luck egalitarian fairness.

Dan Moller has recently argued, against a Lockean justification of egalitarianism in contemporary societies, that

> [e]mpirically speaking, in modern economies, wealth is overwhelmingly the product of *services*, not of the initial acquisition of natural resources. For countries like the contemporary USA, the distribution of natural resources has almost nothing to do with who has what property, or who is rich or poor and why. This means that the Lockean approach to explaining private property is largely irrelevant, as are left-criticisms that are focused on it, be they strictly Lockean, or Georgist, or other kinds of offshoots. What really needs to be explained is private property deriving from transfers following services. This might seem trivial if we imagine those transfers themselves go back to wealth in natural resources a step or two removed, but as I show that is not the case. For most contemporary wealth, it is services or something close enough all the way down.[33]

These claims are not, however, established in Moller's ensuing discussion.

One argument he offers on their behalf is that the proportion of economic value traceable to services as compared with land (and other natural resources)[34] is much higher than it was in agricultural societies of Locke's times. Moller writes that

> about 80% of the value of American economic output (by GDP) derives from *services*. The US is toward the high end of the spectrum – modern European economies are closer to 70% – but the trend toward GDP being dominated by service sector work in advanced economies is unmistakeable. ... The economic importance of the kinds of agricultural activity that so preoccupied Locke and that feature prominently in philosophical discussion has plummeted until now it is completely trivial ....[35]

But the ratio of the economic value of services to that of land does not settle the matter.

First, one would need to establish how much of the economic value of such services should be attributed to labour versus land. This, as G.A. Cohen notes, is a conceptually tricky matter.[36]

[33] Moller 2017, p. 2.

[34] I shall henceforth drop the parenthetical reference to 'other natural resources', which shall be taken as read in subsequent references to 'land'. See the opening paragraph of this paper.

[35] Moller 2017, pp. 5–6. He defines a service as corresponding 'roughly to tertiary sector output not the result of primary resource extraction, farming or secondary manufacturing including construction. It includes fields such as banking, retail, hospitality, dining, entertainment, law, healthcare, education, design and computer programming'. (Moller 2017)

[36] See Cohen 1995, ch. 7.

Second, even if we stipulate that labour is responsible for a vast multiple of economic value, in comparison with land, that does not justify a suspension of the constraint on our acquisition of land by the proviso that we leave enough and as good for others. On the contrary, as Locke argued, such responsibility of labour for this vast multiple provides an explanation for how it is possible to satisfy the proviso rather than grounds for its supersession. He wrote:

> ... he who appropriates land to himself by his labour, does not lessen, but increase the common stock of mankind: for the provisions serving to the support of human life, produced by one acre of inclosed and cultivated land, are (to speak much within compass) ten times more than those which are yielded by an acre of land of an equal richness lying waste in common. And therefore he that incloses land, and has a greater plenty of the conveniencies of life from ten acres, than he could have from an hundred left to nature, may truly be said to give ninety acres to mankind: for his labour now supplies him with provisions out of ten acres, which were but the product of an hundred lying in common. [He adds:] I have here rated the improved land very low, in making its product but as ten to one, when it is much nearer an hundred to one ... (II.37)

Here Locke is saying that, when one compares the amount of commonly owned land which people must use in order to sustain themselves as hunter-gatherers with the lesser amount of enclosed land on which they can subsist, we can see that taking land out of common ownership and privatizing it in no way lessens the stock available to others. Far from depriving people of enough and as good for their comfort and sustenance, enclosure of subsistence plots of farmland increases the opportunities for others to sustain themselves.[37] Hence we, so to speak, leave more than enough and as good for others by retreating from the wilds in which we hunt and gather in order to becoming subsistence farmers.

There would remain a compelling case to provide people with equal opportunity to transform natural resources into welfare, in accord with a strongly egalitarian interpretation of the proviso. We would therefore still need to know to what extent differences in opportunity for welfare trace to land. Moller therefore must establish the claim that people's inequalities in opportunity for welfare in a service economy are not, or are only trivially, a function of their ownership of land.

Moller does not establish this claim. He maintains that:

> Vast amounts of wealth get created without natural resources playing an important role. It is true that some of that wealth involved manufacturing

[37] See Cohen 1995, pp. 187–8.

> or processing physical assets, but even then the reasons for the sudden wealth-creation weren't discovering some extra trees and rocks to make into houses and aeroplanes, but technical innovation, specialization, trade, and the other appurtenances of modern capitalism.[38]

Even a very high contribution by innovation, specialization, and trade to the economic value of society does not, however, establish the truth of the above claim. Even in the absence of the discovery of extra natural resources, one's enjoyment of the value of improved resources may be a function of one's access to land. Consider the simple case of agricultural land which Locke discusses. Locke maintains that the improved value of a given unit of such land is near to 100 times greater than its unimproved value. Let us grant this claim for the sake of argument. Let us also suppose that any increase in the total value of all land is not at all down to the discovery of new land but entirely down to innovation in farming techniques. It would remain the case that differences in people's opportunities for welfare would be a non-trivial function of their access to land. This would hold true whether or not access to innovative farming techniques was equal. In order to realize equality, opportunities for welfare that arise from improvements of the value of land would need to be equalized.[39]

This sensitivity of opportunity for welfare to access to land applies to an economy dominated by services as well as an agricultural economy: land makes a significant difference to one's ability to generate income and therefore welfare, even in an economy dominated by services. For many service providers, the location of the place where one provides one's service or resides will make a large difference to the amount of income one is able to generate. To take a banal example, shops and restaurants on the high street (or main street) will achieve much more foot traffic than more out of the way places. There are various other advantages that location also confers. As Noah Smith writes:

[38] Moller 2017, pp. 8–9.

[39] This is one respect in which the Lockeanism under discussion is more egalitarian than a Georgist tax on the unimproved value of land, according to which, on Peter Vallentyne's formulation, 'agents must pay the full competitive value of the natural resources that they appropriate'. As Vallentyne explains, an upshot of such a tax is that 'agents who produce more – because they work longer hours or because they are more efficient producers owing to greater productive talents – pay the same taxes (rent) as those with less advantageous unchosen personal endowments who own equally valuable natural resources. Those with strong egalitarian inclinations will reject this view, and hold that persons with greater unchosen advantage should pay higher taxes, since they can reap greater benefits from natural resources' (Vallentyne 2000, p. 8).

> for most of human history, the value of land came mainly from the value of its natural productive power – the fertility of the soil, or the minerals beneath the earth. But in the modern age, land has value for a very different reason, summed up by the real estate mantra: location, location, location.
>
> In a city or suburb, land's value comes from location. People want to be close to the companies where they work. Companies want to be close to the people they employ. Stores want to be close to the consumers they serve, and consumers want to be close to the stores. Companies in the same industry want to be close to one another, so they can keep an eye on rivals, absorb ideas and poach talent ...
>
> As our economies become more complex, there are more kinds of stores ... and more industries to cluster together. Therefore, the value of location increases, which pushes up the value of land. It doesn't matter how much empty land is out there – who wants to live on the Kansas prairie? What matters for the value of modern land is the incentive to locate close to other people. And unless we all start telecommuting and living entirely online, location will become more and more valuable as our economy becomes more complex.[40]

In other words, locations – spatial regions independently of what they contain – are natural resources which are of high value in present-day circumstances. The passages from the *Second Treatise* which I quoted in my earlier discussion of the significance of money show that, for Locke, proximity of human beings to one another makes the following difference: if one is able to engage in commerce with others, that will make it easier to generate a surplus on large landholdings without violating the spoilage proviso. The possibilities for accumulation without spoilage become greater with the introduction of money. These passages demonstrate that Locke was attentive to facts about proximity and its relevance to possibilities for trade and industry which are akin, albeit in more bucolic form, to the considerations that Noah Smith mentions in the passage above. There is, therefore, a Lockean case for egalitarianism grounded in claims to land, which applies to the post-industrial service economies of today as well as the agrarian societies of Locke's day.

[40] Smith 2015.

7

Rights, Distributed and Undistributed: On the Distributive Justice Implications of Lockean Property Rights, Especially in Land

JAMES PENNER

7.1 Introduction

Locke famously claimed that first appropriations of the material resources of the world was subject to a proviso, that there be 'enough and as good' left for others similarly to appropriate. Both Gopal Sreenivasan and Michael Otsuka argue that in conditions of scarcity Locke's proviso properly modified or elaborated[1] justifies an 'equal shares' right to which every individual is entitled. That is, every individual is entitled to a right to access the material resources of the earth to an extent which is calculated by dividing the material resources of the earth by the number of individuals living at any one time.

Besides the helpful comments of the other contributors to this volume, I am grateful to James Gordley, Dennis Klimchuk and Gopal Sreenivasan for helpful comments. I am especially grateful for the searching criticisms and suggestions of my co-editor, Mike Otsuka. This chapter is a kind of companion piece to another (yet unpublished paper) of mine on Lockean theories of appropriation leading to scarcity of land: 'Locke on Equality and Inequality: The Consent to Value Money and 'Positional' Goods' (Penner 2018). In that paper I try to solve a mystery in Locke's claim that the consent to value money leads to scarcity of land, i.e. that all or most land is appropriated leaving not enough and as good land available for appropriation by all persons. I claim to solve that mystery by treating the 'consent' to value money as the recognition or acceptance of the value of positional goods, i.e. goods where the value of the good turns on the fact of its exclusivity, and thus on the fact that other persons don't have it. Arguably, the valuing of positional goods is irrational and immoral on any perspective, but I claim that it is particularly problematic for Locke on both bases. So the claim is that while Locke could rightly and plausibly explain the appropriation of all land (and hence its scarcity), framing the 'tacit consent' to value money as the tacit consent to value positionality in the holding of worldly resources and the products of industry, and that this would result in more or less total appropriation of land, from Locke's own moral perspective, i.e. the perspective of 'Lockean' morality, the ensuing scarcity will not be legitimate.

[1] See text to n. 21 and 22.

I offer an alternative and, I think, superior Lockean perspective on the issues at stake.[2] By (1) attributing to Locke what I think would plausibly be his views on contractual fairness, (2) examining the stringency of his 'spoilation' proviso on legitimate appropriation, and (3) taking seriously Locke's views on the value of labour, I argue that the 'equal shares' right is unnecessary for the achievement of economic, or 'distributive' justice, and it would not, I suggest, be Locke's own solution to the problem of economic injustice. Indeed, I shall claim that the distribution of titles to land, even in conditions of scarcity, is irrelevant to the question of distributive justice in holdings. Where the real action lies is in a just distribution of the fruits of a division of labour, which, under the developed Lockean theory of just contractual exchange, does not allow first acquirers of titles in land to exploit the landless.

In order to substantiate these claims, I have first to step back and consider what a person might mean by 'distributive' justice, which is to ask, I think, what sorts of things are ones of which we can ask whether their distribution amongst persons is fair or just. Since our concern here is with powers to acquire exclusive rights to holdings of material resources and powers to create rights under contracts, we can narrow this question to: what sort of *rights* and *powers* are ones of which we can ask whether their distribution amongst persons is fair or just.

7.2 Undistributed Powers and Rights

The basic thought underlying the concept of an undistributed right or power (henceforward I shall use 'right' to cover both, unless the context requires otherwise), in particular what we might call a 'natural' right, is that one's having such a right is not the result of a distributive *choice*, in the sense that a society could, whilst complying with basic moral requirements, deny anyone that right. Of course this does not mean that everyone agrees on what these 'natural' rights may be.[3] The point is rather that the considerations that go to justify the recognition of such rights do not turn on the idea that they reflect a fair or just allocation of rights amongst persons.

One way in which rights can be thought of as distributed rights is on the contractarian models of Rawls and Scanlon. The idea behind both of these

[2] This alternative may be consistent with Sreenivasan's and Otsuka's views on where a Lockean argument might take us. See text to n. 23 and 24.

[3] Someone might, for example, deny that one had any natural rights, or very minimal such rights, as for example does Hobbes in his characterisation of one's single right of self-defence in the state of nature. Hobbes 1991, pp. 91–2.

models is that the rights we have owe their existence to our ability to agree on some set of claim rights and liberties that we can all equally hold. I don't think I can do better than Otsuka in addressing this sort of distributive or allocative model of basic rights:

> A contractualist device such as Rawls's original position that constructs principles of justice out of the self-interested choices of individuals who have been placed behind the 'veil of ignorance' will fall short of generating principles that reflect the existence, importance, and stringency of natural rights of self-ownership. It will fall short because, when it comes to our convictions regarding the circumstances in which it is unjust to harm others, we are moved by a variety of ethical considerations that are far too subtle to be captured by any such contractual device that reduces the choice of principle (sic) to a procedure of self-interested choice in conditions of ignorance. A contractualist device such as Scanlon's that endows the parties to the contract with the ethical motivation to arrive at principles that are unreasonable to reject might, by virtue of endowing them with this motivation, ensure that the parties arrive at those principles that give natural rights their due. But this greater accuracy in choice of principles of justice is bought at the price of a reduction in the usefulness of the contractual device as a means (distinct from ordinary forms of moral reasoning) of arriving at the right principles of justice. Although we can figure out what people would choose in their self-interest in conditions of ignorance without engaging in ordinary forms of moral reasoning, the same cannot be said regarding principles it would be unreasonable to reject. In order to determine which principles would be unreasonable to reject, one cannot avoid engaging in the familiar sort of moral argumentation ...[4]

This thought regarding 'the familiar sort of moral argumentation' can be fleshed out, I think, by drawing upon what is sometimes called 'value theory', which has been most thoroughly explored by Raz[5] and Gardner.

In a recent article, Gardner has developed these thoughts in terms of 'basic responsibility'. Gardner writes:

> Basic responsibility is what it sounds like. It is an ability. More fully, it is the ability and propensity to have and to give self-explanations in the currency of reasons. The ability and the propensity are but two sides of the same coin. As beings who are able to respond to reasons we cannot avoid being disposed to respond to them. There is nowhere to hide from them ...
>
> Basic responsibility, I suggest, cannot be assigned or allocated by anyone. There is no normative power, by the exercise of which anyone can add to or subtract from it. That is not because it is impossible for any of us not to have it. Some of us lack it altogether. Well, actually, that depends on who

[4] Otsuka 2003, pp. 5–6.

[5] Raz 1990.

> counts as 'us'. But assuming we mean 'human beings', we might doubt the basic responsibility of very young children, those with advanced forms of dementia or severe mental illnesses, and those in comas. Surely basic responsibility is entirely lacking in at least some such cases? Yes, and that is already a matter of regret. Human beings ought to be answerable to reasons. That is part of their human ergon, to use the Aristotelian term, sometimes translated as 'function' but perhaps better as 'destiny'.[6]

The basic idea is that we are 'valuing' creatures. We respond to or react to or understand facts *as reasons*. We see the world, in part, in terms of values (physical pleasure, social and aesthetic values, and so on) that we have reason to realize, and also in terms of disvalues (pain, actions which we regard as cruel or debased or pointless), which we not only have reason to avoid but also to prevent. Reasons underpin rights and duties in a straightforward way on this perspective; X has against Y a right to q if the value of q gives rise to a reason for action which is 'categorical' in the sense that it prevails over Y's otherwise innocuous plans to realize values. Y cannot push X out of the way, thus interfering with X's right to bodily security, in order to hasten himself on the way. Very roughly, X's interest in bodily security is of a strength and stringency such that it imposes a categorical (which is not to say absolute) duty on Y not to infringe it.

If this way of looking at things is right, then the idea that our natural rights are a matter of distribution or allocation is awry. We have the natural rights we have because of the kind of creatures we are. We have these rights as against each other (aberrant circumstances aside) because we are all capable of recognizing the values[7] and disvalues the world presents us with and responding accordingly in our practical reasoning, i.e. in reasoning about how to act. Natural rights, then, are undistributed rights.

However, in formulating this way of thinking about natural rights in terms of self-ownership, it seems to me that Otsuka, and Cohen upon whom Otsuka draws, retain a tinge of distributive thinking which mars their formulations. Here are the relevant passages, first from Otsuka:

> I shall adopt the following plausible definition of a full right of self-ownership: a person's right of self-ownership is full if and only if that person

[6] Gardner 2017, pp. 7–8.

[7] As has been pointed out to me by James Gordley, Locke seemed to entertain two different views about the nature of values a person might choose to realise. At points in the *Essay Concerning Human Understanding*, Locke seemed to distinguish between values of greater and less intrinsic worth, whereas at other points he seemed to treat the choice to pursue one value rather than another as a matter of mere personal taste; Locke 1975: compare II.xxi 51, 52, with II.xxi 55. See further James Gordley, *The Eclipse of Classical Thought in China and the West*, draft, September 18, 2017, on file with the author.

> possesses, to the greatest extent and stringency *compatible with the same possession by others*, the aforementioned rights 'to decide what would become of himself and what he would do, and ... to reap the benefits of what he did.[8]

And here is the passage from Cohen that Otsuka[9] cites, in which Cohen defines the full right of self-ownership as:

> [T]he fullest right a person (logically) can have over herself *provided that each other person also has just such a right.*[10]

The question is what is the significance of the italicized passages? They can be read in a number of ways, but here's a plausible folksy one: 'your right to swing your fist ends where my nose begins', which invokes the familiar trope of spatial boundaries. But this trope is clearly *distributive*, in the sense that the object of the right, our space of liberty, is divided so that each of us has an equal share of the space of liberty, and this equality of division is part of what makes the right legitimate for each of us to have.

To my mind this trope is misguided in two ways. First, it suggests a distributive way of thinking about natural rights which is in fact absent on the natural rights perspective that I have just set out. That is, it suggests that my having a right to x depends upon someone (or everyone) else's having that right. It turns a right concerning the sort of creature I am, i.e. one which looks to my intrinsic properties, into a right which is inherently relational, based on maintaining an equivalence between me and others. The difference can be seen by noticing two of Kant's formulations of the categorical imperative. On one, which to my mind embraces the misguided trope I am drawing attention to, it is formulated as a principle of universalizability: Act only where the maxim of your action can be regarded as a universal law (binding oneself and all others).[11] This gives rise to the notorious problem that different people with different levels, say, of toughness or physical strength, could perfectly plausibly propose different universal laws with which they would be happy to live. On the other formulation, there is no universalizability or 'equal' treatment element: Treat anyone who belongs to the kingdom of ends never only as a means but also as an end.[12] The two formulations have different implications. Assume that chimpanzees belong in the kingdom of ends. That is to say no more, I think, than that

[8] Otsuka 2003, p. 12, my italics.

[9] Otsuka 2003, p. 12, fn. 7.

[10] Cohen 1995, p. 213 (my italics).

[11] Kant 1994, 30, AK 421.

[12] Kant 1994, 36, 39; AK 429, 433. It is clear that Kant himself thinks that only humans populate the kingdom of ends.

chimpanzees' lives are of intrinsic value. On the latter formulation, this would be morally significant for how we should treat chimpanzees. But it would not dictate that we treat them *in the same way that we treat our fellow humans*, whose lives might have more or different intrinsic value. That is, this formulation would not entail that humans and chimpanzees would have the same rights. The second formulation allows us to take these considerations into account straightforwardly. But the first formulation does not, as it could only apply, presumably, to persons, not chimpanzees, as would of course Cohen's formulation that x has a right only 'provided that each other [member of the kingdom of ends] also has just such a right'. Furthermore, abusing humans and chimpanzees (not treating them as within the kingdom of ends) would be wrong even if they had no fellows, i.e. neither had any rights equal to those of any other being; it would be wrong for God to abuse the first or last human and chimp on earth, despite the fact that there would be not equal rights as between humans, chimps and God on the plausible presumption that God has different intrinsic properties from both humans and chimps.

But more importantly, this *sort* of distributive perspective undermines the principle underlying the appreciation of natural rights that I, following Gardner, endorse. On this spatial distributive model, the idea is that it would somehow be to my advantage to have the greatest liberty to do whatever it occurs to me to do, irrespective of whatever values *or disvalues* my acting realizes. But that is misconceived. It is not to my advantage to have the liberty to punch you in the nose, take your life, or steal your goods, however much I might mistakenly *want* to have such freedom of action available to me. On the value theory I am endorsing, one has no (rightful) liberty to realize disvalues; equivalently, one can have no right to such a liberty. A duty not to assault or kill others is not, on this account, a normative *burden* of any kind, since one rightly appraised of the values and disvalues out there should have no interest in pursuing such actions in the first place.[13] Of course, given the sort of person I might be, the absence of such liberties, or contrariwise, the presence of such duties 'not to', could chafe, for example, psychologically. I might be naturally careless or have a

[13] This point is not to be confused with Hart's point when criticising Rawls 1999, that the contours of our liberties could vary upon what might be called ethical considerations, about the sort of lives people see as better in some ways – e.g. some 'tougher' types might be glad to endorse a broad freedom of expression in which, e.g. defamation was not prohibited, leaving the response to defamation to be more expression. See Hart 1972–73, pp. 545–52. See also Mendus 2008, pp. 309–13; Rawls 2005, Lecture VIII.

quick temper, or be alienated from others, and so on. But my psychological dispositions are obviously not to the point.

On a non-distributive reading, the phrase 'compatible with the same possession by others' seems to be otiose. The reason we all have the *same* rights has nothing to do with 'compatibility' with the rights of others but merely reflects the fact that we are all relevantly the same creatures, i.e. are relevantly the same in terms of what we can demand of each other in terms of the requirements of morality. We have the same rights because we are all tokens of the same type of intrinsically valuable being. Of course one could put the idea of 'same' rights in terms of 'equal' rights but the danger of doing so should now be obvious: 'equal' suggests a division or distribution.

7.3 Is There a Natural, i.e. Undistributed, Right to Property?

Putting to one side Locke's theological premise that persons have a duty to God to exploit worldly resources to preserve themselves,[14] it seems fairly uncontroversial that individuals have a liberty (in Hohfeldian terms, have no duty not) to appropriate and make use of wordly resources, and a claim right that others, in general, not interfere with their doing so. This follows, plausibly, from the fact that we are actors, agents, who appropriately seek to realize values and avoid or prevent the realization of disvalues. That is the essence of what it is to be a human living a human life. We are situated in a world where life requires engagement with the external world. I think the Kantian perspective on this, in particular as expounded by Ripstein,[15] is quite compelling. The idea is that the right to property is essentially about taking parts of the external world into one's sphere of agency, such that, no less than one's own body, these external resources become part of one's own *means*. The function of the natural right to property is to make exclusive to any individual certain bits of the world; they become X's means, rather than Y's. This story is 'simple or even boring', as Ripstein would have it,[16] with regard to the modes of appropriation or acquisition of external resources, and hence to their resultant distribution amongst persons. The point is that human agency is impossible without a right to realize one's agency in the world by way of exclusive rights to some of the world's resources. One thus acquires property by taking control of it, and making it part of one's means. Having done so it is, as a matter of right, not available to others.

[14] Locke 1970, pp. 26–7, section 26.

[15] Ripstein 2009, ch. 4; Ripstein 2013.

[16] Ripstein 2009, p. 90.

As with Lockean theories of property, this way of conceiving of property rights is not, in the first instance, one that raises concerns about a just distribution of property rights. This is one of the points of first conceiving of property rights in a state of plenty. In such a state there can be no possible good reason for interfering with another's means in so far as that other's means comprises worldly resources any more than there is a possible good reason for interfering with another's body, her bodily 'means'. Of course, differences remain between this Kantian spin on the issue of first appropriation, and Locke's. Even in the absence of the theological premise one might say that Locke's question of first appropriation is more austere or urgent in a way that Kant's is not. For Locke the question is not so much a matter of finding a realm in which human agency rightfully operates, but a realm in which human existence can happen at all in a rightful way, i.e. how anyone can appropriate so as to consume what was otherwise held in common.[17] For the purposes of this chapter, however, I think the difference is not so great as to detract from the 'Lockean' flavor I purport to find in the arguments below, which concern less the justice of first appropriation than the justice inherent in the spoilation proviso and in 'Lockean' barter and exchange.

So far so good, I trust. I shall proceed on the basis that there is a natural, i.e. undistributed, right to property as set out above. We now consider how this right is contoured or curtailed in a world where external resources are scarce. In particular, our focus will be on property rights in land.

7.4 Sreenivasan and Otsuka on Property Rights in a State of Scarcity

Sreenivasan's *The Limits of Lockean Rights in Property*[18] is a subtle and powerful exploration of Lockean justifications of property rights, which repays reading. For our purposes here one point needs emphasizing. Sreenivasan considers Locke's arguments in two stages. First, which involves an intricate exploration not only of the Second Treatise but other of Locke's writings, Sreenivasan presents what he claims to be Locke's own theory of property. He then criticizes this theory, and develops not the theory of property of Locke himself, but a *Lockean* theory of property, which purports to make better sense of Locke's various arguments and insights than Locke himself did.

[17] I thank Dennis Klimchuk for pressing this point with me.

[18] Sreenivasan 1995.

For Sreenivasan (and, as we shall see below, also for Otsuka), the aspect of Locke's theory which is of greatest relevance to the question of how scarcity affects the strength and scope of an individual's property rights is Locke's 'enough and as good' condition, which I shall follow him in calling [S], for sufficiency.

For Locke himself, according to Sreenivasan, [S] does not require that every individual has the opportunity to acquire property in land herself:

> Having property in land is simply not a precondition of the exercise of [the right to the means of preservation]. Certainly, for the able-bodied, it is a sufficient, and arguably the most desirable, manner of exercising one's right to the means of preservation, but it is not the only one. For it is equally true that for Locke labouring on someone else's property for payment which is, or enables one to purchase, the means of subsistence and comfort also exercises this same right.[19]
>
> [S] is consistent with the scarcity of land because that scarcity does not per se imperil any of the rights which the condition is intended to safeguard. Naturally, there are contexts in which scarcity of land would do just that. To begin with, if those without land were denied the opportunity to labour on someone else's land, then clearly they would be prevented from exercising their natural rights and in that degree would be injured. Hence, under conditions of scarcity, there attaches to property in land, as a condition of its continuing legitimacy, the obligation to employ those without land of their own. As we have said, no one may be denied access to the materials necessary to produce the direct means of subsistence. This is a matter of natural right.[20]
>
> Hence, for the sufficiency condition to be satisfied, appropriated land must be able to sustain at least as many people as it was capable of sustaining while held in common. This is just to say that appropriation is only legitimate where *enough and as good direct means of subsistence are available for others.* In ensuring this much, the sufficiency condition discharges its task of securing the material preconditions of the right to the means of preservation. It will thus be observed that what must be left for others need not be left in kind.[21]

At this point I only want to make one comment in relation to these passages. Assuming that Sreenivasan's exegesis of Locke is correct, it is noteworthy that for Locke the possibility of contractual exchange, and arguably a division of labour, is essential for compliance with [S] when there is a scarcity of land.[22] That is, compliance with [S] does not require that all are

[19] Sreenivasan 1995, p. 51. The point is essentially repeated at p. 53.

[20] Sreenivasan 1995, p. 54.

[21] Sreenivasan 1995, p. 55, italics original, my underlining.

[22] Strictly speaking, the entitlement itself is not dependent on or mediated by exchange. But realizing that entitlement does depend on some sort of exchange.

landowners, but rather compliance is afforded because non-owners, via contractual exchange, are *entitled* to labour on others' land for payment.

But this construal of [S], according to Sreenivasan, leads to unjust results:

> Locke fails to recognise two salient differences between the position of commoners generally under common ownership and the position of landless commoners under land scarcity that justify the complaints of the latter. The first difference is that unlike landless commoners, commoners generally were formerly *at liberty* to enjoy the fruits of the full potential of their labour. In other words, commoners were formerly at liberty to produce not merely subsistence but a surplus. ... The upper bound on their standard of living was therefore, in a manner of speaking, internal: set 'by the Extent of Mens Labour, and the Conveniency of Life'[23] and by the limits inherent in natural property.
>
> This manifestly is *not* the position of the landless commoners under land scarcity, for their standard of living is further constrained by an external limit set by the minimum measure of subsistence. A right of employment entitles them (in either sense) to no more than this. Landless commoners are not at liberty even to produce a surplus, since their access to the necessary materials depends upon the permission of the landowners. Furthermore, where they are permitted to produce a surplus, not only do landless commoners have no claim-right to keep most, or perhaps even any, of the surplus they produce, but they are not at liberty to keep it either. The benefit of labour's abundance – which Locke so celebrates – is therefore placed at the disposal of the landowners.
>
> The second difference is that under common ownership the access to the common materials enjoyed by the commoners generally is the same for each commoner. That is, they all enjoy *equal* access, whereas the access to those materials enjoyed by any and every landless commoner is, *ex hypothesi*, radically unequal to that enjoyed by any and every landowner. ...
>
> Clearly, then, the natural property regime fails to preserve the access to the materials necessary to produce the means of comfort and support to which each commoner was originally entitled. ...
>
> Locke's sufficiency condition is therefore too weak to discharge the function assigned to it in his larger argument, namely, the resolution of the consent problem [ie the right to appropriate worldly resources without requiring the consent of all others].[24]

Sreenivasan then considers whether a 'Lockean', though not Locke's, property entitlement might satisfy a more robust version of [S] such that the problems identified in the last passages can be overcome, and he thinks one can be found.

[23] Citing Locke 1970, section 36.

[24] Sreenivasan 1995, pp. 114–5, his italics, my underlining.

> [A] prima facie case can be made that at least one form of Lockean property would satisfy an adequate sufficiency condition. ...
>
> In a Lockean state of nature, the sufficiency condition would be satisfied by a regime of Lockean property in land in which each able-bodied commoner had a claim right to a share of land equal to that of every other able-bodied commoner. This is *not* to say, of course, that vesting such a claim right in every able-bodied commoner is a *necessary* condition of satisfying the Lockean sufficiency condition, but only that it is a sufficient condition of doing so.
>
> Under such a form of Lockean property, each commoner would evidently have sufficient access to the materials necessary to produce the means of subsistence. Significantly, each commoner would be at liberty to enjoy the fruits of the full potential of their labour: the benefit of labour's abundance would be at everyone's disposal. Equality of access would also be guaranteed by definition, and thus adversity would be absent along this dimension of power relations amongst commoners. In short, it would appear that no one would have any relevant grounds for complaint.[25]

Let me state the premises which Sreenivasan does not make explicit but which seem to underlie his characterization of Locke's position. The first, which I shall spend a fair amount of time on below, is that landowners are necessarily in a bargaining position such that they can, in effect, extract any surplus value from any economic activity performed on their land by the landless commoner – in this sense contractual exchange has no moral constraints beyond giving effect to the landless commoner's entitlement to labour on the land of others': in every other respect, a person, such as a landowner, is entitled to consider only their own self-interest in entering into bargains, and in particular, in this case a landowner is essentially able to hold the landless commoner to ransom: work for a subsistence wage or survive on charity. For now let me just say that this strikes me as a rather anachronistic premise to attribute to Locke, writing as he did a century before Adam Smith and two and half centuries before Marx.

The second premise, which I think is correct (second instance of underlining, above), is that Sreenivasan's 'equal shares of land' solution to meeting [S] in conditions of scarcity is not the only possible solution. He does not himself suggest alternatives but, as I said at the outset, I shall propose one below which I claim could plausibly be attributed to Locke, or at least better matches his explicit pronouncements in 'Of Property'.

Finally, the premise underlying the first and third underlined passages I also agree with, which is that the point of any property regime's satisfying [S] is to ensure that each and every individual is able to set 'internally'

25 Sreenivasan 1995, pp. 116–7, his italics, my underlining.

the extent to which they labour to produce a surplus above what is necessary for bare subsistence. That is, within the bounds set by technology, the available material resources, and the talents and inclinations of her fellows, each and every individual retains significant (though never absolute) mastery of herself in the sense of being able voluntarily to choose how she will exploit the means at her disposal to realize whatever values she chooses.

Otsuka treads a similar path and reaches a similar conclusion. He first considers [S] as Nozick construes it, and then counters with his own version of [S] which avoids the defects of Nozick's version of [S]:

> *Nozick's proviso.* You may acquire previously unowned land (and its fruits) if and only if you make nobody worse off than she would have been in a state of nature in which no land is privately held but each is free to gather and consume food and water from the land and make use of it.
>
> As a means of ensuring that nobody is placed at a disadvantage, Nozick's version of the Lockean proviso is too weak, since it allows a single individual in a state of nature to engage in an enriching acquisition of all the land there is if she compensates all others by hiring them and paying a wage that ensures that they end up no worse off than they would have been if they had continued to live the meagre hand-to-mouth existence of hunters and gatherers on non-private land. Such acquisition would pre-empt others from making any acquisition of their own that would improve their situation over that in which they live no better than a meagre hand-to-mouth existence. This acquisition is objectionable both because it condemns others to such a miserable existence and because it is manifestly unfair that a first grabber be allowed to monopolise all opportunities to improve one's lot through acquisition.
>
> ...
>
> The following version of the Lockean proviso provides a remedy to these defects in Nozick's version:
>
> *Egalitarian proviso.* You may acquire previously unowned worldly resources if and only if you leave enough so that everyone else can acquire an equally advantageous share of unowned worldly resources.
>
> The egalitarian proviso has prima-facie plausibility for the following reason: One's coming to acquire previously unowned resources under these terms leaves nobody else at a disadvantage (or, in Locke's words, is 'no prejudice to any others'), where being left at a disadvantage is understood as being left with less than an equally advantageous share of resources. Any weaker, less egalitarian versions of the proviso would, like Nozick's, unfairly allow some to acquire greater advantage than others from their acquisition of unowned land and other worldly resources.[26]

[26] Otsuka 2003, pp. 23–4.

Unlike Sreenivasan, Otsuka does not spell out this egalitarian proviso by claiming it is Lockean by a chapter and verse exegesis of Locke's texts, but given that he says on the first page of *Libertarianism without Inequality* that his views are inspired by Locke's *Second Treatise*, doubtless he could do so. In any case Otsuka converges with Sreenivasan on an 'equal shares' solution to the injustices created by an unregulated right of first acquisition.

Regarding the three premises underlying Sreenivasan's thought I identified above, Otsuka more or less explicitly adopts the first premise, i.e. that first acquirers, or 'first grabbers' as Otsuka would have it, are in a position to extract the entirety of the surplus generated by the work of labourers on their land, leaving the latter to a subsistence existence.

It is not clear whether Otsuka agrees with the second premise, that an 'equal shares' solution to meeting [S] in conditions of scarcity is not the only possible solution, but it would appear not; that is, it seems as if he presents the equal shares version of [S] as one which exclusively avoids the defects of the sort of version of [S] which Nozick holds.

It does seem that Otsuka would endorse the third premise as a corollary of his dedication to self-ownership, i.e. that the point of [S] is to ensure that each and every individual is able to set 'internally' the extent to which they labour to produce a surplus above what is necessary for bare subsistence; self-ownership would seem to require that, again within the bounds set by technology, the available material resources, her dealings with others, etc., each and every individual retains significant (though never absolute) mastery of herself in the sense of being able voluntarily to choose how she will exploit the means at her disposal to realize whatever values she chooses.

7.5 Why the Ownership of Land in Unequal Shares, Such that Some May Have No Property Rights in Land, is not Necessarily Unjust

Let me begin here with an observation I have made elsewhere,[27] which is that theorists of contract do not typically concern themselves with questions of distributive justice, despite the fact that contractual exchange is an actual *mode* of distribution, whereas property theorists typically do concern themselves with issues of distributive justice. I think this is clearly a bit odd. In any case, the relevance of a theory of just contractual exchange will be the focus of this part of the chapter. It cannot but be if we are concerned with the legitimacy, or justice, of individual private

[27] Penner 2013, p. 267.

property holdings of worldly resources, in particular land, if we accept, as I think we should, that Locke was committed not only to the view that labour generates 999/1,000ths[28] of the value inherent in external resources in so far as they contribute to meeting human needs or wants, but to the important way in which a division of labour and just contractual exchange works hand in hand with his view about the value of labour. Locke's use of the word 'industry' is not meant to be restricted to the individual agency of any particular individual working with or upon wordly resources, but embraces and endorses a division of labour, a division mediated by fair contractual exchange.

It is clear that Locke endorses the trade of surpluses, i.e. goods gathered or created.[29] At the same time, whilst trade can be seen to avoid the strictures of the spoilation proviso [SP], there is nothing in Locke that suggests that where, for example, someone speculatively gathers or produces more than she can use *or trade* for something else which she can use fully, she can escape [SP]. If this is right then, I submit, the best way of understanding how the right to trade within the continuing bounds of [SP] operates is by thinking of a *division of labour*. On this understanding of Locke, the co-operative production of goods makes sense even in a world of plenty if one assumes even fairly low efficiency gains from economies of scale and from the specialization of labour, because then the total amount of labour each individual has to expend to obtain a commodious existence is reduced. Although Locke does not explicitly endorse a division of labour, he certainly recognized its existence and implicitly the benefits of specialization.[30]

This is particularly important to recognize in the exploitation of land, again, even in conditions of plenty. Although it is conceivable that tilling or animal husbandry or mining or building can be carried on by individuals on their own, this is surely atypical, and nothing in Locke's writing suggest that he thinks otherwise. In speaking of agriculture, Locke refers to the activities of 'families',[31] not individuals, and Sreenivasan too thinks that the 'unit' for the application of the right to employment, appropriation, etc., is the 'family'.[32]

Now again, for the moment, restricting our attention to a world of plenty, upon what basis would the fruits of this co-operative 'industry', i.e. a production of useable goods, be divided amongst the parties to the division

[28] Or whatever fraction: Locke fluctuates in his estimate in 'Of Property'.

[29] Locke 1970, p. 301, section 48.

[30] Locke 1970, p. 298, section 43.

[31] Locke 1970, p. 301, section 48.

[32] Sreenivasan 1995, p. 102, n. 15.

of labour? Given Locke's claim that labour is by far the most important factor in realizing the value for persons of wordly resources, it would appear obvious that individual labourers should receive roughly in proportion to their input in terms of labour. Locke admits to differences in particular individuals' 'industry', allowing some rightly to have more than others.[33] He does not in fact distinguish between the differential value of one sort of labour over another, but I think it would be fair to expect Locke to understand that certain kinds of specialized, skilled, labour would be a greater factor in realizing the value of the world in relation to some other forms of labour. In any case, however, though it could never be precise, it would appear that there is a basis for determining whether the division of outputs arising from co-operative processes typified by a division of labour is just or not. Assuming the relations of co-operation and division are entered into consensually, i.e. are made of a network of contracts, a fair contractual exchange would be one in which each participant receives their due – that fraction of the output which represents their fraction of the input.

Moreover, in conditions of plenty, it is likely that fairness in these consensual economic exchanges will be realized, since every party can, if he so chooses, refuse to participate, 'hold out' as it were, by deciding to act on their own, that is, acting directly on the plentiful, unowned, worldly resources for themselves (though at the same time foregoing the efficiencies of cooperating with others).

This is not to say that each and every bargain which contributes to an extensive division of labour will actually be just, just that there will be an 'idea' of just contractual exchange, each receiving his due, that will animate consensual participation. At the time Locke was writing, those interested in the nature of contracts, in particular in making sense of the Roman law of contracts, accepted the idea of 'equality of exchange'.[34] This was particularly so because of the adoption of Aristotelian and Thomistic notions of fairness in contractual dealing.[35] In the Nicomachean Ethics Aristotle famously distinguished between commutative and distributive justice.[36] Contracts were a case that fell within the former. As such, the idea of equality of exchange was based not on the idea of some equal intrinsic value in the objects or services which formed the subject matter of a contract, but rather on the idea that contracts were not intended to serve

[33] Locke 1970, p. 301, section 48.
[34] Gordley 1981, 1991.
[35] Gordley 1991, ch. 2.
[36] Aristotle 2009, pp. 84–91.

as a means for the redistribution of wealth. If a man wanted to distribute his wealth to another, he would not enter into an exchange; he would make a gift. Therefore contracts in which there was a gross disparity in the values exchanged would not be valid, as they would effect a redistribution of wealth. In the case of sales, this idea of fairness was embodied in the doctrine of the 'just price'.[37] We know that Locke was aware of these ideas because he contributed to the literature on them. Thus, in his 1695 *Venditio*[38] he gave his own views on the doctrine of the just price. There is only one point from this piece that I need to mention here, which is that Locke agreed that 'price discrimination', i.e. tailoring the price one would charge so as to take advantage of the particular circumstances of a particular buyer, is unjust. Locke says:

> He that makes use of another's ignorance, fancy, *or necessity* to sell ribbon or cloth, etc, dearer to him than to another man at the same time, cheats him.[39]

This strongly indicates, I would suggest, that Locke would not have allowed as a matter of morality or law a first-acquirer of land to bargain harshly with a landless person for his labour, providing him with a mere subsistence wage, in so far as that wage did not reflect equality in exchange, i.e. amounted to a redistribution of wealth. That would be to take advantage of the latter's necessitous situation, and would flout the general principle of equality of exchange. Now one might object to this thought along the following lines: the above *Venditio* passage suggests that Locke places two conditions for violating the principle of the just price: (1) that someone is taking advantage of another's necessity and (2) that the person engages in price discrimination. Therefore, without falling afoul of the quoted passage, one could charge everyone the same price that only those who are desperate will pay. That is, in fact, what landowners, sweatshop owners, etc., often do: they offer *everyone* the same wage for a lousy job, where this wage is set as low as it is because they know that some will be desperate enough to accept it.

However, it seems to me that this *is* an example of price discrimination. That there is a class of needy individuals, rather than just one, is not the issue. If a just price is one which relates to the value of work as understood

[37] Gordon 1981, 1991; Baldwin 1959. I thank Johan Olsthoorn for bringing this latter reference to my attention.

[38] Locke 1695. See also Locke 1970, p. 170, para 42, 'a Man can no more make use of another's necessity, to force him to become his Vassal [by withholding charity] ... than he that has more strength can seize upon a weaker, master him to his Obedience, and with a Dagger at his Throat offer him Death or Slavery'.

[39] Locke 1695 my italics. Thanks to Mike Otsuka and Gopal Sreenivasan for helping me to clarify my thoughts on the following passages.

by all possible market actors, but a landowner sets his price deliberately so that only the desperately needy would be moved to accept it, then it seems to me that that landowner is setting a price so as to discriminate against those in need. The same could be said of a seller of bottled water who sets the price at $10 a bottle but is able to target a group of the desperately thirsty, say refugees who are at sea. Of course the seller is offering the same price to everyone in one sense, but in reality he is relying on the need of the refugees to price the water in a discriminatory way. This claim can be elaborated in different ways. First, we might apply a counterfactual test. If it were not for the presence of the necessitous, would the seller or employer set a different price or offer a different wage? If the answer is yes, then the 'at first glance' equal offer to all is duplicitous – it is targeting the price elasticity of the necessitous. In other words, just because you profit more from contracts with the necessitous, and adjust your price so only they will pay it, foregoing the rest of the market, does not mean you are not engaging in price discrimination; rather, this sort of behavior epitomises it (think of the 'pay-day loans' industry). Another way of seeing the point is by considering the concept of a 'price-setter'. In an efficient market everyone is a 'price-taker', that is, cannot unilaterally raise or lower the price of goods (including the 'price' of labour). By contrast, where, for example, a person has a monopoly, she is a price-setter, allowing her to extract monopoly 'rents'. The parallel here is obvious. The person taking advantage of others' necessity is able to set a price, relying upon the desperation of these people, allowing her to extract 'necessity rents'.

There is one further point that will become significant in a moment. Not having the insights of modern economics, theorists of the just price, or of equality in exchange more broadly, never satisfactorily related this idea to the market price, which they took as prima facie evidence of the just price.[40] But it is important to understand how they understood the just price. As Gordley has noted,

> Not having a mechanism to determine how need, scarcity, and cost [of production] affected the market price, they ascribed this role to human judgment, to the communis aestimatio. ... In their simpler account, the market price depended on as many factors as the persons making the judgment. ... Regulated prices, however, were legitimate and, on occasion, wise. In setting a price, the public authority was simply substituting its own judgment about the price that would best reflect need, scarcity and cost for the judgment or aestimatio of buyers and sellers.

[40] Gordley 1981, pp. 1607–8.

Given what Locke says about the contribution that labour makes to the value of goods, e.g. that labour contributes at the least 9/10ths of their value, it would be difficult to ascribe to Locke the view that the communis aestimatio of the value of that labour would be a subsistence wage for the labourer, all remaining value in the resultant good going to the owner of the raw materials. This will be even clearer when I point out below that first acquisition can simply be regarded as one form of labour amongst others under a just division of labour.

With this notion of Lockean contractual fairness in mind, we can now pursue Locke's views on the value of labour and his 'spoilation proviso', [SP], and see how they work together to shape a Lockean idea of justice in exchange, though not one found specifically in *Venditio.*

The first thing to notice about the world about which Locke was writing was that the resources of the world were not then, and are not now, scarce, in the following important sense: given industry and the division of labour, it is clear that there is enough to go around so that no one needs to starve. Moreover, for Locke, given the tenor of his discussion of money,[41] which I have addressed elsewhere,[42] it is not clear that land would be scarce in the sense of being fully privately appropriated, but for our valuing of things useless to the life of man but which are desired because of their positional value, that is goods where the value of the good turns on the fact of its exclusivity, i.e. on the fact that other persons don't have it.[43] It is an empirical question. The point of raising these considerations is this: what has become scarce is land, *in the sense that there is not enough and as good land left such that every person has the opportunity to appropriate land for herself.* It is not true that there is a scarcity of land in the sense that some people are necessarily destitute because the fruits of exploiting the resources found on land are simply too few to support the population of the earth. Rather, what has occurred has been a kind of 'division of labour' specialization with respect to land exploitation. Not all participants in the exploitation of the fruits of the earth under a division of labour can make land acquisition, or more accurately 'direct land exploitation', their role or one of their roles under the division of labour.

The difference between these two notions of scarcity, what we might call 'absolute scarcity' and 'artificial scarcity', and the importance of seeing that Locke is concerned to justify the continuing property rights in land in the

[41] Locke 1970, pp. 299–302, sections 46–51.
[42] Penner 2018.
[43] Locke 1970, p. 293, section 36.

latter, but not the former, can be brought out with the toy example of the desert island.

A, B, and C wash up on a desert island. Given that the island is resource poor and has a bad climate, however much A, B, and C labour it will only produce enough to feed, clothe and shelter three people. The only benefit that A, B, and C will achieve by engaging in a division of labour is the efficiency of reducing their combined workload to produce the subsistence level of sustenance the island can afford. It will not generate any *surplus* that might be spoiled or traded away.

Now D washes up. Nothing that Locke says in his passages on property rights addresses this 'planks in a shipwreck' situation. In this condition of scarcity, at least one of A, B, C, or D will die, and I see nothing in Locke to provide some sort of solution to this problem, in particular one which regards A's, B's, and C's current rights to the land of the desert island as becoming illegitimate with D's arrival.[44]

Now consider a second case, which I think Locke does have the resources to address. As before, A, B, and C wash up on a desert island, but this one is fertile, and its resources easy to exploit – say fruit trees and easily captured game and fresh water are abundant, and the climate is so equable that clothing is unnecessary.

Let as also assume that for matters of convenience, A, B, and C divide the island into thirds, each having his own 'territory', so to speak. Now D washes up. According to Locke's proviso as interpreted by Sreenivasan, and the Nozickian proviso provided by Otsuka, A, B, and C have D over a barrel. Each can refuse D entry to his territory on pain of D's death, and whilst D may have some competitive advantage in this situation, that is, he can try to get a better bargain from one of them – in this sense A, B, and C have to 'compete' for D's labour – any bargain that is actually struck is valid irrespective of their positions in terms of bargaining power. This would be so even if A, B, and C form a cartel to ensure they can each reap some labour from D at a wage just high enough to provide D with a level of well-being as he would have had if he had been free to roam, hunt and so on, on the island. Given the plentiful resources of the island, this might be quite a nice wage. Still, however, D will have no right to enclose or generate a surplus. The field will obviously be tilted in A's, B's, and C's favour when, for example, a hundred or a thousand D's turn up, for in that case the bargaining power of any individual D will be reduced. We will have something like a Marxian proletariat.

[44] For discussion of this sort of case, see Mack 1995, p. 193.

This way of looking at the matter seems to underestimate the resources of [SP], as understood by Locke himself. It seems clear that the acquisition of land is not different from the acquisition of other property. Locke says of land,

> I think it is plain, that property in that too is acquired as the former.[45]

In particular, [SP] applies:

> But if either the grass of his enclosure rotted on the ground, or the fruit of his planting perished without gathering, and laying up, this part of the earth, notwithstanding his enclosure, was still to be looked on as waste, and might be the possession of any other.[46]

In other words, if a person encloses more land than he can use, so that its fruits go to waste, [SP] is violated. On what basis, then, can A, B, and C deny D's access to their territories, not just to pick fruit or catch game which none of A, B, and C will themselves acquire, but also to appropriate and improve what A, B, and C are not actually using for their own benefit? Does their denial of D's access to just that extent not consist in the spoiling or letting rot of these resources? That would appear to be in the spirit of [SP], and perhaps within the strict letter given the passage I have just quoted. And the point is even stronger given the empirical premise about scarcity we have accepted, which is that, whilst there may be not enough and as good land left to appropriate, land is not scarce in the sense that there is insufficient worldly resources to provide everyone alive with the means of subsistence (and considerably more). Furthermore, it would appear that the lesson of this story could be generalized, i.e. that though A, B, and C may have strict property rights *inter se*, in the sense that they chose to divide the island up equally as they did,[47] those rights are frail as against any D whose use of any of their land is merely of resources that are not otherwise going to be exploited by A, B, and C themselves for each of their own benefits. From this perspective, the Ds of the world have the likes of *A, B, and C* over a barrel. For unless the land that, e.g. A holds is scarce in sense of the first, resource-poor desert island example (that is, it can only support one individual), A's right in the land must yield wherever it might be more fruitfully exploited, since another can provide for himself from it in a way that leaves A no worse off than he was when he was the only person on the land. That is, simply, the *morality* of [SP].

[45] Locke 1970, p. 290, section 32.

[46] Locke 1970, p. 295, section 38.

[47] This could be understood as them first acting jointly to appropriate the whole island, and then by agreement dividing into equal shares.

Let me consider a variation on this scenario,[48] which reveals the power of [SP] as I have described it, in another way. Let us assume that A, B, and C develop a fondness for lentils, a fondness bordering upon the obsessive. Let us also a assume that lentil plants are very unproductive, so that in order to dine only on lentils A, B, and C each have to raze their individual thirds of this plentiful paradise and plant a monoculture of lentils. Doing so allows them each to harvest just enough lentils to eat; there is no surplus. Now D washes up. We are now back to the planks in a shipwreck situation of the resource poor island, though here one that is created by human folly. I think that in this case, A, B, and C have to stop this nonsense, restrict their lentil consumption and produce more productive crops, and allow D to do the same.

Although at first glance A, B, and C have not violated [SP], I submit that, on Lockean grounds, it can be shown that they have.

First of all, God gave the earth 'to the use of the Industrious and *Rational*.'[49] In the second place, one of Locke's justifications for enclosure of land is that it makes the land more productive, not less.

> [H]e that appropriates land to himself by his labour, does not lessen but increase the common stock of mankind. For the provisions serving to the support of human life, produced by one acre of enclosed and cultivated land, are (to speak much within compass) ten times more, than those, which are yielded by an acre of Land, of an equal richness, lyeing waste in common. And therefor he, that encloses Land and has a greater plenty of the conveniencies of life from ten acres, than he could have from an hundred left to Nature, may truly be said to give ninety acres to Mankind.[50]

A, B, and C have done the opposite. By their acts of environmental destruction, they might be truly said to have taken from Mankind, not given, and done so for no rational reason. Locke equates the idea of spoilage with the idea of taking more than one's share,[51] and one could argue that by taking land and making it less productive, A, B, and C have taken more than their rightful share, and thus have committed an act of spoilation, as well as despoilation.

But does taking seriously the resources of [SP] lead to something like the 'equal shares' solution? It seems to me that it does not.

On this account, first acquisition is best seen as a form of labour, as would be trading raw materials and finished goods. 'Labour' is not restricted to

[48] Prompted by Mike Otsuka.

[49] Locke 1970, p. 291, para 34, my italics.

[50] Locke 1970, p. 294, para 37.

[51] Locke 1970, p. 295, para 37.

'direct' resource application (gathering, mining, fishing, tilling) or manufacturing goods from raw materials. On this understanding, first appropriation is not a matter of 'staking a claim', but is itself a kind of labour, a form of economically valuable activity like any other. (If this is right then Sreenivasan's workmanship theory of Locke's theory of labour[52] is under-inclusive.)

And from this perspective, the position of first-acquirers is distinctly limited in terms of their contribution to the usable things created by application of human labour to worldly resources. We should bring together Locke's acceptance of the doctrine of the just price, or more broadly, equality of exchange, with his labour theory of value. It would seem out of keeping, if not flatly contradictory, to allow a first-acquirer to set the terms of his dealing with, say, employees who labour on his land, such that he might be entitled to the lion's share of the value created. Recall again that, for Locke, labour contributes (at least) 90 per cent of any usable thing's value. If appropriation counts for so little, why is it assumed that landowners can rightly enter into contracts with labourers so as to capture the lion's share of the physical product? Any such contracts would clearly violate the principle of equality of exchange, in the sense that they would be contracts that redistribute wealth to the landowner from the labourer. It is only under the threat of what we have seen to be an illegitimate, that is [SP]-violating,[53] denial of access to a landholder's land that a unfair bargain could be struck such that the landholder would acquire by way of contract most of the value of a non-landholding labourer's contribution to the creation of usable things. The justice of any such bargain in favour of a landholder would reach the vanishing point if one were entitled to acquire exclusive title to land, i.e. a right of denial of others to access a particular piece of land, just by being the first one to 'stake a claim'.

Given the weak position of first acquirers, both as a matter of justice in contracting and because of the 'morality' or 'moral vision' underlying [SP], in determining the division of surplus under a division of labour, it seems perfectly clear that no one is made worse simply because his place under the division of labour does not involve the first, direct, engagement with material resources, i.e. no right to an equal share of worldly resources by dint of first acquisition. If we withdraw the unprincipled premise under

[52] Sreenivasan 1995, pp. 62–9.

[53] Remember the extent of the spoilation proviso – a person could not simply acquire all the land by 'staking a claim', and if done for trade, would receive minimal remuneration, for if he couldn't strike a bargain he would have to release it back into the common.

which landowners, simply in virtue of their titles, have a just claim to the lion's share of the social product, unprincipled because it seems to have no basis in the Lockean justification of property rights because (1) of the stringency of [SP], (2) Locke's labour theory of value, and (3) the principle of equality in exchange, then properly understood, the differential distribution of titles to land is just a particular facet of the division of labour. Equality of opportunity must be assessed against the comprehensive backdrop of the division of labour more generally. Because bakers are needed does not mean that everyone has the right to be a baker, although there should not, of course, be hereditary titles to practice the trade of baking or any other illegitimate barriers to entry.

So on this accounting, the problem of distributive or economic justice does not lie in regard to Locke's theory of first acquisition, even first acquisition of land, but in our failure to see that the spoilation proviso continues to operate in cases of artificial scarcity of land and in our impoverished notions of justice or fairness when it comes to contractual exchange. My suspicion is that Locke would agree.

8

Lockean Property Theory in Confucian Thought: Property in the Thought of Wang Fuzhi (1619–1692) and Huang Zongxi (1610–1695)

NORMAN P. HO

8.1 Introduction

Two key questions in property theory are understanding how a person legitimately acquires private property rights over objects (in other words, understanding the origins of private property), and why such private property rights should be recognized. Contemporary property theory scholarship has focused much on understanding, developing, and critiquing the answers of primarily – almost exclusively – Western philosophers to these questions. Indeed, this focus cannot be blamed simply on Eurocentrism. Rather, it is first because many leading Western philosophers in history – most famously John Locke – indeed attempted to explicitly answer these questions. Second, property rights and state protection of individual property rights played very important roles in the broader political philosophy of various Western philosophers, such as Locke and Edmund Burke. The sanctity of property rights was seen by such philosophers as key to ensuring individual liberty against state tyranny. Indeed, today, the quality of a country's liberal democracy and rule of law is frequently measured with reference to its government's commitment to recognizing and protecting private property rights. More simply put, the concept of property has been essential to Western political philosophy.

Therefore, the emphasis in property theory scholarship on Western philosophers is not without good reason. However, this emphasis has led to two perhaps unintended consequences. First, the notions of the importance of private property rights and their role as a check on uninhibited government power have largely been credited to the Western

Besides the editors and contributors to this volume, I would like to thank my colleagues at Peking University School of Transnational Law for their helpful comments.

philosophical tradition. Put another way, it is the thought of Western philosophers, such as Locke, Georg Hegel, and Hugo Grotius (just to name a few), which continue to form the main bedrock of these state-inhibiting justificatory theories of property. Second, this emphasis has led to considerably less scholarly attention by contemporary property theorists on the role of property in the political and legal thought of philosophers outside of the West, such as philosophers in the Chinese tradition. In other words, the study of non-Western philosophers as possible sources for such justificatory theories of private property has been relatively underdeveloped. This scholarly deficit has cumulatively led to misunderstandings and overly broad generalizations about the role and status of property in non-Western thought, perhaps most notably in Chinese legal and political thought, both among legal scholars and historians.

The still widely held view of the Chinese Confucian[1] tradition's relationship with the notion of property is that Confucian thought was not supportive of, and even antithetical to, property rights. Numerous scholars have generalized Confucian thought as being opposed to private property, or they portray Confucianism as a scapegoat in order to explain the weakness of private property protection – especially intellectual property rights – in China and East Asia today.[2] These viewpoints are not just limited to scholars working in the West. Indeed, Chinese legal scholars who have worked on property law reform in China have not looked to the Confucian tradition as a resource for justifying property rights protection. Rather, they have emphasized the importance of Western law and legal theory – especially American and German law – as models for property rights reform.[3]

More specifically (and most germane for this chapter), how do many scholars today understand what traditional Chinese Confucian thought[4]

[1] In this chapter, I use the term "Confucian" to refer broadly to the Confucian tradition in dynastic China as a whole; I am not using the term to specifically refer to a type of Confucianism (e.g., pre-Qin Confucianism, the Neo-Confucianism of Zhu Xi, etc.).

[2] For example, Peter K. Yu has noted that it has become "typical" in the past two decades for scholars to argue that "Asian culture, especially Confucianism, is hostile toward intellectual property reforms" (Yu 2012, p. 340). For specific examples of scholarship that have argued that Confucianism is responsible for the lack of property rights in China and East Asia more broadly, see Alford 1995; Lehman 2006; Mo Zhang 2008. Other scholars, notably Daniel A. Bell, do not take as strong a view, but they nevertheless emphasize the Confucian tradition's constraints on property, rather than inquire as to how the Confucian tradition can serve as a justification for property. See Bell 2003.

[3] Potter 2012, p. 51.

[4] In this chapter, by "traditional Chinese" or "traditional China," I refer to dynastic China from antiquity up to 1911 (i.e., up to the overthrow of the last imperial Chinese dynasty – the Qing dynasty – and the establishment of the Republic of China).

had to say with respect to the two questions mentioned at the start of this chapter (i.e., how a person legitimately acquires property rights and why property rights should be recognized)? The widely heard answer is that traditional Confucian political thought held that property rights could not be acquired by a person at all, and therefore no property rights would be recognized. This position was justified by the belief, held by most Chinese for almost 2000 years, that the emperor was theoretically and practically speaking the owner of everything in the empire, especially of the most important form of property in traditional China – real property (land).[5] Therefore, a person in dynastic China did not have property rights in land, because his land was in reality simply a bestowal by the emperor. It has been further asserted that Confucian political thought throughout the entirety of dynastic China (antiquity up to 1911) basically adhered to, as a textual basis for such preceding views on property, a poem in the *Classic of Poetry*[6]; the relevant verse says that "[u]nder the wide heaven, all is the king's land / within the sea-boundaries of the land, all are the king's servants."[7] Moreover, the predominant understanding of traditional Confucian thought's low treatment of property has also been affected by scholarly interpretation of the Confucian concept of the "great unity" (datong 大同); Kang Youwei 康有为 (1858–1927) interpreted this concept

[5] For example, Mo Zhang argues that the "history of China reveals that the concept of private property was never really developed in the country's [China] past, as private ownership scarcely reached the level of being properly respected and legally protected" and that the emperor had "absolute right to determine property and life of citizens, since *governing Confucianism* [emphasis mine] said if a ruler wanted a subject to die, the subject must die" (Mo Zhang 2008, pp. 319–20).

[6] The *Classic of Poetry* (*Shijing* 诗经 in Chinese and also commonly translated as *Book of Songs* or the *Book of Odes* in English) in Chinese history was considered one of the so-called "Confucian Classics," which were among the most important texts in all of premodern Chinese history. The Confucian Classics formed the basis of education throughout much of dynastic China and were used as guides for daily behavior and local, as well as national, governance. The *Classic of Poetry* is comprised of 305 poems dating back to approximately the Western Zhou dynasty (i.e., approximately eleventh to seventh centuries BC); compilation of the *Classic of Poetry* has traditionally been attributed to Confucius himself. In traditional China, the status of the poems in the *Classic of Poetry* was very high, and Confucian thinkers and statesmen studied various poems for moral and political lessons. As such, the *Classic of Poetry*'s influence extended far beyond literature and into individual and collective morality, government policy, and education. Poems in the *Classic of Poetry* are frequently referred to by number under the so-called "Mao 毛" numbering system, named after Han dynasty Chinese scholar Mao Heng 毛亨 who in his commentary work on the *Classic of Poetry* arranged and numbered the poems.

[7] As an example of such an assertion, see Mo Zhang 2008, pp. 319–20. I use James Legge's translation of the verse. See poem *Bei Shan* 北山 (North Mountain) (*mao* number 205) in Legge 2006.

as justifying a utopian society where all work together for a common good with the disappearance of private property.[8]

To be sure, it must be pointed out that historians have recently begun to challenge some of these notions, pointing out that some Chinese dynasties institutionally did respect property rights and enforced land contracts, for example.[9] While such work by historians have been useful in correcting commonly held assumptions and generalizations about traditional Chinese *institutions*, less work has been done on compiling and correcting the widely held generalizations regarding traditional Chinese Confucian *thought* and Confucian *theoretical views* on the origins of property and property rights. For example, Jonathan Ocko, a leading historian of Chinese law, has argued that one substantial difference between Western and Chinese Confucian political thought is that whereas property and property rights played a major, at times pivotal role in the former, they were quite absent in late imperial and early modern Chinese political and legal sociopolitical discourse, which was dominated by the metaphor of the family.[10] Ocko has also asserted that even though at times there were challenges to Chinese "imperial systems," there was never a "Locke to articulate the notion that private property was the guarantor of individual liberty and of freedom from despotic states."[11] In short, the still commonly held view is that property and property rights did not play an important role in traditional Confucian political theory.

This chapter seeks to diversify this generalization of the role of property in Confucian thought. It focuses in particular on the property theory of two famous Chinese thinkers, Huang Zongxi 黄宗羲 (1619–92) (also romanized as Huang Chung-hsi) and Wang Fuzhi 王夫之 (1610–95) (also known as Wang Chuanshan 王船山 and also romanized as Wang Fu-chih), who have been hailed by historians as some of the most important theorists and philosophers in the Confucian tradition. The chapter argues that contrary to continued portrayals of Confucian thought as downplaying, opposing, or not emphasizing the role of property and property rights, Confucian thinkers Huang Zongxi and Wang Fuzhi in many ways radically challenged

[8] Chen 2014, p. 93.

[9] See, for example, the important work of historians Madeleine Zelin and Taisu Zhang. In particular, see Zelin 2004 (arguing that property rights in Qing and Republican China were strong and often enforced by the state); Zhang 2011 (examining, in a comparative framework, property rights in land sales in Qing and Republican China); and Zhang 2014 (arguing that Qing and Republican China institutionally gave greater economic protection to the poor in society than similar institutions in early modern England).

[10] See Ocko 2004.

[11] Ocko 2004, p. 179.

traditional views of the origins of property ownership (namely, land ownership) in traditional China, denying the notion the emperor owned all land in the empire. Furthermore, they both also emphasized the role property rights (and state protection of property rights) could play in limiting despotic rule, thereby making property rights a key concept and component in their broader political theory. Wang, in particular, arguably advanced a theory of property based on natural law ideas.[12] This chapter also will compare Huang's and Wang's views on property and property rights and argue that, contrary to most scholarship which has analogized Huang's broader political thought to Locke,[13] Wang and his theory of the origins of property can be described as more Lockean in nature. Wang's theory of property is also more complete than Huang's as it more explicitly addresses questions concerning the origins of property. To my knowledge, there is basically no scholarship in Western languages, and very little scholarship in the Chinese language, which has discussed Huang and Wang together in one written forum, focusing on their views of property; similarly, no scholarship that I know of has compared Wang to Locke or has situated either Huang or Wang's views on real property ownership in the larger property theory context.[14]

Through setting forth and explicating the above specific arguments, this chapter also hopes to make two broader contributions to the fields of Chinese legal history and property theory. First, with respect to Chinese legal history, this chapter hopes to correct the usual, often-heard narrative of Chinese political and legal thought as not emphasizing property or property rights or as simply operating on the theoretical basis that the emperor owned everything in the realm. This chapter hopes to show that questions of property – such as the origins of property rights and the reach of the emperor's property rights – were very much discussed and debated

[12] I will discuss what I mean by "natural law" later in the relevant section of this chapter.

[13] See, e.g., Lin 1942, p. 199; Yeung 2005; Yongzhong Zhang 2008, 2009; Shi 2011; Ren 2014.

[14] There is scholarship (mostly in the Chinese language) specifically on Huang Zongxi's views on land ownership, as well as scholarship (mostly in the Chinese language) specifically on Wang Fuzhi's views on land ownership. For scholarship on Huang Zongxi's views on land ownership, see de Bary 1993, pp. 42–8; Zhang 2009, pp. 36–9, 2012b; Zhao 2005; Chen 1994; Qiao 2007; Luo 1987; Huang 2008.

For scholarship on Wang Fuzhi's views on land ownership, see McMorran 1992, pp. 167–78; Li 1983; Zeng 1993; Xiao and Liu 2007; Ma 2006; Liu 1982.

For helpful general historiographical overviews of Huang Zongxi which lay out recent scholarship on various facets of Huang Zongxi and his thought (i.e., "state-of-the-field"-type essays), see Liu 2006; Zhang and Huangfu 1996.

For helpful general historiographical overviews of Wang Fuzhi which lay out recent scholarship on various facets of Wang Fuzhi and his thought (i.e., "state-of-the-field"-type essays`), see Liu 2004; Hunan University Press 2009.

by important Confucian thinkers. Second, with respect to property theory, this chapter hopes to develop the sub-field of comparative property theory, putting Eastern and Western property theorists in dialogue with another. More specifically, this chapter hopes to show that Lockean ideas regarding property are not necessarily unique to the Western tradition.

Before delving into the body of the chapter, some remarks about terminology are in order. First, when discussing Huang's and Wang's theory of "property," I am referring to real property – mainly, land – as this was the type of property being discussed by Huang and Wang. Furthermore, land was the most important form of property in traditional China. It should be noted, however, that Huang's and Wang's theory of property need not be confined to real property; it could be equally applicable to personal property, although this chapter does not explore or extend possible interpretations or applications of their theories to personal property. Second, also when discussing Huang's and Wang's theory of "property," I am referring to the idea of private property (in contrast to common or state property), which itself can be understood as rules of property organized around the notion that "contested resources are separate objects, each assigned to the decisional authority of some particular individual (or family or firm)."[15] Second, as to my use of the term "theory" (when I am referring to Huang's and Wang's "theory" of property or property "theory"), I mean a theory of property that is normative and justificatory, in contrast to an analytical or definitional theory of property – in other words, a theory that "attempts to provide a normative justification for allocating rights to material resources in a particular way."[16] More specifically, I mean general justificatory theories – that is, theories that seek to justify the general idea of having things under the control of private individuals or units. The reason for focusing on justificatory theories of property and not definitional theories of property is simple – as I will show and argue, Huang and Wang were setting forth justificatory theories of property.

8.2 Biographical Orientations and Context: Huang Zongxi and Wang Fuzhi

The purpose of this brief section is to provide some biographical orientation and historical context to Huang and Wang so their theories of

[15] Waldron 2010, p. 9. Waldron's parenthetical here is particularly important to keep in mind in the Chinese historical context, because in Ming-Qing China (generally speaking) the main private property-holding unit "was the household rather than individuals who constituted it" – i.e., the "family." See Zelin, Ocko, and Gardella 2004, p. 5.

[16] Alexander and Peña 2012, p. 6.

property can be better understood.[17] However, this section is not simply descriptive. I will also justify why we can and should examine Huang and Wang together, and indeed, why it is worth looking at Huang and Wang in the first place. Additionally, I will briefly explain why a comparison between Huang and Wang with Locke is warranted with respect to historical context.

It is natural to look at Huang and Wang together for several reasons. First, both intellectuals shared similar life backgrounds. They each lived through the tumultuous Ming-Qing transition and witnessed the fall of the Ming dynasty (1368–1644). Despite the Manchu Qing dynasty's (1644–1911) conquest of the Ming, they both retained their loyalties to the Ming dynasty, actively opposing the new Qing government. Wang, a native of Hunan, assembled a small army to fight for the Ming against the Qing army, but he was defeated and went into retirement at the age of 33, refusing to serve the new Qing regime.[18] Huang, a native of Zhejiang, also assembled volunteer soldiers to stem the advance of Qing troops, but ultimately his military efforts were not successful.[19] After the collapse of the Ming, he too refused to collaborate with the new Qing government and retired from public life, devoting his life to research and writing.[20]

Second, both shared a similar intellectual heritage and political orientation. With respect to intellectual heritage, both Huang and Wang were influenced by the Donglin Academy, a late Ming group of scholars and literati who tried to improve the Ming through a vigorous critique of what they saw as Ming despotism.[21] The late Ming was characterized by increasing autocracy and government corruption; eunuch cliques had usurped power at court, the emperor ruled as a dictator, and those who remonstrated to the government were often punished and even beaten to death.[22]

Huang's father was a member of the Donglin Academy,[23] and Wang's father was extremely sympathetic to the Donglin scholars and their mission. Wang also received part of his formative education by a teacher who

[17] This section only briefly covers the life and background of Huang and Wang as is germane for the chapter. For full biographies of Huang in other languages, see Cao 2009; Xu 2009a; Ono 1967. I would like to thank Lynn Struve for directing me to Ono's biography of Huang.
For a full biography of Wang, see Zhang 1997. See also the biographical overview in McMorran 1992, pp. 1–46.

[18] Ouyang 2003, p. 631.

[19] Wang 2012, p. 110.

[20] Wang 2012, p. 110.

[21] Wang 2012, p. 95. For a detailed study of the Donglin movement, see Dardess 2003.

[22] Lou 2012, p. 29.

[23] Wang 2012, p. 108.

became head of the Donglin Academy in 1642.[24] With respect to political orientation, both Huang and Wang's political theory were influenced by the fall of the Ming. They both opposed imperial despotism, blaming it for causing the fall of the Ming.[25] Both sought, in their writings, to reform the imperial system through what some scholars have labeled as "progressive" reforms.[26] Both also staunchly identified as thinkers in the Confucian tradition, and they sought to protect Chinese culture and Confucianism from what they saw as the alien, Manchu Qing invaders.[27]

Finally, both are considered by Chinese historians as thinkers within a similar intellectual tradition, the so-called "proto-Enlightenment" tradition in China, which appeared on the Chinese intellectual history scene in the late Ming to early Qing. According to Chinese historians, the main characteristics of "proto-Enlightenment" thought in China included opposition to autocratic government, a belief in historical progress, dedication to a "spirit of rationality" in government, as well as the introduction of "early versions of democracy and human rights."[28] Both Huang and Wang are considered to have inherited and developed the "proto-Enlightenment" tradition[29]; Huang, for example, has been called by one scholar as an "important predecessor to Enlightenment thinking in China,"[30] while Wang has been described as "unusually analytical for a Confucian philosopher, so much so that one might suspect the influence of Western logic."[31]

Having examined some similarities which would justify examining Huang and Wang together, why should we care about Huang and Wang in the first place? The short answer is that they have both shared similar legacies and reputations in history as two of the most important Confucian

[24] McMorran 1992, pp. 5–6.

[25] McMorran 2000, p. 27.

[26] Wang 2012, p. 109.

[27] McMorran 2000, p. 26.

[28] Wang 2012, p. 80. Whether Huang or Wang should be labeled a "democratic" thinker is a subject of debate. According to Wm. Theodore de Bary, the general consensus among scholars is that Huang does "bespeak a kind of democratic thought" and that he can be seen as a "champion of government for the people," although scholars disagree whether Huang "advocated anything like government by or of the people" (de Bary 1993, p. 80). Similarly, Wang advocated certain democratic ideas, namely that government should be "for the people" and that the ruler must exercise empathy toward his people, but there is some debate whether Wang's political ideas are comparable to democracy. See Liu 2002, p. 754.

[29] Wang 2012, p. 80.

[30] Xu 2009b. The leading scholar in the West on Huang, Wm. Theodore de Bary, has also argued that Huang indeed should be seen as part of an Enlightenment movement in China. See de Bary 1993, p. 77.

[31] Black 1989, p. xiv.

theorists in the Chinese tradition.[32] In other words, neither Huang nor Wang were marginal Confucian thinkers. Huang himself was an important figure for Chinese political reformers in the late nineteenth to early twentieth centuries and has been seen as a "direct progenitor" of democratic and nationalist movements in modern China.[33] His key 1662 work, *Ming yidai fang lu* 明夷待访录 (translated in English often as *Waiting for the Dawn: A Plan for the Prince*; hereafter, "Waiting for the Dawn"),[34] which "embodied [his] most radical and critical reflections on the various problems besetting the Ming regime,"[35] influenced famous late nineteenth to early twentieth century reformer Liang Qichao 梁启超 (1873–1929) (who called Huang "China's Rousseau"[36]) and has been seen as a "landmark work in the history of Chinese political thought."[37] This work has also been appraised as the "most eloquent and comprehensive statement of its kind in Chinese political literature" and "has proved the most enduring and influential Confucian critique of Chinese despotism through the ages, as well as the most powerful affirmation of a liberal Confucian political vision in premodern times."[38] In sum, Huang was a "vastly learned man whose scholarly accomplishments stand out even in a century notable for intellectual giants in China."[39]

Wang and his thought have enjoyed similar influence and assessments. He has been described by Chinese scholars as the "most brilliant and also the most romantic of the late Ming scholars."[40] Similar to Huang, his work influenced late nineteenth-century and twentieth-century Chinese political reformers, including the 1898 reform movement martyr Tan Sitong 谭嗣同 (1865–98), who remarked that Wang was the "only person during

[32] It is important to note that while Huang was very much a public intellectual – consulted by many other thinkers – during his lifetime, Wang retired at the age of 33 literally into the mountains – specifically, he moved to "Stone Boat Mountain," where he lived and wrote for approximately 40 years (Struve 2002, p. 306; Ouyang 2003, p. 631). However, after their death, both were recognized as key political thinkers in the Confucian tradition. For a study which argues that Huang should be seen more "as a culminator rather than an instigator of ideas" but which nevertheless concedes that Huang was "an outstanding intellectual of the later imperial era in China," see Struve 1988.

[33] de Bary 1993, pp. 71–2.

[34] Unless otherwise indicated, I use Wm. Theodore de Bary's full English translation of this text. For the original Chinese version, see Huang 1985b.

[35] Chow 2003, p. 271.

[36] de Bary 1993, p. 80.

[37] de Bary 1993, pp. 71, 79–80.

[38] de Bary 1993, p. 85.

[39] Struve 2002, p. 306.

[40] Wang 2012, p. 120.

the last 500 years who truly understood the ways of man and nature."[41] Wang's influence was also made clear in 1914, when an eponymous academy – the Chuanshan Academy – was founded to specifically focus on studying Wang's thought itself and as a resource for political reform.[42] Even Mao Zedong admired Wang and attended meetings in the Chuanshan Academy.[43] An eponymous journal – *Chuanshan Xuekan* (*Chuanshan Journal*) – was founded in 1915 as a journal focusing exclusively on Wang; the journal continues to be in circulation today and is said to be the oldest continuing journal on philosophy in China. Wang's ideas have and continue to resonate with scholars, as "his metaphysical and historical views reflect a realism that is more akin to modern Western temper than were those of his Confucian predecessors."[44] In sum, both Huang and Wang are worthy of our attention and both can, and should, be examined together due to the similarities they share.

Having introduced Wang and Huang, we can arguably also see similarities between them and Locke with respect to historical context. These similarities, in turn, make a comparison between Wang or Huang and Locke more intellectually justifiable. First, and most obvious, Locke, Wang, and Huang were all contemporaries, living in the seventeenth century. Second, and more specifically, Locke's Europe – similar to the late Ming and early Qing China – also experienced political tumult, with the English Civil War in the 1640s and significant political debates and conflicts between the British monarchy and the British Parliament. More significantly, many of these debates also revolved around issues concerning the proper scope of the British king's power, akin to late Ming debates over the emperor's autocratic governing style and the Donglin Academy's critique of late Ming monarchy. Third, Locke also took general positions against autocracy that can be compared with those of Wang and Huang. Indeed, Locke wrote his *First Treatise of Government* to oppose Robert Filmer's Divine Right of Kings doctrine, arguing against absolute monarchy. In his *Second Treatise of Government*, Locke emphasized government that is built upon the natural rights of the people and whose legitimacy is derived from a social contract.[45] Similarly, as we have seen, Huang and Wang also set forth ideas that have been described as democratic. To be sure, there are not insubstantial differences between Locke on one hand and Wang or Huang

[41] McMorran 1992, p. xiii.
[42] McMorran 1992, p. xiv.
[43] McMorran 1992, p. xiv.
[44] Black 1989, p. xiv.
[45] Uzgalis 2016.

on the other – for example, Huang and Wang never explicitly set out that sovereignty resides in the people and never explicitly suggested that government should be of the people. Nor did they explicitly emphasize natural rights to the same degree as Locke. Nevertheless, there are compelling similarities that make a comparative discussion plausible and justified. We can now turn to their specific, individual, theories of property.

8.3 Huang Zongxi's Theory of Property

If we consider the two questions in property theory posed at the very start of this chapter, Huang's theory of property, on the whole, is arguably less complete than Wang's, since Huang does not clearly answer the question as to the origins of property ownership – i.e., how someone comes to legitimately acquire rights over something.[46] Huang instead focused more on the question of why property rights should be respected and protected, on the whole arguing that such respect and protection would serve as an effective means to protect the ownership rights of landowners and also serve as an effective check against imperial despotism. He was staunchly opposed to government expropriation of private land, and therefore he was a protector of property rights. As we will see in the next section, Wang, by contrast, addressed both questions.

Huang's theory of property can be deduced from his discussion of land reform and land tax reform in *Waiting for the Dawn*. In Huang's view, there was no private ownership of land during the time of the ancient sage kings. All land was shared in common, and land was distributed by the king through the well-field (*jingtian* 井田) system.[47] After the "Three Dynasties of Antiquity" (i.e., Xia (ca. 2100–1600 BC), Shang (ca. 1600–1050 BC), and Zhou (1046–256 BC) dynasties, or collectively known in Chinese as the

[46] Zhang 2009, pp. 38–9.

[47] de Bary 1993, p. 43. The well-field system was a land distribution system in ancient China that was idealized by Mencius. According to Mencius, a square league of land should be divided into a pattern that looks like the Chinese character for "well" (*jing*) – i.e., a total of nine separate fields. The well-fields would be 900 acres, and in the middle would be the public field, a form of common property. However, eight families would each have their own private land – i.e., the other remaining eight fields. They would, in Mencius's view, ideally first farm the public field (and the yields would presumably go to the entire state) before tending to each of their own private fields. The public well would also build camaraderie and affection among the eight families on that particular square league of land. See Mencius 3A13-20 in Van Norden 2008, p. 67. It should be noted that scholars still debate today whether the well-field system actually existed in Chinese history; Huang certainly believed it did. For further discussion on the scholarly debate over the existence of the well-field system in Chinese history, see Zhang 2012a, pp. 220–4; Hu 1988, p. 71.

sandai 三代), the ruler no longer granted or bestowed land to the people.[48] Instead, people acquired land for themselves through purchase and sale, and private landholding was firmly established in the Qin (221–206 BC) and Han dynasties (206 BC–220 AD).[49] Therefore, given that land was no longer given for free by the emperor but purchased by people using their own resources, Huang also proceeded to deny the emperor's automatic right to land in his realm, arguing that the land was no longer the king's land. Indeed, in a passage in his essay "Poxielun" 破邪论 (hereafter, "Arguments to Defeat Evil"[50]), Huang argued:

> During the time of the sage kings, the people were looked after and taken care of by the ruler. After that period, the people looked after and took care of themselves. Afterwards, exorbitant, burdensome taxes were levied on the people, and they therefore did not have the means to take care of themselves. The *Classic of Poetry* says: "Under the wide heaven, all is the king's land / within the sea-boundaries of the land, all are the king's servants."[51] [During the time of the sage kings], land was granted by the king to the people. Therefore, such land can be called the king's land. However, in later periods, land was purchased by the people themselves, and therefore the land is the people's land and not the king's land ....[52]

In this passage, Huang quoted the famous *Classic of Poetry* poem mentioned in the chapter's introduction, in particular the verse which had provided the justification for the king/emperor as the owner of all land. But Huang pointed out that the verse was no longer accurate because after the time of the sage kings, the land was in reality no longer the "king's land" since it was purchased by the people themselves.

Ultimately, Huang's theory of property is more concerned with the protection of property rights and the role of property as checking government despotism. After private landholding was firmly established in the Qin and Han dynasties, Huang pointed out that concentration of land became a major problem – that is, a select few controlled the majority of land.[53] Chinese officials proposed various solutions, including a return

[48] Chow 2003, p. 271.

[49] de Bary 1993, p. 43.

[50] Here, I use Lynn Struve's English translation of the title "Poxielun." See Struve 1988, p. 496. "Arguments to Defeat Evil" was an essay written by Huang which set out his views on a variety of issues, including taxation, religious matters, and the civil service examination system.

[51] I use James Legge's translation of this *Classic of Poetry* verse. See poem *Bei Shan* 北山 (North Mountain) (*mao* number 205) in Legge 2006. For a description of the *Classic of Poetry*, see note 6 and the accompanying text.

[52] This is my translation of the original Chinese. Huang 1985a [17th century], p. 203.

[53] de Bary 1993, p. 44.

to the well-field system or to abolish private property, expropriate all land, and redistribute land.[54] Han dynasty scholar-official Dong Zongshu 董仲舒 (179–104 BC) had proposed a limitation on the amount of land any one person could hold. Huang was a staunch opponent of such policies; in *Waiting for the Dawn*, he excoriated such proposals:

> After the abolition of the well-fields, Dong Zhongshu proposed a limitation on the amount of land a man could hold ... their [officials like Dong Zhongshu who were proposing land reform measures] intentions were good, but whereas in ancient times the wise ruler granted land so as to provide for the people, today people own their own land and if an attempt is made to deprive them of it by decree – it is [what Mencius] called "doing even one act that is not right" and should not be done.[55]

In other words, Huang did not only consider such proposals to be ineffective given the reality of the situation (i.e., as opposed to antiquity, people own their own land today), but he considered them fundamentally immoral (quoting Mencius and labeling such proposals as "not right"). Rather than advocating government expropriation, a return to the well-field system, or limitations on land ownership, Huang strongly believed that the property rights of the rich should be protected and their landholdings – even though expansive – should not be affected. Private property, in other words, should stay.[56] As for land needed for redistribution to those who were well-off, Huang believed the source of such land should not come from wealthy landowners but rather the state – that is, official lands and large estates that had been set up for the emperor's family members or his allies.[57] In other words, official land, and not private land, should be redistributed as necessary to provide subsistence for those who needed it.[58] Huang saw this distinction of land in black and white terms, positing that "[a]ll land is either official or private. Official land cannot be bought and owned by an individual."[59] Therefore, in Huang's view, there should not be an alternative category of land created to justify the seizure of private lands. In sum, Huang himself most accurately characterized his views on land: "[s]o why should there be any fuss over property limitations and equalization, or should one needlessly make a big thing out of causing the well-to-do to suffer?"[60]

[54] de Bary 1993, p. 45.
[55] Quoted in de Bary 1993, p. 131; I use de Bary's translation here.
[56] de Bary 1993, p. 46.
[57] de Bary 1993, p. 46.
[58] de Bary 1993, pp. 47–8.
[59] Quoted in de Bary 1993, p. 133.
[60] Quoted in de Bary 1993, p. 133.

Thus far we have examined Huang's theory of property directly from his writings on land reform. However, I would also argue that the importance Huang placed on property can also be seen his broader political thought and attack on the emperor and the imperial government. More specifically, Huang used the very vocabulary of property in his discourse and his critique of despotism, which itself formed the crux and main aim of *Waiting for the Dawn*. He lamented and despised the emperor's treating his people and everything in his kingdom as his own personal property:

> In ancient times, all-under-Heaven [the people] were considered the master, and the prince was the tenant .... Now, the prince is the master, and all-under-Heaven are tenants ... In order to get whatever he [the prince] wants, he maims and slaughters all-under-Heaven and breaks up their families – all for the aggrandizement of one man's fortune. Without the least feeling of pity, the prince says, "I'm just establishing an estate for my descendants." Yet when he has established it, the prince still extracts the very marrow from the people's bones and takes away their sons and daughters to serve his own debauchery. It seems entirely proper to him. It is, he says, the interest on his estate. Thus he who does the greatest harm in the world is none other than the prince.[61]

As we can see, Huang used the very metaphor of property to criticize autocracy, arguing that rulers were now improperly treating their people as tenants. In reality, Huang argued, the relationship should be reversed – people should be the "masters," or the landlords. In ancient times, the people themselves had actually been the masters of the land, whereas the ruler was a mere "tenant" or servant, but in later periods, emperors became the "masters" while the people became "tenants" without property.[62] Using extremely dramatic corporeal language ("marrow," "bones"), Huang also rebuked the emperors' expropriation of the property, assets, and very bodies of his people in order to build up his own "estate" – i.e., his own property holdings. Indeed, Huang also remarked that emperors "looked upon the world as an enormous estate to be handed on down to his descendants, for their perpetual pleasure and well-being."[63] The dynastic system, in Huang's view, was inherently selfish and desired to own and control everything under the realm.[64]

Huang did not merely (as in the above passage) point out the harms and costs to society of a ruler's selfishness to expropriate all for his own

[61] Quoted in de Bary 1993, p. 92; I use de Bary's translation here.
[62] de Bary 1993, p. 18.
[63] de Bary 1993, p. 92.
[64] de Bary 1993, p. 16.

enjoyment. Perhaps even more radically, he also couched his critique of imperial and dynastic despotism and the emperor's expropriation of people's land in explicitly moral terms, believing that dynastic rule was indeed the "prime incarnation of political and economic evil."[65] Indeed, Huang also specifically attacked the immorality of the emperor himself, arguing that the "biggest evil in the world is nothing but the ruler."[66]

Not only was the emperor's interference in, and expropriation of, the people's lands harmful to the people and evil, it was also unnatural. Simply put, Huang argued that it was natural for men to pursue their own self-interest and to satisfy their needs. To prove this, Huang advanced a "state of nature" argument. In the original state of nature, Huang argued that "[i]n the beginning of human life each man lived for himself and looked to his own interests."[67] Huang's state of nature, in other words, was one where humans in their earliest, original state managed and satisfied themselves without a leader. People managed their own affairs and looked out for themselves, and it was a rational society where individuals supported themselves. Furthermore, this was not a state characterized by selfishness, but *self-interest*. It is important to note that Huang believed in the dignity of the individual – he believed human nature was fundamentally good, and he believed that human desires (such as those to pursue self-interest) were rational and natural. In making these points, Huang was in essence emphasizing the individual autonomy of each person to pursue his own benefit.[68] However, at the same time, such a society lacked a sense of cohesion and relationships, and so rulers eventually came onto the scene to consider things such as the common benefit and common harm and to unite everyone into a political society.[69] Therefore, expropriatory actions and attitudes on the part of the ruler – such as "extracting the very marrow from people's bones"[70] in order to fatten his own estates – were unnatural because they interfered with the people's natural desires and ability to take care of themselves. Huang's ultimate point was that if society was not better off with a ruler, people could simply revert to their original state.[71]

To sum up, we can see that Huang's theory of property focuses more on the question of why property rights should be respected and protected,

65 de Bary 1993, p. 18.
66 Chow 2003, p. 271.
67 Quoted in de Bary 1993, p. 91.
68 Zhang 2012b, p. 116.
69 Sun 2008, pp. 165–7.
70 Quoted in de Bary 1993, p. 92.
71 Sun 2008, p. 166.

arguing that expropriation of property by the ruler would be harmful, immoral, and unnatural. Huang's theory of property also emphasizes the importance of property generally as a check on imperial despotism. He even used the metaphor of property (language such as "tenants" and "master") in his polemic against imperial autocracy. At the same time, we must point out some weaknesses in Huang's theory. As one scholar has pointed out, Huang ultimately did not address the question regarding the origins of property – even if we accept the Huang's notion that the ruler owned the land during the "Three Dynasties of Antiquity," where did the ruler's right to the land derive from?[72] Huang did not give an answer, instead solely relying on the previously quoted verse from the *Classic of Poetry*. As we will see in the next section, Wang's theory addresses this issue more explicitly and persuasively. In this sense, Wang's theory of property is more complete than Huang's. At the very least, however, Huang represents an example of a prominent thinker in the Confucian tradition who saw protection of property rights as paramount in his broader political thought.

8.4 Wang Fuzhi's Theory of Property and Comparisons with Locke

Wang's theory of property, in contrast to Huang, explicitly addresses the question of the origins of property ownership while also answering the question of why property rights should be respected and protected. I want to also show that Wang's theory of property can be understood as couched in natural law principles and is in some respects Lockean in nature.

As a starting point and to provide more context, it is important to note that Wang strongly emphasized the importance of property in his political thought. He believed that the most urgent problem in his time was the land system.[73] Given that the economy and society was based upon agriculture, the regulation of land was of key importance, and Wang believed that previous dynasties had implemented deficient land policies.[74] As a result, the wealth disparity in society became more pronounced, with the rich accumulating huge estates while smaller landowners and farmers were forced to sell off their land and work the fields of the rich.[75] Thus, similar to Locke, Wang saw property as serving important political goals.

[72] Zhang 2009, p. 39.
[73] McMorran 1992, p. 166.
[74] McMorran 1992, p. 167.
[75] McMorran 1992, p. 167.

Like Huang, Wang rejected the notion that the emperor ruled all the land in his realm. He even went further than Huang, denying the right of the emperor to tax the nation's land, since he did not own it.[76] Wang set out the main components of his theory of property in a passage from his 1687 work *Du Tongjianlun* 读通鉴论 (*On Reading Sima Guang's Comprehensive Mirror in Aid of Governance*[77]), an important essay which set forth Wang's analysis of Chinese history and his own proposals on pressing issues of his day:

> The emperor may make the people of the empire his subjects, but he may not arrogate unto himself the land of the empire .... The people depend on the emperor for political order and to be able to live out their lives, so they devote their labors to the service of the emperor and he[78] accepts them without hesitation. As for the land, however, then it definitely belongs to the universe and natural world. Emperors may rise and fall one after another, but the mountains and rivers, the plains and marshes remain unchanged. They produce all the various kinds of grain, plants, trees, metal, and stone to support man. Emperors too depend on these for their support, but none of them depends on emperors, and so the emperor cannot arrogate them unto himself .... [79]

Unlike Huang, who simply denied the right of the emperor to the land but did not express who the true original owner of the land was, Wang argued that land ultimately belonged to nature, not to the emperor. Therefore, despite the famous verse from the *Classic of Poetry* which had claimed that all the land under Heaven was the emperor's, in Wang's view, the emperor had absolutely no right and no basis for expropriating land for himself. Land was simply naturally occurring in the world, "owned" by the "universe" and the "natural world." I believe that we can, in turn, understand the "universe" and the "natural world" as basically referring generally to the concept of Heaven, which Wang understood as the "totality of nature," comprising natural phenomena and natural objects without metaphysical

[76] McMorran 1992, p. 167.

[77] The *Comprehensive Mirror in Aid of Governance*, or *Zizhitongjian* 资治通鉴, is a chronicle history of China written by Sima Guang (1019–86) and others, which covers Chinese history from the fifth-century BC to the mid-10th century AD. The work was commissioned by the emperor at the time and was intended to be a definitive history of China.

[78] I use Ian McMorran's translation here. Quoted in McMorran 1992, p. 168. For the original Chinese text, see Wang 1996b [1687].

[79] I use Ian McMorran's translation here, with some of my slight modifications. Quoted in McMorran 1992, p. 169.

status or inherent morality – just like the "natural world."[80] Simply put, for Wang, Heaven is nature itself.[81] He continued:

> The land, like Heaven, cannot be claimed by any one man as his possession. Heaven cannot be divided up, nor can the land be partitioned. Although the emperor is the Son of Heaven, how could he possibly regard the land or Heaven as his private property, or convey its everlasting riches and annex it as his own territory![82]

Here, Wang again rejected the ruler's right to ownership of the land. However, a question must be addressed: if, according to Wang's theory, Heaven is the ultimate owner of all the land and therefore the emperor has no right to the land, can a person ever really own the land? Doesn't Wang's theory simply replace the "emperor" figure with "Heaven" in the *Classic of Poetry* poem verse? Must land ownership actually only been seen as a bestowal of land from Heaven on someone? Wang certainly did acknowledge the existence of land ownership. He accepted the reality that land acquisition and land sales could not be stopped.[83] For example, in his 1691 work *Song lun* 宋论 (*Discussions on the Song Dynasty*), Wang described the various historical stages of land taxation. He noted that in ancient times, "land did not have a fixed owner" and the state "did not have a fixed land tax."[84] People were taught by the sage kings how to farm and the people selected the land and relied on their own efforts to take care of themselves.[85] This taken with some of Wang's other statements suggest he, like Huang, believed people had a right to self-preservation and for taking care of themselves, satisfying their own needs. Wang believed, for example, that man cherished and valued life, as well as producing and sustaining life.[86] He further believed that men's desires – e.g., their biological needs – are natural, inalienable from their bodies, and in accord with Heavenly Principles, and therefore it is natural to try to satisfy them through self-sustenance and the like (although of course it is important to exercise self-restraint when appropriate).[87]

[80] Liu 2002, p. 750. The concept of Heaven (*tian* 天) in Chinese philosophy is quite complex and has changed over time and with different thinkers. For a brief overview of the concept of Heaven in Chinese philosophy, see Fu 2002.

[81] Liu 2001, p. 322.

[82] I use Ian McMorran's translation here, with some of my slight modifications. Quoted in McMorran 1992, p. 169.

[83] Liu 1982, p. 74.

[84] Wang 1964 [1691], p. 51.

[85] Wang 1964 [1691], p. 51.

[86] Tan 2010, p. 82.

[87] Tan 2010, pp. 174–5.

This stage of history – i.e., the ancient times – however, soon changed. With population increases[88] and the advent of enfeoffments of land and title to feudal lords and a dizzying array of different land tax standards, the rulers in the "Three Dynasties of Antiquity" had no choice but to set up artificial land boundaries and to unify land taxes.[89] People did not set the boundaries of their land themselves, but relied on government officials to do so.[90] However, by the time of the Han and going forward, private land holdings had been established, and people were getting allotments from their ancestors and were thus able to determine the borders of their own land.[91] Thus, how does Wang's theory of property account for the people's ownership of land? Put more directly, how does a person legitimately acquire property rights over land?

As leading Wang scholar Ian McMorran has pointed out, Wang's answer is not completely clear.[92] However, it appears that Wang adopted a Lockean response to his question; Wang's theory, like Locke's, seems to use labor to justify the acquisition of property. According to McMorran, in Wang's view, only people who labored on the land had a special right to it.[93] In a 1682 essay entitled *E Meng* 噩梦 (*Strange Dreams*), where Wang set forth specific positions on policy issues, Wang argued:

> The empire receives its government from the emperor, and so the latter makes the people of the empire his subjects, and labors at his tasks, but, as far as the land is concerned, he certainly cannot regard it as his private property ....[94] Between heaven and earth there is the land, and men live upon it, and rely on its resources to support themselves. It is the able-bodied who work the soil, and while dynasties may rise and fall, the people own their own allotments of arable, worked land, and do not wait for an emperor to give land to them.[95]

Above, Wang emphasized the importance of people "working" the soil in order to provide for themselves and also that people owned their own allotments especially of arable, *worked* land, suggesting therefore that those who labored on the land had a special right to it. Furthermore, similar to Huang, Wang also emphasized the autonomy of individuals. Wang

[88] Li 1987, p. 75.
[89] Wang 1964 [1691], p. 51.
[90] Wang 1964 [1691], p. 51.
[91] Wang 1964 [1691], p. 52.
[92] McMorran 1992, p. 170.
[93] McMorran 1992, p. 170.
[94] Quoted in McMorran 1992, p. 163. I use McMorran's translation here. For the original Chinese text, see Wang 1996a [1682], p. 551.
[95] Quoted in McMorran 1992, p. 170; I use McMorran's translation here.

also believed the human nature was innately good and that we should view human efforts and human work (i.e., equivalent to the notion of human labor) as positive, instrumental forces in transforming and improving society (as opposed to the view – held by other Confucians – that the emphasis should not be on individual and collective current human achievements but rather the accomplishments of the ancients).[96] And, in another passage in *On Reading Sima Guang's Comprehensive Mirror in Aid of Governance*, Wang discussed the well-field system in antiquity, stressing the importance of people's adding labor to land:

> According to the well-field system there were eight private fields for every one public field. The ruler, his ministers, and officials were all supported by the produce from the public field, but the ruler did not presume to regard it as his private property. He could only cause the people to cultivate it for him. As regards the land which the people cultivated for themselves, the ruler could never encroach on it. The ruler could employ the lab[o]r of the people, but he could not possess their fields.[97]

Above, Wang used his understanding of the well-field system to again deny the right of the emperor to own the land in the empire, but he also stresses cultivation and adding labor to land, noting that "[a]s regards the land which the people *cultivated for themselves* [emphasis mine], the ruler could never encroach on it."[98] Finally, I believe this interpretation of Wang as setting forth a Lockean labor theory of property is historically tenable, because during the Wang's time there were in fact legal practices which in fact awarded property rights to those who labored on the land. For example, Qing law distinguished between abandoned land and virgin (unopened, unworked) land. For both types of land, one who added value was generally seen as establishing a right in the land, and it was also common for land grabbers who failed to cultivate their virgin land to actually lose their rights because they did not work and improve the land.[99]

With respect to the question of why property rights should be respected and protected, Wang also shared Huang's emphasis on property rights protection, arguing that expropriation of property by the state would be harmful to society and would also be unnatural, because it would be against the principles of Heaven. Despite feeling sympathy for peasants and small landowners and expressing disquiet at the large landholdings of the rich, similar to Huang, Wang strongly opposed any expropriation and

[96] Liu 2002, pp. 751–2.
[97] Quoted in McMorran 1992, p. 169; I use McMorran's translation here.
[98] Quoted in McMorran 1992, p. 169.
[99] Zelin 2004, pp. 20-1.

redistribution of land proposals.[100] He even argued that those who reallocated land – even if they had the best of intentions to help the poor – should be "punished mercilessly."[101] In Wang's view, expropriation and reallocation would ultimately harm society because they would fundamentally not solve the problem of unequal land holdings.[102] Rather, Wang believed the key was to reform the tax system so that it was not based on land but rather based on men and which discriminated based on occupations – for example, extra taxes would be implemented on large landowners or speculators, while smaller taxes would be implemented on farmers.[103] Therefore, the property rights even of the rich had to be protected.[104] Wang also emphasized that such an approach – a discriminatory tax and not expropriating private property – would also be natural, because not taxing the land would be following the "essence and body of Heaven," which itself would be tantamount to following Heavenly Principles."[105] By "Heavenly Principles," Wang referred to a certain rational order of nature.[106] Therefore, Wang's theory of property holds that state expropriation and redistribution of private property would basically be unnatural and not aligned with the order of nature and the universe.

Thus, to recap, Wang's theory of property covers both issues of the origins of property and the importance of property rights protection. To summarize the main points in Wang's theory: he argued that land was naturally occurring in the world and therefore owned by Heaven (nature). There was no ownership in the beginning. Land was from Heaven, and people worked the land and took care of themselves. Human action and human efforts – i.e., human labor – were forces of good in transforming and improving society. Wang also suggested that humans need, and have a right, to take care of and preserve themselves. Because land was naturally existing and from Heaven, Wang proceeded to deny the emperor's right to own the land or to transfer the land to others. How then could people acquire property rights over land? Wang argued that one can acquire land through the fruits of his/her labor (working the land). He also argued that the property rights of the people should be protected and spoke out against

[100] McMorran 1992, p. 173.
[101] McMorran 1992, p. 173.
[102] McMorran 1992, p. 174.
[103] McMorran 1992, p. 176.
[104] Xiao and Liu 2007, p. 6.
[105] Wang 1996b [1687], p. 511.
[106] Liu 2001, p. 322.

government expropriation and redistribution of land, arguing that such moves would be both harmful and unnatural, against Heaven's principles.

Having set out Wang's theory of property, we can proceed with two broader observations by extension. First, Wang's theory of property was grounded in natural law ideas and principles. First, what do I mean by "natural law," especially in the Chinese context? I adopt China legal historian Geoffrey MacCormack's explanation:

> When we find that the Chinese data disclose ways of thinking about law that advert to an ultimate standard or absolute norms grounded either in the cosmos or in man's own nature, we may reasonably translate these ways of thinking as "natural law." A further idea, properly conveyed by this term, is that such an ultimate standard ought to form the basis for the laws enacted by the ruler for the regulation of the state.[107]

What does "cosmos" mean in the above passage? MacCormack explains that the term "cosmological" refers to "those theories predicated upon the notion of a law governing the universe (cosmos) and all its constituent parts, both human and non-human."[108] Applying this framework to Wang's theory of property, we can see that Wang built his understanding of land ownership and the origins of property on the absolute, cosmologically informed natural law rule that land was naturally occurring in the universe, and therefore the emperor had no right to claim automatic ownership of it. As Wang argued, emperors come and go, but one thing never changed – the land, such as "mountains and rivers" and "plains and marshes." I would add to MacCormack's framework by suggesting that Wang's cosmological basis is akin to natural law in the sense that it is discoverable by human reason – we can see that mountains and rivers are naturally occurring. And, in Wang's view, these natural law standards formed the basis for regulation of the state in the sense that the emperor had no right to simply expropriate or grant land, because he could not be considered the original owner in the first place.

Second, Wang's theory of property can be described as Lockean in nature. There is a huge, voluminous literature on Locke's view on property, and I do not want to repeat what has already been said[109]; in particular I shall not attempt to engage with the manifold critiques of Locke's theory. For the purposes of this chapter, a very brief, general outline of Locke's

[107] MacCormack 2013–14, p. 105.

[108] MacCormack 2013–14, p. 105.

[109] For an overview of the relevant literature (as well as different scholarly interpretations) of Locke's property theory, see Stapelbroek 2014.

theory of property will suffice.[110] Locke – similar to Huang and Wang – was trying to lay out a broader political theory and critique of despotism, and property was only one component of that theory.[111] He was trying to answer the questions of both how a person could legitimately acquire property rights in something (i.e., origins of property), and also why such rights should be protected. Locke's starting point is creation – Locke was a Christian, and he believed that the Christian God created all men and the world.[112] Humans, as God's creations, should be preserved and they must preserve themselves; this human duty and right of self-preservation was possible because God created the world, which contains the things humans need for survival.[113] Specifically, God gave all these things to all men in common, since human needs and desires (e.g., food, water, shelter) needed to be satisfied.[114] This was, in other words, a world marked by the "equal right and duty of self-preservation."[115] There was no private ownership – in Locke's words, initially, "nobody has originally a private dominion ...[116] Locke, however, wanted to understand how people could "come to have a property in several parts of that which God gave to mankind in common"[117] – in other words, how people could make "private use of the resources that God gave them?"[118] How could someone rightfully originally "appropriate" to himself something that originally given by God in common (like an acorn, an apple, or a piece of land?[119] Locke's answer focused on the role of human labor. First, Locke argued that every human

[110] A helpful summary of the main points of Locke's labor theory of property are set out in Penner 1997, pp. 188–90.

[111] For an overview of Locke's political theory as a whole, see Ashcraft 1994.

[112] As Edward Feser notes, some scholars – notably Leo Strauss – have "held that Locke was no more a sincere believer in God than Hobbes was, and that his reference to a divine source of rights is a mere smokescreen intended to veil from the *hoi polloi* his true, quasi-Hobbesian agenda." But Feser also notes that "while this thesis still has defenders today, it has been rejected by most Locke scholars ..." (Feser 2007, pp. 104–5). For a brief discussion of the scholarly debates surrounding the role of theology and Christian faith in Locke's political thought, see the helpful summary in Myers 1995, pp. 629–30. Some scholars have attempted to set forth secular versions of Locke's theory of property. See, for example, Widerquist 2010; Brown 1999. I am grateful to Widerquist's article for directing me to the Brown and Myers articles cited in this note.

[113] Alexander and Peña 2012, p. 37.

[114] See Locke 2003, Chapter 5.25–26, pp. 273–4. All citations to "The Second Treatise of Government" will be to this source.

[115] See Locke 2003, Chapter 5.25, p. 273.

[116] Locke 2003, Chapter 5.25, p. 274.

[117] Locke 2003, Chapter 5.25, p. 274.

[118] Alexander and Peña 2012, p. 37.

[119] Locke 2003, Chapter 5.26, 5.28, p. 274.

being has property in his own person – a man owns his own body.[120] Second, if a man owns his own body then he naturally owns his labor. Once he removes something out of the commons which God created and mixes it with his labor, he makes it his own property, subject to certain provisos (namely, that he does not take more than he can use before the thing spoils, and he must also leave enough and as good in common for other people).[121]

Locke also specifically discussed the acquisition of land. Like Huang and Wang, he believed in the importance of land, calling it the "chief matter of Property."[122] For Locke, land is acquired in the same way as other property forms.[123] Land is acquired through man's labor on the land: "[a]s much land as man tills, plants, improves, cultivates, and can use the product of, so much is his property. He by his labour does, as it were, enclose it from the common."[124] Locke even added that "it cannot be supposed He [God] meant it [the Earth and its fruits in common] should always remain common and uncultivated. He gave it to the industrious and rational (and labour was to be his title to it), not to the fancy or covetousness of the quarrelsome and contentious."[125] Of course, Locke was fully attune to the problem of monopolization of land ownership by a select few, and so he made clear that the acquisition of land was also subject to the two provisos of avoiding waste and leaving land in common for others that is enough and as good.

We can see that Wang's theory – more so than Huang's – possesses Lockean characteristics. Wang also believed that land was originally unowned in antiquity. Land was owned and given to the people by Heaven – although Heaven is not analogous to a God-creator in Locke's sense, Wang nevertheless similarly attributes the origins of ownership to a non-human entity or force. Both establish their theories of property on a natural law foundation – Wang on cosmological principles and Heaven, Locke on God and God's will to provide for humans and to have humans engage in self-preservation. In other words, both Wang's and Locke's theories of property acknowledge human beings' natural law "right" to preserve themselves and take care of themselves. More specifically, both Wang and Locke portray Heaven and God (respectively) as forces which

[120] Locke 2003, Chapter 5.27, p. 274.
[121] Locke 2003, Chapter 5.27, p. 274; Chapters 5.31 and 5.33, pp. 276–7.
[122] Locke 2003, Chapter 5.32, p. 276.
[123] Goldwin 1987, p. 487.
[124] Locke 2003, Chapter 5.32, p. 276.
[125] Locke 2003, Chapter 5.34, p. 277.

treat humans equally. For Wang, Heaven is a naturalistic, amoral force. It does not have specific preferences for certain types of people – in other words, it does not discriminate. The land ultimately belongs to it, and the land is available for people to use and live on. All people have any equal right to self-preservation, as Huang explicitly noted in his brief state of nature discussion. Similarly, for Locke, God gave the earth and its fruits to all men, who were created by God equally.

Most notably, Wang also suggested that only individuals who labor on the land and improve it can acquire the land. It is through adding one's labor that one gains special rights in the land. Furthermore, like Locke, Wang did not support unlimited land acquisition. While he did not explicitly lay out something akin to the so-called "Lockean proviso," Wang lamented monopolization of land by the rich, and he supported instituting a man-based and occupation-tax system to discourage such acquisitions. Finally, like Locke, Wang shared a similar belief that the state should seek to protect private property rights. Although it should be pointed out that Wang did not go as far as Locke as suggesting that sovereignty lay in the people, he did share the belief that the state had a duty to protect property and the people's welfare.

8.5 Conclusion

This chapter is a work in comparative property theory. I have set out the property theory of Huang Zongxi and Wang Fuzhi, two important political theorists in the Confucian tradition. I have argued that both Huang and Wang bestowed an important role on property in their broader thought, challenging traditional Chinese views of the origins of property ownership and denying the emperor's automatic, natural right to own all the land in the realm. Both Huang and Wang, as I have shown, also stressed the importance of property rights and state protection of property rights, as well as property's role in limiting imperial autocracy. I have also attempted to put Huang and Wang's theories in dialogue with one another and with John Locke, a key figure in Western property theory. I have argued that Wang's theory of property is Lockean in nature.

What might be some of the more far-reaching implications of the findings in this chapter? First, it is hoped that often-heard description of the Confucian tradition as being antithetical or opposed to private property and/or not emphasizing property can be complicated and corrected. Key thinkers in the Confucian tradition – such as Huang Zongxi and Wang Fuzhi – explicated theories of property which deserve our attention.

Second, given the importance property played in the political thought of Confucian thinkers like Huang and Wang, it is hoped that there can be more scholarly dialogue between our study of theories of property emanating in the Western and Eastern traditions. At the very least, we can see that theories of property in non-Western traditions shared much in common with Locke's theory of property, itself regarded often as the most symbolic and significant theory of property in the Western tradition. Third, this chapter may also have a broader, normative impact on modern Chinese rule of law and property law reform today. Reformers in China today who are fighting for more state protection of property rights and opposing unlawful local government expropriation of private property may find important resources in the Chinese Confucian tradition and, more specifically, in thinkers like Wang and Huang. These reformers can look to Wang and Huang – thinkers staunchly in the Chinese Confucian tradition – as justificatory and rhetorical sources for their property law reform agendas. By using the language and substance of Confucian theories of property as opposed to Western (and what is perceived frequently by the Chinese government as imported and foreign) property concepts, these reformers may make their pro-property arguments more palatable to Beijing. Given that the current Chinese administration has shown a penchant for looking to the Chinese Confucian past itself for governance models, Wang's and Huang's theories of property may find a willing audience in many Chinese officials today.

9

Two Ways of Theorizing 'Collective Ownership of the Earth'

JOHAN OLSTHOORN

9.1 Introduction

The natural resources and spaces of the earth belong to humanity collectively. In *On Global Justice* and numerous smaller writings, Mathias Risse spells out the implications of that claim for global distributive justice. Risse makes a forceful and persuasive case for regarding humanity's Collective Ownership of the Earth (henceforth: COE) as a ground of justice – 'a reason why claims of justice apply to a certain population'.[1] Any property arrangement that fails to provide the global population with an equal opportunity to satisfy basic needs is unjust: it violates natural rights of common ownership. As a ground of justice, COE has a wealth of applications. It establishes rights of asylum; of relocation; and of access to water and other basic necessities of life; obligations to future generations; and obligations arising from climate change. In addition, COE is a contingent source of human rights: their status as co-owners of the Earth gives individuals living under a coercive global order specific rights vis-à-vis that global order.

In developing the idea of COE, Risse revitalizes and secularizes a relatively neglected tradition of thinking about the relation between private property and the global commons. Early modern natural law theorists such as Hugo Grotius (1583–1645), Samuel Pufendorf (1632–94), and John Locke (1632–1704) made common ownership of the earth, grounded in a divine donation, the starting point of reflections on the nature, extent, and justification of private property. Risse aspires to reveal in particular the modern relevance of Grotius's theory of property. 'What is perhaps most distinctive about my approach [to global justice] is the significance I give to humanity's collective ownership of the earth, inspired by the work

Besides the editors and contributors to this volume, I would like to thank Peter Niesen, Jakob Huber, and participants in the 2016 ECPR panel on international political theory in Prague for their helpful comments on this chapter.

[1] Risse 2012, p. 2.

of the seventeenth-century Dutch jurist and philosopher Hugo Grotius.[2] Grotius is Risse's main interlocutor throughout *On Global Justice*, informing many a discussion.[3]

This chapter argues that Risse's fascinating and highly sophisticated account of COE is considerably more original than he himself claims. Risse's interpretation of the Dutch philosopher, though on the whole rich and nuanced,[4] obscures the fact that COE plays a fundamentally different normative role in Grotius's theory than in Risse's. That, in turn, has important implications for how we think about the legitimating conditions of property and territorial rights. The aim of this chapter is not to quibble about matters of textual exegesis but to enrich contemporary thinking about global justice by revealing that we have at our disposal two rival conceptual models for theorizing original collective ownership of the Earth, each with distinct philosophical potential.

What are these two models? Both Grotius and Risse employ COE as a vantage point from which to assess the acceptability of two coercive and exclusionary social institutions: private property and territorial states. Which conditions need to be met for exclusion from originally collectively owned resources and spaces to be justified? The two philosophers, I argue, approach this conundrum in diverging ways. Risse develops a theory of *justice*.[5] His driving question is: does humanity's collective ownership of the Earth generate any moral rights that restrain the acceptability of particular exclusionary regimes? He answers affirmatively: any property or territorial arrangement that fails to provide the global population with an equal opportunity to satisfy basic needs violates natural rights of common ownership (henceforth: NRCO) and is hence unjust. Grotius, by contrast, advances a theory of *property*. Property rights, Grotius claims, are conventional all the way down. Which shape, he wonders, would it have been rational for us to give to individual property rights against the background of collective ownership of the earth? How extensive a set of rights can reasonably be granted to private property owners? Grotian retained rights of

[2] Risse 2012, p. 17; Risse 2013a, p. 1038.

[3] Risse 2012, pp. 12, 18. Risse is not the only prominent political philosopher who has recently found inspiration in Grotius. In her Tanner Lectures on cosmopolitan justice Marta Nussbaum declares: '[Grotius's] natural law approach to basic principles of international relations is the one I shall attempt to revive' (Nussbaum 2006, pp. 36, 230).

[4] Risse's main exegetical discussions of Grotius are Risse 2009a, pp. 279–82; Risse 2009b, pp. 284–6; Risse 2012, pp. 89–107, 234–7. Risse emphasizes several dissimilarities between Grotius's concept of COE and his, including the absence of religious and historical dimensions in his own account (Risse 2012, pp. 92, 133).

[5] Following Risse (2012, p. 4), I shall use 'justice' as short for 'distributive justice'.

common ownership are themselves property rights. As such, they directly limit the extent of existing property and territorial rights.

How can they do so? In the wake of Hohfeld[6] and Honoré,[7] property rights are commonly and un-controversially thought of in terms of bundles of legal incidents.[8] Suppose I own an apple. My property rights in this apple consists of a set of privileges, claims, immunities, and powers – of various strengths – which I have against the world with respect to my apple. The conjunction of these legal incidents determines the *internal structure* of my property rights in the apple.[9] As the adjective 'internal' indicates, what is at stake are not patterns of holdings, but rather the specific bundles of legal incidents composing property. Theories of property may rule out certain logically possible conjunctions of legal incidents (as morally impermissible or otherwise unavailable). For instance, it can be argued that, morally speaking, property rights cannot possibly be so absolute as to permit property-holders to bar the destitute from using privately owned goods in times of dire need. The bundle of legal incidents making up private ownership cannot, in that case, include the right to categorically exclude the severely deprived.[10] Restrictions to private property generated by theories of property are *internal* to property rights – the theory renders the bundle of rights composing private property less extensive than it could otherwise have been. Internal restrictions are definitive of property rights: they confine the rights of property-holders by determining the set of legal incidents constituting property rights.[11]

By contrast, the limits that theories of justice place on the acceptability of private property arrangements are *external* to property rights. Theories of justice do not state that property rights cannot have such-or-such an internal structure; they do not directly fix the content of these rights. Rather, they deal with the higher-level question of which distributions of holdings are morally acceptable. Justice may grant the destitute a claim to the surplus of the rich. But these claims do not take the form of property rights, nor do they alter the internal structure of the property rights of the affluent. Rather, justice provides the severely deprived with a general

[6] Hohfeld 1923 [1913].

[7] Honoré 1987a [1961].

[8] What is controversial is whether 'ownership' can be exhaustively captured by a conjunction of legal incidents. For an excellent critical discussion, see Penner 1996.

[9] The term 'structure' is taken from Christman 1991, 1994.

[10] Legal theorists have criticized political philosophers for failing to realize that the structure of property rights by itself has distributive implications (Honoré 1987b [1977]).

[11] The moral and non-moral reasons we have for adopting such restrictions are not themselves internal to property theory.

right to be brought into a particular condition, while imposing on others duties to bring closer a just state of affairs. This chapter draws on the concept of rights of necessity to bring out the difference between these two models. In Grotius's profoundly conventionalist model rights of necessity curtail each and every property right, thus obliging all property-holders. In Risse's model, the obligations corresponding to rights of necessity are not built into the internal structure of individual exclusionary rights, but superimposed on a limited set of agents (generally, 'the global order as such'). As we shall see, while Risse's theory is overall vastly more sophisticated, the question of who is obligated to do what by remnant rights of common ownership is resolved more parsimoniously by Grotius.

9.2 Risse on Collective Ownership of the Earth

This section sets out Risse's account of COE and its place within his wider theory of global justice. Risse defends a pluralist theory of the grounds of global distributive justice, combining relational and nonrelational grounds. Relational grounds of justice are essentially practice-mediated. COE is a nonrelational ground of justice: it gives rise to principles of justice that apply globally, to all humans, regardless of what relations they happen to stand in.[12] Principles of justice explicate necessary conditions for the fairness of a distribution of particular goods within a population (consisting of all individuals falling within the scope of the principle). COE grounds several principles of justice. Each expounds conditions which territorial and property arrangements must respect on pain of violating the NRCO of any global denizen. 'Common ownership rights', in turn, 'are natural and pre-institutional'.[13] Individuals do not have these rights as members of political communities. The existence of states exercising border control must consequently be justified not only internally, to citizens, but also to individuals beyond the borders.[14]

Risse secularizes Grotius doctrine by purging it of its theological and temporal aspects.[15] Grotius had defended COE by appeal to a divine

[12] Risse's terminology is somewhat idiosyncratic. Sangiovanni 2016, another prominent global justice theorist, employs the terms 'relational' and 'nonrelational' as predicates of *principles* of justice. Risse's 'grounds' seem equivalent to what Sangiovanni calls 'triggers'. A ground of justice is a reason *R* why a particular principle *P* applies to a population; and *R* refers to the very fact or principle that triggers *P*.

[13] Risse 2009b, p. 291; Risse 2014a, p. 191.

[14] Risse 2013a, p. 1041.

[15] Risse 2012, p. 92.

donation. Risse proffers non-parochial arguments in support instead. The *distribuenda* relevant to COE, he argues, are those resources and spaces of the Earth that exist independently of human activities.[16] Nobody can make privileged claims to these resources and spaces by appeal to accomplishments. The Earth's resources and spaces have not been created by humans and subsequent improvements do not alter their original status. This constitutes one non-parochial reason why these resources and spaces are best regarded as collectively owned.[17] Two other reasons are the resources' value for unfolding human activities and importance for satisfying basic human needs.[18] Only goods that satisfy all three conditions qualify as originally collectively owned. External goods not valuable for human life (e.g. remote galaxies) and goods, however valuable, produced from scratch by humans (e.g. ideas and inventions)[19] fall outside the domain of COE. Risse further restricts the content of NRCO to having *an equal opportunity* to satisfy basic human needs. 'The core idea of common ownership is that all co-owners ought to have an equal opportunity to satisfy their basic needs to the extent that this turns on obtaining collectively owned resources'.[20] In short, Risse deems COE 'plausible because the resources and spaces of the earth are nobody's accomplishment, but are required for human needs to be satisfied'.[21] None of these stipulations about which *distribuenda* are relevant to COE is found in Grotius (Section 9.3).

Risse further departs from Grotius in denying that 'original' common ownership refers to some historical condition.

> Asking about original ownership is not asking about a certain period but about whether the resources and spaces that exist independently of human activities are owned in a sense that is prior to moral claims individuals or groups have to resources based, say, on first occupancy or the mixing of labor with resources, as well as prior to any kind of legal claims they may have.[22]

The earth should be regarded as humanity's *continuing* collective possession, belonging to all humans living now as well as to future generations.

[16] Risse 2012, p. 11, 89, 93; Risse 2014a, p. 181.
[17] Risse 2013b, p. 63.
[18] Risse 2012, pp. 113–4.
[19] Cf. Risse 2012, pp. 233–44. Human artefacts count in a discounted manner (Risse 2012, pp. 155–6).
[20] Risse 2009a, p. 288; Risse 2012, p. 111.
[21] Risse 2014a, p. 195.
[22] Risse 2012, p. 92, 108.

Collective ownership expresses the idea that 'in some sense' all humans have symmetrical claims to original resources and spaces.[23] In what sense? Risse distinguishes four possible conceptions of collective ownership. He defends as the most reasonable conception a minimal one, branded Common Ownership. Common Ownership conceptualizes co-ownership in terms of an *equal right to use* collectively owned objects (within constraints).[24] Individuals in a hypothetical original position, Risse argues, will opt for Common Ownership since it captures the kind of permissions we need to give and receive for original appropriation to be legitimate better than rival conceptions.[25]

The Earth and its original resources and spaces are not so owned that privatization of natural resources and creation of territorial states with coercive border regulations are morally impermissible. Common Ownership differs from more demanding conceptions of collective ownership by not rendering lawful privatization dependent on the consent of every co-owner. Unilateral privatization of original resources and spaces is permissible as long as co-owners retain an equal opportunity to satisfy basic needs 'insofar as such needs require collectively owned resources'.[26] The reason consent is unnecessary is that co-owners can sometimes 'be *reasonably expected* to waive their liberty right to resources within, or entry to,' some area.[27] It would be unreasonable for individuals to refuse to waive their liberty right to use in common resources I seek to appropriate, if my act of

[23] Risse 2014b, p. 520. Stilz 2014, pp. 501–2 argues that COE serves three distinct theoretical functions in Risse's theory. It is an ideal of moral justification, an original natural right, and a legitimacy constraint on property arrangements. Kant conceptualized COE in yet different ways, and with yet different aims, as Huber 2017 reveals in an illuminating comparison of Grotius and Kant.

[24] Risse 2009a, p. 287; Risse 2012, p. 110. Compare the slightly revised categorization in Risse 2014a, pp. 187–90. The term 'ownership' may seem out of place. Abizadeh 2013, pp. 35–7 avers that mere equal rights to use in common are insufficient to establish a form of '*ownership*'. In reply, Risse reiterates his reasons for thinking that the Earth should be seen as collectively owned without taking up Abizadeh's challenge to show that Common Ownership establishes ownership rights (Risse 2013b, pp. 62–3). In an earlier text, Risse maintains that talk of 'ownership' is justified since 'claims individuals have to resources' are involved (Risse 2009a, p. 286). The argument is infelicitous: not all claims to resources presuppose ownership. If humans indeed collectively 'own' the Earth in anything resembling the ordinary sense of the term – over and above mere equal use rights – then, like Abizadeh 2013, pp. 37–9, I deem it plausible that in the original position people would opt for a set of restrictions on property that are stricter and fairer than the principles of justice and reasonable conduct advocated by Risse.

[25] Risse 2012, p. 121.

[26] Risse 2012, p. 111.

[27] Risse 2012, p. 125.

privatization is consistent with everyone else retaining an equal opportunity to satisfy basic needs.[28] Besides disallowing certain acts of privatization as unjust, NRCO also generates less onerous *demands of reasonable conduct*. Agents may reasonably be expected to perform certain actions in virtue of humanity's COE, without owing such conduct to fellow co-owners.

How to reconcile Risse's claim that liberty rights to use external resources in common can sometimes be reasonably expected to be waived with his insistence on humanity's continuing co-ownership of the earth? The answer is that the right established by COE is not a simple use right. It is rather

> a more complicated disjunctive right either to use (in the narrow sense) resources and spaces to satisfy one's basic needs or else to live in a society that does not deny one the opportunity to satisfy one's basic needs in ways in which it otherwise could have been done through original resources and spaces.[29]

The disjunctive nature of NRCO explains why consent is not required for legitimate privatization. As co-owners of the Earth – our collective home – every human has an 'immunity from living under arrangements where an equal opportunity to satisfy basic needs is not realized'.[30] In modern industrialized societies, most humans are entirely barred from using directly originally commonly owned resources. This is morally permissible as long as robust equal opportunities exist for satisfying basic needs in other ways. In industrialized societies, Risse contends, having such an opportunity requires certain labor rights and rights to elementary education. NRCO thus generates social rights whenever direct access to original resources has been rendered unavailable.[31]

Risse's disjunctive NRCO generates the following principle of justice associated with COE, constraining the legitimacy of property and territorial arrangements:

> The distribution of original resources and spaces of the earth among the global population is just only if everyone has the opportunity to use them to satisfy her or his basic needs, or otherwise lives under a property arrangement that provides the opportunity to satisfy basic needs.[32]

[28] Observe that the limits NRCO sets to justified original appropriation does not include the (neo-)Lockean requirement that co-owners shall not be made 'worse off' by acts of appropriation: losing an equal opportunity for fulfilling basic needs is not the only way in which unilateral appropriation can make individuals worse off (cf. Risse 2012, p. 127). Cf. Locke 1988 [1690], §33; Nozick 1974, pp. 175–8. Risse does not flesh out a comprehensive set of conditions about when privatization is morally justified.

[29] Risse 2012, p. 112; Cf. Risse 2014b, p. 519.

[30] Risse 2012, p. 126.

[31] Risse 2012, p. 137; Risse 2014b, pp. 517–8.

[32] Risse 2012, p. 124, 133, 145, 181; Risse 2013a, p. 1052.

Distributions violating this principle of justice defeat the 'core purpose' of NRCO, namely 'to preserve the ability of co-owners to meet basic needs'[33] Two further and related principles of justice follow from COE: a principle of intergenerational justice and a principle requiring satisfaction of everyone's membership rights in the global order.[34]

Risse employs COE to help specify the nature and extent of duties of international justice. Moral rights and obligations generated by COE include rights of asylum,[35] a 'residual right of necessity',[36] rights of relocation[37] and of access to safe drinking water and sanitation,[38] as well as a right that climate change regulation is provided.[39] COE also informs duties of reasonable conduct short of obligations of justice, including duties to admit migrants to relatively underused territories[40] and duties to future generations.[41] These weaker moral demands express what humans, as co-owners of the Earth, may reasonably expect others to do, on pain of social criticism.[42]

In addition, COE is a contingent source of human rights, conceived as membership rights in the global order. It so happens that humans nowadays live under a coercive global order that affects them *qua* co-owners of the planet. In virtue of this contingent fact, NRCO generate human rights vis-à-vis that global order. Every entity within the global order owes it to global denizens 'to do what it can, within limits, to bring about the necessary conditions of just distributions'.[43] States and global institutions have a further duty 'to *give account* for what they do to realize their obligations of justice' to those within the scope of the relevant principles of justice.[44]

A perennial quandary in international political theory concerns the allocation of responsibilities for ensuring justice is realized worldwide. If rights are to be more than merely aspirational (thus justifying the moniker 'rights'), then we must specify the agents upon whom these corresponding

33 Risse 2012, p. 136.
34 Risse 2012, p. 133.
35 Risse 2014b, p. 518.
36 Risse 2014b, p. 519.
37 Risse 2009b; Risse 2012, pp. 145–6.
38 Risse 2014a.
39 Risse 2012, pp. 187–206.
40 Risse 2012, pp. 152–66.
41 Risse 2014a, pp. 177–86, 332.
42 On the difference between obligations of justice and less-onerous demands of reasonable conduct, see Risse 2012, p. 6, 132, 173, 192; Risse 2014b, pp. 520–22.
43 Risse 2012, p. 349; Risse 2013a, p. 1052.
44 Risse 2012 pp. 325–45; Risse 2013a, p. 1055.

obligations are incumbent.[45] The disjunctive character of NRCO problematizes attribution of strict corresponding duties. NRCO disallows those acts of privatization that wrong humans *qua* co-owners of the Earth. Yet NRCO can be realized in modern industrialized societies – where few original resources are left for common use – through basic structures designed so that each global denizen has a robust and equal opportunity to satisfy basic needs. States have a shared responsibility to bring about the necessary conditions for globally just distributions. But this responsibility only requires of states 'to do what [they] can, within limits, to bring about the necessary conditions of just distributions'.[46] Risse maintains that human rights can be aspirational insofar as their immediate realization cannot be reasonably expected. It is 'possible for rights to be unsatisfied and yet for nobody to have done anything wrong'.[47] Moreover, once achieved, the conditions for globally just distributions can arguably be eroded over time by collective actions without any individual wrongdoing.[48]

With respect to human rights, including those springing from COE, 'the duty holder is always the global order as such'.[49] This further weakens the kinds of claims co-owners can make on one another. Consider the case of Kiribati, a Pacific archipelago in danger of disappearing due to rising sea levels. Climate change has altered Kiribateans' living conditions such that their NRCO are now no longer met. Risse argues that inhabitants of Kiribati have a human right of relocation vis-à-vis the global order in virtue of COE: a 'basic claim of each to emigrate *somewhere*' (emphasis added).[50] But against individual countries, Kiribateans only have a weaker demand of reasonable conduct to be admitted. Section 9.4 analyses these claims in greater detail.

I have highlighted five features of Risse's interpretation of COE which, as we shall see, set it apart from Grotius's. For Risse:

1. COE is a ground of justice: it establishes inalienable natural rights with distributive implications. These rights determine which territorial and property regimes are morally acceptable.
2. 'Original common ownership' does not express a historical condition but rather refers to those external resources and spaces existing

[45] Risse 2012, pp. 228–31.
[46] Risse 2012, p. 349.
[47] Risse 2012, p. 250.
[48] On the possibility of structural injustice brought about without individual wrongdoing, see Young 2011, pp. 95–122.
[49] Risse 2014a, p. 183.
[50] Risse 2012, p. 146.

independently of human accomplishments. The principles of justice generated by COE only govern the access to those resources and spaces (or their equivalents).

3. NRCO do not generate entitlements to access goods beyond what is required for satisfying basic needs.
4. As human rights, NRCO are held vis-à-vis the global order as such.
5. Reflections on common ownership are guided by the question: what is the point of having rights of common ownership? Rather than by the question: what is the point of having private property?

9.3 Grotius on Original Common Ownership of the Earth

Time to turn to Grotius.[51] Any exposition of Grotius's theory of property must consider the significant changes between his earlier and later works. In *Mare Liberum*, the young Grotius writes that the introduction of private property 'was the result, not of any sudden transition, but of a gradual process whose initial steps were taken under the guidance of nature herself'.[52] In the later *De Jure Belli ac Pacis* we read that

> the Original of Property … was derived not from a mere internal Act of the Mind, since one could not possibly guess what others designed to appropriate to themselves, that he might abstain from it; and besides, several might have had a Mind to the same Thing, at the same Time; but it resulted from a certain Compact and Agreement, either expressly, as by a Division; or else tacitly, as by Seizure. For as soon as living in common was no longer approved of, all Men were supposed, and ought to be supposed to have consented, that each should appropriate to himself, by Right of first Possession, what could not have been divided (2.2.2.5).[53]

[51] Since my ambitions are primarily systematic, I will analyse Grotius's ideas using modern terminology, at the cost of some anachronisms. My reconstruction nonetheless stays faithful, I hope, to the logical and conceptual structure of Grotius's theory. Indeed, the proffered analysis allows me to correct, in passing, several misconceptions plaguing the existing literature on Grotius.

[52] Grotius 2009 [1609], V.16; Grotius 2006 [1868], XII.101. The 1609 *Mare Liberum* [ML] is a slightly revised version of the twelfth chapter of *De Jure Praedea* [DJP]. The latter manuscript, on which Grotius worked throughout the period 1604–8, was not published until 1868. To facilitate cross-referencing, I shall give references to both ML and DJP. On the compositional history of the two texts, see Van Ittersum 2005, 2009. ML is cited by chapter and page number of the original 1609 edition; DJP by chapter and page number of the 1868 edition. *De Jure Belli ac Pacis* [DJBP] Grotius 2005 [1625] is cited by [book-chapter-paragraph-subsection]. For reasons of brevity, I shall omit the acronym [DJBP] in my citations.

[53] See also Grotius 2005 [1625], 2.10.1.2–4; 3.2.1.1. The right of first seizure results in property rights in virtue of this (tacit) agreement. The principle of first seizure should be

Risse deems it 'peculiar that Grotius would offer two accounts of the origins of private property of which only one stresses agreements'. Rather than examining why he changed his mind about this subject, Risse advances 'an interpretation that minimizes tensions between Grotius's two accounts'.[54] His interpretation attributes to Grotius the view that, regardless of how the institution of private property emerged (spontaneously or by convention), current property arrangements are legitimate only insofar as they 'serve the society's socioeconomic purposes in a reasonable way while remaining consistent with original ownership rights'.[55] This principle, and not consent, determines the legitimacy of property arrangements: 'Grotius does not make consent basic'. Contrary to the non-conventionalist reading advocated by Risse and others,[56] this section shows that the social contract plays an essential role in *DJBP*'s theory of property. A social contract specifically relating to property – what might be called the 'social contract instituting property' (SCIP) – determines the normative status of common ownership rights.

Grotius provides a theistic justification for COE. God has given the Earth and all that it contains to humanity in common. This divine donation grounds NRCO.[57]

> Almighty GOD at the Creation, and again after the Deluge, gave to Mankind in general a Dominion over Things of this inferior World. *All Things*, as *Justin* has it, *were at first common* … From hence it was, that every Man converted what he could to his own Use, and consumed whatever was to be consumed; and such a Use of the Right common to all Men did at that Time supply the Place of Property, for no Man could justly take from another, what he had thus first taken to himself (2.2.2.1).

distinguished from mere occupation, which has place under conditions of communality of goods as well.

54 Risse 2012, p. 103.

55 Risse 2012, p. 104.

56 E.g. Buckle 1991, pp. 42–4; Tuck 1993, p. 199; Tuck 1977, p. 77: 'Grotius's theory in *De Iure Belli* is not radically different from his earlier view: the tacit agreement, to which all men are *supposed* to have consented, is a very weak condition, for it would in principle be impossible to say that men could not have made such an agreement; and as we shall see, it must always be supposed to be rescinded in emergencies'. In fact, no agreement is 'rescinded' in emergencies. Rather, the agreement *contains* the qualification of rights of necessity. The contractarian character of Grotius's theory of property is duly emphasized by Salter 2001, 2010, pp. 11–2; De Araujo 2009; Shimokawa 2013, pp. 564–6. Cf. Haakonssen 1985, pp. 242–3.

57 Buckle 1991 argues that the right to use the Earth in common *is* what it means to own the Earth collectively. On this reading, NRCO are not an implication of collective ownership of the Earth, as Risse has it, but an expression of it. Buckle argues that NRCO are an expression of natural rights of self-preservation which we have in virtue of our common humanity. On this reading two distinct Rissean grounds of justice – COE and Common Humanity – collapse into one.

The right to use the Earth in common is an individual right: 'There are some Things which are ours by virtue of a Right *common* to all Men' (2.2.1). Its violation is by definition unjust. Grotian NRCO are enforceable, actionable in courts and on the battlefield. When no common arbitrator is available, individuals may use force against anyone preventing them from exercising their common right (e.g. 2.2.13.2). Grotian NRCO differ in this respect from Hobbes's and Pufendorf's non-exclusionary natural rights to use the Earth in common. According to Pufendorf, 'others might lawfully take from us, what we had before actually mark'd out for our own Use'. Humans are by nature 'under no obligation to forbear invading and plundering'.[58] Hobbesian agents likewise exercise their natural right to everything – extending 'even to one anothers body' – without wronging other humans.[59]

As noted above, humanity's COE does not in Risse's opinion generate individual entitlements beyond having an equal opportunity to satisfy basic needs. Risse ascribes similar needs-confined NRCO to Grotius. Grotian agents would have a liberty-right to use external resources, but a claim-right only 'to appropriations necessary to satisfy a person's basic needs'.[60] This interpretation of Grotius is doubly wrong. First, there is no *natural* right of appropriation in Grotius. Grotian NRCO certainly justify exclusion of goods from the commons for private consumption. To consume *is* to exclude: consumed goods are no longer available for use by others. Yet exercising the right to use the Earth in common neither requires nor entails a title to acquire private property. In contrast to Locke and Pufendorf, Grotius does not consider it a conceptual truth that all rights to exclude are property rights.[61] Grotius's conception of property right is more fine-grained. Property inseparably involves the right to recover – an element not present in rights to use in common.[62] Grotius can thus coherently reject the contention that lawfully exercising NRCO requires a further right of appropriation – a right that could have been either natural (Locke) or conventional (Pufendorf) in origin.[63] Risse fails to appreciate

[58] Pufendorf 1729 [1672], 4.4.5.

[59] Hobbes 2012 [1651], 14.4.

[60] Risse 2012, p. 112; Risse 2009a, p. 288; Risse 2014a, p. 190.

[61] Cf. Pufendorf 1729 [1672], 4.4.12: '*Property* in its strict and general Sense ... denotes the Exclusion of all Others from a particular thing already assign'd to One'; Locke 1975 [1689], 4.3.18: 'the *Idea* of *Property*, being a right to any thing'.

[62] In an earlier text Grotius writes 'ownership [*eigendom*] consists in the right to recover lost possession' (Grotius 1926, 2.3.4).

[63] Lockean readings of Grotius on appropriation proliferate (e.g. Buckle 1991), as do Pufendorfian ones (e.g. Olivecrona 1971).

the Grotian distinction between appropriation and use. He repeatedly slips from talking about using resources to appropriating them.[64] Indeed, he prefers Common Ownership – granting an equal right to *use* – on the grounds that it best captures the permissions needed for *acquisition* of original resources and spaces.[65]

Second, precisely because exercising NRCO does not generate private ownership, there is no reason to confine valid claims generated by NRCO to what is taken out of need. It is always unjust to prevent individuals from exercising their NRCO through dispossession, regardless of whether they had taken resources to serve basic needs (1.2.1.5; 2.2.2.1). A Lockean anti-spoilage proviso restricting original acquisition is likewise superfluous for Grotius.[66] Whatever is left unused in conditions of common ownership simply becomes common again. Common ownership had initially even extended to the products of human labor. The introduction of industry upended primitive communism but not because labor creates property titles. No traces of a labor theory of property à la Locke are found in Grotius.[67] Rather, private property was introduced soon after industry arose to compensate for the widespread lack of equity and love, a shortcoming which generated undesirable disproportionalities between individual production and consumption ('free-riders') (2.2.2.4).

The social contract serves a double purpose in Grotius's theory of property.[68] First, agreement is needed to institute private property to begin with: a bundle of legal incidents, including rights to manage, to the income and capital, to private use, and above all to recover.[69] Second, the social contract determines the internal structure of private property rights. Which set of legal incidents property rights shall be composed of is determined conventionally. Which goods are liable to privatization and which

[64] Risse 2012, p. 121, 127. On Risse's conception of appropriation, see Risse 2012, p. 111.

[65] Risse 2012, p. 121, 125–6.

[66] Locke 1988 [1690], §31, §37.

[67] Olivecrona 1971, p. 279. Grotius claims that 'he who is the Owner of the Thing, is naturally the Owner of all its Produce' (2.10.4). It does not follow that labor is a source of *appropriation.*

[68] The social contract theory of property fulfils a rather different function in Pufendorf. The German natural lawyer introduces this agreement to justify the exclusion implicit in using up consumables: 'we cannot apprehend how a bare Corporal Act, such as Seizure is, should be able to prejudice the Right and Power of others, unless their Consent be added to confirm it' (Pufendorf 1729 [1672], 4.4.5). Grotian NRCO *already* justify exclusion of goods from the commons for private consumption.

[69] The suggestion by, e.g. Salter 2001, p. 542; Risse 2012, pp. 96, 98; and Miller 2011, p. 87, that Grotius, writing prior to Honoré's development of a bundle theory of property, did not distinguish between the various incidents of property, is false.

exclusionary practices are permissible is determined by a historical agreement all then-living individuals are supposed to have made against the background of common ownership. This original agreement is not penned down but expressed in customs found worldwide (2.2.6.1).

Commentators have generally failed to appreciate that the same consideration underpinning *DJBP*'s 'Law of Non-resistance' against sovereign injustice applies to original rights of common ownership as well (1.4.7).[70] The two doctrines share a common premise: neither natural law nor natural rights mandate any restrictions on coercive social institutions. Individuals may entirely give up rights of resistance and of original common ownership. 'For Nations, as well as private Persons, may give up not only that Right which is properly their own; but that also which they have in common with all Mankind, in Favour of him for whose Interest it may be' (2.3.15.2). It was this consideration, I argue, that logically compelled Grotius to introduce the SCIP in *DJBP*.

In Grotius's juvenile works, the law of nature directly confines private property rights. *Mare Liberum* deemed the right of free passage, sanctioned by natural law, to be inalienable.[71] In *DJBP*, by contrast, all restrictions on private property and sovereign power result from consent: which restrictions on property rights in the state of nature, if any, have those individuals who have set up the social institutions of property and government agreed to retain? No restrictions are entailed by the concept of property. Which legal incidents property is composed of is determined entirely conventionally. According to Grotius, humans *could* have had instituted private property conventions so stringent that the destitute would have been compelled to rely on charity or suffer starvation, rather than to have an enforceable right of necessity. Likewise, a people may introduce a legal constitution that renders it impermissible to forcibly resist the government. Grotius outdoes Hobbes

[70] An exception is Salter 2005, pp. 289–90. My argument does not assume that Grotius's social contracts of government and property are structurally identical. One notable difference between the two is that many different contracts of government have been instituted over time, whereas there has been only one SCIP.

[71] The young Grotius develops a position akin to that of the Italian humanist jurist Alberico Gentili (1552–1608). Gentili grounds restrictions on property and territorial rights in natural law. By the law of nature, he argues, individuals have rights of free passage and of trade and navigation. These rights may not be denied to them except for reasons of security (Gentili 1933 [1598], pp. 86–8). The natural right of self-defence permits waging war against those who refuse to grant asylum or to marry off their daughters (Gentili 1933 [1598], p. 79). In *Mare Liberum*, Grotius likewise claims that the 'sacrosanct law of hospitality', entailing rights of travel and free trade, is grounded in human sociability and therefore inalienable (Grotius 2009 [1609], I.3).

by maintaining that humans may rationally decide to accept 'this rigorous Obligation to suffer Death, rather than at any Time to resist an Injury offered by the Civil Powers'.[72] Witness Jesus Christ on the Cross (1.4.7).

To understand Grotius's position – which is not easy – more needs to be said about his conception of 'rights'. Grotius recognizes two kinds of rights: perfect and imperfect. Both are species of *ius* understood as 'a *moral Quality* annexed to the Person, *enabling him to have, or do, something justly*' (1.1.4). I have so far been talking exclusively about perfect rights. Perfect rights are essentially titles to coerce. Their violation is a potential *casus belli*. Imperfect rights, by contrast, merely express that an individual is fitting or deserving to receive a perfect right (2.2.20.2). Imperfect rights are not enforceable: 'from a mere Aptitude or Fitness, which is improperly called a Right... arises no true Property, and consequently no Obligation to make Restitution; because a Man cannot call that his own, which he is only capable of, or fit for' (2.17.3.1). Perfect rights provide right-holders with the potential standing to hold others' accountable; imperfect rights do not. To say that the destitute have an imperfect right to have their basic needs satisfied is merely to say that it would be morally appropriate for their basic needs to be met. To say that the destitute have a perfect right to basic needs satisfaction is to say that they are in principle entitled to take coercive measures to achieve it. This includes, as a last resort, a right to wage war against property-holders who prevent them from obtaining the requisite resources. It is possible for agents to have a perfect right to χ even if it is morally better for them not to have or to exercise χ. On Grotius's conception of justice, it is not possible in that case for *justice* to deny them χ.

What does this mean for rights of resistance? Grotius deems it possible for individuals and entire peoples to rationally deprive themselves of any right to take coercive measures in response to sovereign injustice. Giving up all rights of resistance does not, on Grotius's account, entail alienation of natural rights to one's life, body, limbs, and reputation (1.2.1.5; 2.17.2.1). The sovereign does not become the owner of citizens' lives and limbs. Citizens merely become obliged to patiently undergo whatever harm the sovereign inflicts upon them.[73] Moreover, certain things remain morally

[72] Cf. Hobbes 2012 [1651], 14.8, 14.29–30, 21.10–17. Hobbes accepts individual rights of resistance while denying the possibility of sovereign injustice.

[73] According to natural reason, the right to life may like any other property title be voluntarily transferred to another party. But the Gospel teaches us that we have no such absolute right over our life; that ultimate *dominium*, revelation reveals, belongs to God (Grotius 2005 [1625], 2.19.5.4; 3.2.6; 3.11.18.1). Our life is not fully our own – it includes no *jus alieni*. Had we had an absolute right over our life, then suicide would have been lawful (cf. 2.17.2). Like

due to citizens: humans deserve to be treated equitably and respectfully even if they have voluntarily forgone the right to hold the government accountable by force. In Grotius's terminology, citizens retain an *imperfect* right to be treated respectfully. Since imperfect rights are not things people 'own', but merely statuses of moral fittingness, they cannot be transferred even in principle. Grotius does not morally commend forgoing all rights of resistance. Yet he does advocate its *legal* permissibility, in the process of developing an encompassing constitutional theory that can account for widely diverging European legal practices.

Whether resisting the supreme leader is permitted within a particular state depends

> upon the Intention of those who first entered into Civil Society, from whom the Power of Sovereigns is originally derived. Suppose then they had been asked, Whether they pretended to impose on all Citizens the hard Necessity of dying, rather than to take up Arms in any Case, to defend themselves against the higher Powers; I do not know, whether they would have answered in the affirmative: It may be presumed, on the contrary, they would have declared one ought *not* to bear with every Thing, unless the Resistance would infallibly occasion great Disturbance in the State, or prove the Destruction of many Innocents (1.4.7, *emphasis added*).

Grotius argues here, cautiously, in favour of a right to resist the sovereign in extreme necessity.[74] The peculiar nature of his argument bears stressing. Unlike Hobbes and Locke, Grotius does not argue that natural rights of self-preservation either rationally or morally *require* this exception. The right of self-government may in principle be alienated entirely, in some circumstances even rationally.[75] Instead, Grotius argues that the assumption that the founding fathers had meant to impose such harsh conditions on citizens is implausible.[76] We should hence not so interpret the social contract. Which constitutional rights and obligations citizens have is thus determined exclusively by the original covenant.

Similarly, humans *could* have instituted rules of property so absolute as to leave the destitute dependent on charity. Such rules would not have been equitable. But they would have been legally binding.

Hobbes, Grotius maintained that agreements made under conditions of extreme duress are naturally binding (Grotius 2005 [1625], 2.11.7.2; Hobbes 2012 [1651], 14.27).

[74] On grounds of natural reason. The Christian Gospel categorically prohibits resisting the sovereign (Grotius 2005 [1625], 1.4.7).

[75] Von Platz 2013.

[76] On the role of gauging the founders' intentions for discovering constitutional rights and duties, see also Grotius 2005 [1625], 2.6.4.

> Let us now see whether Men may not have a Right to enjoy in common those Things that are already become the Properties of other Persons; which Question will at first seem strange, since the Establishment of Property seems to have extinguished all the Right that arose from the State of Community. But it is not so; for we are to consider the Intention of those who first introduced the Property of Goods. There is all the Reason in the World to suppose that they designed to deviate as little as possible from the Rules of natural Equity; and so it is with this Restriction, that the Rights of Proprietors have been established (2.2.6.1).[77]

'Equity', Grotius points out, is an equivocal term. It may signify [Equity A]: 'every Thing which is better done than not done, tho' not according to the strict Rules of Justice, properly so called'. In its second signification, equity means [Equity B]: 'that Part of Justice which restrains the Generality of the Terms of a Law, according to the Intent of the Law-maker' (3.20.47).[78] Those who have introduced property must be understood to have intended to stick to Equity A as much as possible (2.2.6.1; 2.2.9). To suppose differently, would be to advance an uncharitable and unfavorable interpretation of the founders' intentions (2.2.6.1).[79] Equity thus signifies both a natural normative standard targeted by the social contract of property [Equity A] *and* the jurisprudential norm which demands that law be interpreted reasonably – not according to the letter, but to its spirit (the lawmaker's intention) [Equity B]. In sum, Equity B requires interpreting the social contract of property according to Equity A.

Risse misconstrues the meaning of 'equity' in this passage and elsewhere. He thinks equity expresses a principle of reasonable conduct grounded in COE. The demands of reasonable conduct which equity imposes on individuals as co-owners are weaker than obligations of justice. Maxims of natural equity would provide 'room for social criticism' – short of injustice – 'if private property is not arranged in a manner that takes seriously the original moral equality'.[80] This creative interpretation has some textual warrant. Equity A indeed imposes a moral demand on agents not always to press their rights to the fullest. Sometimes it is morally preferable to forgo what is rightfully ours (what we may claim as a matter of justice) (e.g. 2.24.1–2; 3.1.4.2). Since Equity A does not generate enforceable rights, it

[77] Grotius envisions the right of necessity as a return to the primitive communism of the state of nature: 'in all Matters of human Institution, Cases of extreme Necessity, by which all Things return to a mere State of Nature, seem to be excepted' (Grotius 2005 [1625], 2.6.5).

[78] Also Grotius 2005 [1625], 1.2.7.4; 1.3.4; 2.20.27. The distinction between these two senses of equity was commonplace. See e.g. Suárez 1944, 1.2.9–10.

[79] On the duty to interpret charitably, see also Grotius 2005 [1625], 2.4.8.1.

[80] Risse 2012, p. 133; cf. Risse 2012, p. 99, 104.

may be duly labelled a 'demand of reasonable conduct'. However, Equity A does not exhaust the role of equity in confining private property rights. Equity B further specifies which enforceable rights of common ownership are retained – i.e. with which reservations private property should be understood to have been instituted. Equity A demands, for instance, that humans not withhold their property from those in dire need. The severely deprived cannot claim a right to use the surplus of the well-off on the basis of Equity A. The existence of such an enforceable right of necessity is, however, revealed by Equity B. That principle of equitable interpretation attests that humans have been granted a right of necessity in the SCIP.[81] Since Risse defends a non-contractarian reading of Grotius on property, he has no place for Equity B.[82]

We are now in the position to see that Risse misconstrues Grotius's theory of property quite dramatically. Risse highlights the set of prescriptions proscribing 'unacceptable use of collectively owned resources' which Grotius 'derive[s] from original ownership of the earth'.[83] He treats these prescriptions as on a par with the principles of justice and demands of reasonable conduct ('equity') he himself derives from COE. In fact, Grotian rights-shaped[84] restrictions on private property and territorial rights differ from Risse's NRCO with respect to their: (1) nature, (2) normative ground, and (3) theoretical function.

For Grotius, rights-shaped restrictions take the form of Retained Rights of Common Use (henceforth: RRCU). Any such restriction follows from human consent, namely from a decision not to depart from common ownership in certain areas. RRCU permit individuals to use privately owned goods without the owner's consent (within constraints). It bears stressing that such RRCU are perfect rights – a matter of justice, not charity (2.2.6.4). They are hence enforceable – their violation is a *casus belli*.[85] RRCU come in two sorts. The first, already discussed, are rights of necessity (2.2.6–10). The second, more heterogeneous, group consists of rights

[81] General laws must be generally interpreted favourably or equitably, so as to exclude cases of extreme necessity (Grotius 2005 [1625], 3.23.5.3).

[82] Klimchuk similarly misconstrues the role of equity in Grotius's theory. His claim that equity poses 'non-conventional constraints' on the form that the institution of private property may take (Klimchuk 2013, pp. 52–6) should be rejected.

[83] Risse 2012, p. 93.

[84] I introduce the neologism 'rights-*shaped*' to make clear that these restrictions, while taking the form of 'rights', are not rights-*based* (grounded in, or derived from, rights).

[85] Misled by his mistaken belief that the right of necessity is a mere liberty-right, Salter advances the textually unwarranted claim that Grotius's right of necessity 'certainly does not permit the use of force against the owner' (Salter 2005, pp. 301, 288).

of innocent use. It would have been irrational, Grotius claims, not to have permitted common use of private property, insofar as such use benefits the user without harming the owner. No moral norm prohibits this permission. By the principle of equitable interpretation, therefore, we know that these restrictions exist: 'the Right of Property may have been established with the Reservation of such a Use, as is advantageous to some, without injuring others; and therefore the Authors of that Establishment are to be supposed to have done it on that Foot' (2.2.13.1). The right of innocent use entails rights of free passage (2.2.13.1), of free trade (2.2.13.5), of sojourning (2.2.15.1), to cultivate waste lands abroad (2.2.17), and of asylum (2.2.16).[86]

As the concept of innocent use reveals, all these reservations are rights to make use of goods *privately owned* by others. Commentators have not always realized that the lawful exercise of rights of necessity and innocent use does not alter ownership status; goods remain privately owned even if in certain conditions they may be used in common.[87] 'This then is a Sort of Right to take, without a Right of acquiring' (3.13.1.1). For this reason, Grotius can coherently impose a duty of restitution upon anyone compelled to invoke rights of necessity – the owner has a right to be compensated for the use of what remain *her* goods (2.2.9; 3.12.1.1; 3.17.1).[88] However, the owner's consent is not required and force may be used against the owner in defence of rights of necessity and innocent use. Furthermore, no property rules are suspended in cases of necessity. For 'the Fact was never comprehended under the Intention of the Law' (2.20.27).[89]

[86] It is noteworthy that Grotius categorizes rights of asylum under rights of innocent use and not under rights of necessity. Grotius also defends the existence of 'common Right[s] to Actions', actions that ought as a matter of justice be permitted everywhere. They include universal rights to buy at a fair price (2.2.19), to marry foreigners (2.2.21.1), and to not be discriminated against when legal permissions are granted to strangers (2.2.22).

[87] The scholarly confusion is partly due to a failure to distinguish between two kinds of 'use-rights'. The concept of a right to use collectively owned goods should not be confused with the concept of a right to make use of privately owned goods.

[88] We may think, with Thomson 1986, p. 41, that the reason the destitute should compensate owners for using their goods is that the owner's rights are infringed. But as Klimchuk 2013, p. 62, rightly notes, Grotius does not justify the duty of restitution as a 'redress for a wrong'. Rather, Grotius argues that the rationale behind instituting a right of necessity does not require making the right 'absolute' (i.e. without a duty of compensation) (Grotius 2005 [1625], 2.2.9). Modern defenders of the right of necessity, including Mancilla 2016, have found it difficult to make sense of an accompanying duty of restitution, precisely because they examine the right through the lens of a theory of justice.

[89] Salter misreads this passage (Salter 2005, pp. 285, 302).

Risse's NRCO express individuals' rights not to be excluded from the earth's natural resources and spaces in virtue of being co-owners of this planet. They are thus developed from the perspective of the rights of those left out. Grotius, by contrast, settles the extent of RRCU from the perspective of the property-holder: how extensive a right to exclude does private ownership generate? The right of innocent use reveals that not every consideration favouring curbing an owner's right to exclude is based on others' rights not to be excluded. The right to innocently access land privately owned by others is no corollary of original co-owners' natural right not to be excluded from the earth's natural resources and spaces. According to Grotius, we have no such inalienable right not to be excluded. Humans *could* have set up property rights so absolute that we may no longer freely travel 'over any Lands and Rivers, or such Parts of the Sea as belong to any Nation' (2.2.13.1). Rights of innocent use are rather established by a decision on how extensive a set of rights to exclude humans could have rationally allotted to property-holders in a condition of collective ownership. Why grant to land-owners the right to prevent harmless incursions of their property? RRCU are *internal* restrictions on property and territorial rights: they partly *define* the set of legal incidents constitutive of property rights. Rissean NRCO and Grotian RRCU thus fulfil a different theoretical role. Risse's NRCO determine, *inter alia*, whether acts of original appropriation are acceptable. Grotian RRCU do not; they help determine the internal structure of all existing property and territorial rights. Original appropriation is instead governed by the SCIP.

RRCU also differ from NRCO with respect to their normative ground. NRCO are grounded in original collective ownership of the Earth, and RRCU in the SCIP. Humans have RRCU because the SCIP is best understood as having included these reservations. This, in turn, affects the normative status of these rights. Remarkably, RRCU are not *moral* rights. They are conventional rights, introduced by human decisions.[90] The jurist Grotius envisions the SCIP as an historical event. The customary rules adopted in the SCIP should be interpreted, as much as possible, in line with natural equity. But customary rules are not themselves rules of equity. They cannot be, since equity does not generate enforceable rights. Natural equity grants the destitute only an imperfect right: it declares them *worthy*

[90] Salter 2010, pp. 11–2: 'It is important to stress, against interpreters who have tried to downplay the importance of the agreement in Grotius' mature theory in order to ascribe to him a natural rights theory of property, that the right of necessity depends on the existence of such an agreement. Without it, those who have not acquired their own property through either division or occupation face starvation'. Cf. Salter 2005, pp. 285, 301.

of receiving a perfect right of necessity. Enforceable rights of necessity exist solely in virtue of the SCIP.[91]

I have argued that for Grotius private property rights are not grounded in moral principles but rather in a supposed historical social contract. This significantly diminishes its modern appeal. A historical contract is a highly infelicitous starting point for any normative theory. There never has been such a contract. And even had there been one, why should we think that humans today are bound by morally arbitrary customs introduced by our ancestors millennia ago?[92] I shall not defend Grotius against such devastating objections. Instead, I will highlight a flipside of this critique. Grotius raises a theoretically important question precisely by treating property rights as wholly conventional. What internal structure can we rationally assign to individual property rights, given that the Earth originally belonged to humanity in common? Recognizing the significance of this question neither requires endorsing the existence of a historical SCIP, nor of other unpalatable aspects of Grotius's theory (such as a norm of non-resistance).

9.4 Comparing the Two Models

In January 2016, the Italian Court of Cassation upheld the right to steal in dire need. It declared a homeless person arrested for attempting to steal sausages and cheese (worth a grand total of €4) not guilty of the crime of theft. The Court reasoned that the man had taken 'possession of a little food to cope with an immediate and unavoidable need to feed himself, thereby acting in a state of necessity'.[93] The Court seems to have treated necessity as an *excusing* condition, rendering blameless an action that is otherwise morally wrong. Both Risse and Grotius view the right of necessity rather as *exculpatory*.[94] The homeless person did not commit any action in need of excusing in their view – his right of necessity morally justified his action.

Both Risse and Grotius conceive of rights of necessity as individual rights with corresponding obligations. But the two propound rather

[91] One major innovation of Grotius is his radical decoupling of moral ('imperfect') from enforceable and justice-governed ('perfect') rights, subject to human jurisdiction. Individuals may even have enforceable rights which they do not morally deserve.

[92] According to Grotius, future generations cannot be injured 'because they have not as yet obtained any Right' (Grotius 2005 [1625], 2.4.10.2).

[93] Corte di Cassazione, sez. V Penale, verdict of January 7, 2016, n. 18248/2016. I am indebted to Alessandro Mulieri for retrieving the court documents and translating them for me.

[94] On Grotius's distinction between extenuation and exculpation see Grotius 2005 [1625], 2.1.14.

different views on the deontic status of the property-holders to whose resources the deprived may claim a right. For Risse, the lawful exercise of rights of necessity leads to reasonable infringements of property rights, which owners are obliged to accept. The infringement is not morally wrong (which would make it a rights-violation) because of the justificatory presence of a right of necessity. The owner is either obliged to waive his right against the world to exclusive use of the resource in question, or can reasonably be expected to do so. For Grotius, there is no infringement of property rights at all, and no right to be waived. Since the claims of the destitute are conceptualized as internal restrictions on ownership rights, no rights are overridden. Property rights were never so expansive as to include the right to categorically exclude the severely deprived to begin with.[95] For this reason, lawful exercise of RRCU does not in principle require seeking the consent of property-holders whose goods are targeted.[96] By conceptualizing RRCU as property rights themselves rather than as claims of justice, Grotius thus solves theoretically more neatly the question of who are the relevant duty-bearers. RRCU directly limit the rights of *every* individual property-holder. No property-owner has rights so extensive by dint of private ownership. Risse's NRCO, by contrast, primarily have 'the global order as such' as duty-bearer.

An example may elucidate this further. According to Risse, refugees fleeing a devastating civil war have a claim of justice against the global order to be given asylum 'somewhere'. But against individual countries, refugees only have a weaker demand of reasonable conduct to be admitted – and

[95] The distinction between infringing and violating rights is developed by Thomson 1986, pp. 40–1, Thomson 1990, p. 122. I interpret Risse as subscribing to a *pro-tanto* theory of rights: claims to justice *override* claims to property. The rival specificationist theory portrays rights as absolute but not as general. Rather than accepting the idea of permissible infringements of rights, specificationists delimit the content of rights in each particular case to what it is impermissible to do to the right-holder. Reconstructing Risse along specificationist lines would bring his views closer to Grotius. However, the contrast I draw between Grotius and Risse does not hinge on attributing a *pro-tanto* theory of rights to Risse. It hinges on the claim that Risse's NRCO cannot be seen as internal restrictions on exclusionary rights. That claim follows from two commitments of Risse: (1) NRCO do not entail corresponding duties on each and every property-holder; (2) NRCO may remain unrealized without anyone having done anything wrong. On the distinction between *pro-tanto* and specificationist theories of rights, see Wellman 1995; Frederick 2014 and the above-cited works by Thomson.

[96] Grotius recognizes three conditions for lawful exercise of the right of necessity: (1) it must be a last resort, (2) the property-owner must not find herself in like necessity, and (3) restitution must be made afterwards (Grotius 2005 [1625], 2.2.7–9). The last resort condition arguably implies that the deprived must ordinarily first seek the consent of property-holders for using their goods, but not because such consent is required for its own sake.

only against those countries that are relatively under using their resources and spaces.[97] Refugees can reasonably demand that such countries waive their liberty-right to exclude non-nationals. According to Grotius, territorial rights of states are not so absolute as to permit exclusion of refugees to begin with. The well-off can build fences, guard the borders, stow away their property, and pretend not to hear the cries of the desperate outside the gates. But they cannot justify such conduct by claiming that their property is 'theirs'. The social institution of property did not set up rights so absolute as to permit excluding the severely deprived from enjoying privately owned property in common. Insofar as the legal system permits such exclusion, the law is an expression of force, and not of right. In the words of the English radical Gerrard Winstanley (1609–76), the affluent exclude the destitute 'by club law, but not by righteousness'.[98]

Grotian rights-shaped restrictions on private property are more demanding than Risse's in a second way as well, due to *DJBP*'s peculiar conceptualization of 'rights'. For Grotius, 'rights' are essentially titles to take coercive measures – including, if courts are unavailable, bellicose ones. 'Rights' express what humans may legitimately demand of one another, rather than what is their due in a morally perfect world. According to Grotius, refugees may back up their rights by force whenever asylum is unduly refused to them. States have no right to resist the just war waged against them. (This shows that the prevailing interpretation of Grotius as the prime theorist of Westphalian external sovereignty requires qualification.) Similarly, in Grotius's view, the destitute are morally entitled to wage war against property-holders if the latter prevent them from using in common their possessions (where legal redress is unavailable). Property-holders are not allowed to resist this show of force.

Risse is silent about which measures individuals may take to enforce their NRCO. He is unlikely to endorse a corresponding right to wage war. Not because his is a theory of *justice* – other such theorists have argued that subsistence wars can in principle be morally justified[99] – but rather because the responsibility for realising NRCO, *qua* human rights, lies primarily with the global order as such. Risse offers a study of the necessary conditions for a just global basic structure. He accepts that rights may be aspirational: it is 'possible for rights to be unsatisfied and yet for nobody

[97] Risse 2012, p. 146.

[98] Winstanley 2009, p. 285.

[99] Fabre 2012, pp. 97–129; Fabre 2014, pp. 416–25, has argued that dereliction of duties of global distributive justice is a possible cause of just war.

to have done anything wrong'.[100] The rights Grotius recognizes in *DJBP* – a systematic exploration of when coercion may legitimately be used – are in no way aspirational.

Grotius's theory of property, I hope to have made clear, provides us with a rather different conceptual framework than the one implicit in modern theories of justice. The restrictions with which private property has been introduced are in Grotius's view *themselves* property rights. Not titles of ownership, to be sure, but certainly rights to make use of resources. Above, I have emphasized that Grotius's social contract theory of property determines the shape property rights shall have (their 'internal structure'). We can see now that any such restrictions take, remarkably, the form of property rights as well. These restrictions reflect that humans sometimes have a right to make use of resources privately owned by others without their consent.

This brings us to a further conceptual difference between Grotius's and Risse's theory. All Grotian rights are of the same sort and placed at the same deontic level. Property rights and claims of justice are conceptually identical on Grotius's account. Every right justice order respects for *is* a property right (understood in an expansive sense as including rights to life, liberty, and actions) (1.1.4–5). Insofar as Grotius recognizes a distinction between legal and moral rights, the distinction is placed elsewhere – at the level of perfect vs. imperfect rights. Risse, by contrast, conceptualizes NRCO as moral rights, and justice as a norm regulating moral rights, invoked to criticize and evaluate existing patterns of holdings. These moral rights are not, on Risse's account, definitive of individual property rights. Rather, they determine which patterns of holdings are morally acceptable.

Let me conclude my analysis by highlighting a philosophically important question rendered salient by Grotius's theorization of COE. Unlike Risse, Grotius does not treat COE as a ground of justice (as a source of pre-institutional rights constraining acceptable exclusionary regimes). Rather, he portrays COE, plausibly, as the moral default position with respect to such regimes: the burden is on us to justify any departures from natural common ownership towards coercive and exclusionary social institutions.[101] Such justifications are not out of reach – philosophers have advanced sundry compelling arguments in defence of the moral permissibility of private

[100] Risse 2012, p. 250.

[101] Robert Filmer (1588–1653) was one of very few thinkers to argue in print for the position that private property in external things exists by nature. He did so on the basis of a shaky argument drawn from Scripture.

ownership, both consequentialist and rights-based in nature.[102] Grotius's justification is a contractarian one. He invokes COE to ask which, if any, conventional arrangements of exclusionary rights – including the set of legal incidents these rights shall be composed of – may be reasonably adopted against the background of original common ownership of the Earth? Equity commands us to assume that the set of rules which would have been most rational for individuals to adopt, as reflected in the actually existing customary norms of international law, determines the shape of existing property and territorial rights.

Grotius's contractarianism further determines which resources and spaces are available for privatization. Due to their teleological nature, contractarian theories render theoretically central the question of what the point is of having exclusionary and coercive social institutions.[103] Consider ownership of the sea. Departing sharply from his juvenile *Mare Liberum*, Grotius does not think it morally impermissible to privatize the oceans in *DJBP*: 'it was yet in Consequence of an arbitrary Establishment, and not by Vertue of any Prohibition of the Law of Nature, that the Sea was not then possessed, or that it could not be lawfully possessed' (2.3.10.1).[104] Rather, the Dutchman argues that international custom ('the law of nations') should not be interpreted as permitting privatization of the oceans, on the grounds that such privatization serves no purpose: 'the Cause which obliged Mankind to desist from the Custom of using Things in common, has nothing at all to do in this Affair: For the Sea is of so vast an Extent, that it is sufficient for all the Uses that Nations can draw from thence' (2.2.3.1).

Risse primarily aims to show that humanity's continuing COE provides each human earthling with natural and pre-institutional rights that restrict the range of morally acceptable exclusionary regimes. What the point is of consenting to institute a regime of exclusive holdings he leaves largely undiscussed. Largely, but not completely: in his discussion of intellectual property rights, Risse develops a justification for property regulation *prima facie* in the spirit of Grotius's contractarianism. Inspired by *Mare Liberum*, Risse explores 'what sort of private property rights in ideas it is

[102] Waldron 1988 offers a seminal analysis of many such arguments, both historical and contemporary.

[103] Recall that Grotius does not restrict NRCO, as Risse does, to the right to satisfy basic needs 'insofar as such needs require collectively owned resources' (Risse 2012, p. 111). Doing so would have made little sense for Grotius, given that he invokes COE to examine what the point is of any exclusionary social institution.

[104] Cf. Grotius 2009 [1609], VI.37; Grotius 2006 [1868], XII.108: 'it is repugnant to the law of nature for any person to possess the sea, or use thereof, as private property'. Also Grotius 2006 [1868], VII.43, XII.110.

legitimate for a legal system to recognize'.[105] To be sure, the right he 'eventually derive[s] does not emerge from common ownership but from the distinctively human life'.[106] Common Humanity – a nonrelational ground of justice – requires that 'intellectual property... not be regulated in a way that recognizes far-reaching private rights (beyond what is justifiable in terms of incentives and fair compensation)'.[107]

It is worth stressing that Risse is not here taking up the Grotian question of what set of legal incidents property rights should be composed of. Risse's concern is with how much legal protection intellectual property should have. How long may a patent reasonably last?[108] Furthermore, Risse's reflection on whether we should have intellectual property rights at all takes shape 'in light of the point that ideas originally belong to a Common'.[109] Common Ownership – his preferred conception of COE – permits unilateral original appropriation (within constraints); the contractarian question of what the *telos* is in setting up private property and territorial states with coercive border control is thereby decisively set aside. For Risse, it is not COE that determines whether privatization is permissible; rather, judgments about which forms of privatization are reasonable determine the shape that COE shall take. Far from uncovering common ground, Risse's discussion of the intellectual common thus reveals how different are his and Grotius's ways of theorizing collective ownership of the Earth.

9.5 Conclusion

This chapter aimed to contribute to modern thinking on global justice by analyzing different ways in which the idea of collective ownership of the Earth may implicate normative theory. I hope to have shown that Grotius's contractarian employment of the idea is fundamentally different from Risse's, notwithstanding the latter's own declaration of allegiance. The difference between their two models of theorizing COE reaches far beyond the issue of contractarianism, however. I have argued that the Dutchman advances a theory of property rather than a theory of justice. I have sought

105 Risse 2012, p. 232.
106 Risse 2012, p. 232.
107 Risse 2012, p. 244.
108 For Grotius, 'duration' is not a legal incident, but a way ('modus') of having ownership. This is evinced by his discussion of another bundle of legal incidents – 'sovereignty' (Grotius 2005 [1625], 1.3.11).
109 Risse 2012, p. 233.

to defend neither Grotius's conceptualizations of rights and justice, nor his substantive conclusions. What I have suggested is that a question absolutely central in Grotius's theory – what shape shall we give to particular exclusionary rights? – is worth reviving.[110] This question is of philosophical importance even if we reject Grotius's contention that property is conventional all the way down. Which internal structures, we should then ask ourselves, are *morally* acceptable? Risse's magisterial theory has found inspiration in centuries-old normative ideas. This chapter has suggested that by probing deeper still, into the underlying conceptual framework, we can unearth unfamiliar viewpoints through which we can reflect on the possibilities and impediments of prevailing ways of approaching moral quandaries.

[110] This question receives little attention in modern political philosophy. Welcome exceptions include Christman 1991, 1994 and work by left-libertarians such as Steiner 1994; Otsuka 2003, pp. 11–40.

REFERENCES

Abizadeh, Arash. 2013. "A Critique of the 'Common Ownership of the Earth' Thesis," 8 *Les ateliers de l'éthique / The Ethics Forum* 33.

Alchian, Armen A. 1965. "Some Economics of Property Rights," 30 *IL Politico* 816.

Alexander, Gregory S. 2009a. "The Complex Core of Property," 94 *Cornell Law Review* 1063.

2009b. "The Social-Obligation Norm in American Property Law," 94 *Cornell Law Review* 745.

Alexander, Gregory S., and Eduardo M. Peña. 2012. *An Introduction to Property Theory*. Cambridge: Cambridge University Press.

Alford, William P. 1995. *To Steal a Book is an Elegant Offense: Intellectual Property Law in Chinese Civilisation*. Stanford, CA: Stanford University Press.

Allen, W. W. 2014. "Accountability of Cotenants for Rents and Profits or Use and Occupation," 51 *American Law Reports* 388.

Aquinas, Thomas. 1947. *Summa Theologica*. New York, NY: Benziger Bros.

Aristotle. 1999. *Nicomachean Ethics III.2*. Upper Saddle River, NJ: Prentice Hall.

2009. *The Nicomachean Ethics*. Oxford: Oxford University Press.

Arruñada, Benito. 2011. "Property Titling and Conveyancing," in Kenneth Ayotte and Henry E. Smith, eds., *Research Handbook on the Economics of Property Law*. Cheltenham: Edward Elgar.

Ashcraft, Richard. 1994. "Locke's Political Philosophy," in Vere Chappell, ed., *The Cambridge Companion to Locke*. Cambridge: Cambridge University Press.

Austin, John. 1869. *Lectures on Jurisprudence or the Philosophy of Positive Law*. London: J. Murray.

1875. *Lectures on Jurisprudence, or, The Philosophy of Private Law*. London: John Murray.

Austin, Lisa M. 2014a. "The Power of the Rule of Law," in Lisa M. Austin and Dennis Klimchuk, eds., *Private Law and the Rule of Law*. Oxford: Oxford University Press.

2014b. "Property and the Rule of Law," 20 *Legal Theory* 79.

Bagchi, Aditi. 2008. "Distributive Injustice and Private Law," 60 *Hastings Law Journal* 105.

2014. "Distributive Justice and Contract," in Gregory Klass, George Letsas and Prince Saprai, eds., *Philosophical Foundations of Contract Law*. Oxford: Oxford Univesity Press.

Baldwin, J. W. 1959. "Medieval Theories of the Just Price: Romanists, Canonists, and Theologians in the Twelve and Thirteenth Centuries," 49 *Transactions of the American Philosophical Society New Series* 1.

Balganesh, Shyamkrishna. 2008. "Demystifying the Right to Exclude: Of Property, Inviolability, and Automatic Injunctions," 31 *Harvard Journal of Law & Public Policy* 593.

Barak, Aharon. 2006. *The Judge in a Democracy*. Princeton, NJ: Princeton University Press.

Brandon, Douglas Ivor et al. 1984. "Self-Help: Extrajudicial Rights, Privileges and Remedies in Contemporary American Society," 37 *Vanderbilt Law Review* 941.

Beckett, Katherine, and Steve Herbert. 2010. "Penal Boundaries: Banishment and the Expansion of Punishment," 35 *Law & Society Inquiry* 1.

Bell, Daniel A. 2003. "Confucian Constraints on Property Rights," in Daniel A. Bell and Chaibong Haim, eds., *Confucianism for the Modern World*. Cambridge: Cambridge University Press.

Bell, Stepahnie A., John F. Henry, and L. Randall Wray. 2004. "A Chartalist Critique of John Locke's Theory of Property, Accumulation, and Money," 62 *Review of Social Economy* 51.

Benson, Peter. 2002. "Philosophy of Property Law," in Jules L Coleman, Kenneth Eimar Himma and Scott J. Shapiro, eds., *The Oxford Handbook of Jurisprudence and Philosophy of Law*. Oxford: Oxford University Press.

Black, Alison. 1989. *Man and Nature in the Philosophical Thought of Wang Fu-chih*. Seattle, WA: University of Washington Press.

Blackstone, William. 1765–1769. *Commentaries of the Laws of England*. Oxford: Clarendon Press.

Breakey, Hugh. 2009. "Without Consent: Principles of Justified Acquisition and Duty-Imposing Powers," 59 *Philosophical Quarterly* 618.

Brown, Vivienne. 1999. "The 'Figure' of God and the Limits to Liberalism: A Rereading of Locke's 'Essay' and 'Two Treatises,'" 60 *Journal of the History of Ideas* 83.

Brownstein, A. E. 1985. "What's the Use? A Doctrinal and Policy Critique of the Measurement of Loss of Use Damages," 37 *Rutgers Law Review* 433.

Buckle, Stephen. 1991. *Natural Law and the Theory of Property: Grotius to Hume*. Oxford: Oxford University Press.

Burk, Dan L. 2013. "Intellectual Property in the Cathedral," in Dana Beldiman, ed., *Access to Information and Knowledge: 21 Century Challenges in Intellectual Property and Knowledge Governance*. Cheltenham: Edward Elgar.

Calabresi, Guido, and A. Douglas Melamed. 1972. "Property Rules, Liability Rules and Inalienability: One View of the Cathedral," 85 *Harvard Law Review* 1089.

Cao, Guoqing 曹国庆. 2009. *Huang Zongxi ping zhuan* 黄宗羲评传 *[An Critical Biography of Huang Zongxi]*. Beijing: China Social Press.

Chen, Albert H. Y. 2014. "The Concept of 'Datong' in Chinese Philosophy as an Expression of the Idea of the Common Good," in David Solomon and

P. C. Lo, eds., *The Common Good: Chinese and American Perspectives*. Dordrecht: Springer.

Chen, Zhaohui 陈朝晖. 1994. "Lun Ming Qing shixue sichao zhong de tudi jingji sixiang" 论明清实学思潮中的土地经济思想 ["Land in Ming-Qing 'Practical Learning' Thought"], 4 *Yantai Daxue Xuebao (zhexue shehui kexue ban) [Journal of Yantai University (Philosophy and Social Sciences Edition)]* 15.

Chow, Kai-Wing. 2003. "Huang Zongxi," in Xinzhong Yao, ed., *The Encyclopedia of Confucianism*. Abingdon/Oxon: Routledge.

Christman, John. 1991. "Self-ownership, Equality, and the Structure of Property Rights," 19 *Political Theory* 28.

1994. *The Myth of Property: Toward an Egalitarian Theory of Ownership*. New York, NY/Oxford: Oxford University Press.

Claeys, Eric R. 2009. "Property 101: Is Property a Thing or a Bundle?," 32 *Seattle University Law Review* 617–31.

2014. "Intellectual Usufructs: Trade Secrets, Hot News, and the Usufructuary Paradigm at Common Law", in Shyamkrisha Balganesh, ed., *Intellectual Property and The Common Law*. Cambridge: Cambridge University Press.

Cohen, G. A. 1995. *Self-Ownership, Freedom and Equality*. Cambridge: Cambridge University Press.

Cohen, Morris R. 1927. "Property and Sovereignty," 13 *Cornell Law Quarterly* 8.

Dagan, Hanoch. 1999. "The Distributive Foundation of Corrective Justice," 98 *Michigan Law Review* 138.

2011. *Property: Values and Institutions*. Oxford: Oxford University Press.

Dagan, Hanoch, and Avihay Dorfman. 2016. "Just Relationships," 116 *Columbia Law Review* 1395.

Dardess, John W. 2003. *Blood and History: The Donglin Faction and its Repression (1620–1627)*. Honolulu, HI: University of Hawaii Press.

De Araujo, Marcelo. 2009. "Hugo Grotius, Contractualism, and the Concept of Private Property: An Institutionalist Interpretation," 26 *History of Philosophy Quarterly* 353.

De Bary, Wm. Theodore. 1993. *Waiting for the Dawn: A Plan for the Prince – Huang Tsung-hsi's Ming-i-tai-fang lu*. New York, NY: Columbia University Press.

Demsetz, Harold. 1967. "Toward a Theory of Property Rights," 57 *American Economic Review* 347.

Dickey, Anthony. 1972. "Hohfeld's Debt to Salmond," 10 *University of Western Australia Law Review* 62.

Douglas, Simon, and Ben McFarlane. 2013. "Defining Property Rights," in James Penner and Henry E. Smith, eds., *Philosophical Foundations of Property Law*. Oxford: Oxford University Press.

Dukeminier, Jesse, et al. 2010. *Property*. New York, NY: Wolters Kluwer Law & Business.

Dworkin, Ronald. 1996. "Do Liberty and Equality Conflict?," in Paul Barker, ed., *Living as Equals*. Oxford: Oxford University Press.

Ellickson, Robert C. 1991. *How Neighbours Settle Disputes*. Cambridge, MA: Harvard University Press.

2014. "The Affirmative Duties of Property Owners: An Essay for Tom Merrill," 3 *Brigham-Kanner Property Rights Conference Journal* 43.

Emerich, Yaëll. 2014. "Why Protect Possession," in Eric Descheemaeker, ed., *The Consequences of Possession*. Edinburgh: Edinburgh University Press.

Epstein, Richard A. 1979. "Possession as the Root of Title," 13 *Georgia Law Review* 1221.

2006. "Weak and Strong Conceptions of Property: An Essay in Memory of Jim Harris," in Timothy Endicott et al., eds., *Properties of Law: Essays in Honour of Jim Harris*. Oxford: Oxford University Press.

Essert, Christopher. 2013. "The Office of Ownership," 63 *University of Toronto Law Journal* 418.

2014. "Property in Licenses and the Law of Things," 59 *McGill Law Journnal* 559.

Fabre, Cécile. 2012. *Cosmopolitan War*. Oxford: Oxford University Press.

2014. "Rights, Justice and War: A Reply," 33 *Law and Philosophy* 391.

Fennell, Lee Anne. 2007. "Property and Half-Torts," 116 *Yale Law Journal* 1400.

2011. "Commons, Anticommons, Semicommons," in Kenneth Ayotte and Henry E. Smith, eds., *Research Handbook on the Economics of Property Law*. Cheltenham: Edward Elgar.

Ferrara, Peter J. 1993. "Social Security and Taxes," in Donald B. Kraybill, ed., *The Amish and The State*. Baltimore, MD: Johns Hopkins University Press.

Feser, Edward. 2005. "There is No Such Thing as an Unjust Initial Acquisition," 22 *Social Philosophy & Politics* 56.

2007. *Locke*. Oxford: Oneworld Publications.

Fichte, J. G. 2000. *Foundations of Natural Right, According to the Principles of the Wissenschaftslehre*. Cambridge: Cambridge University Press.

Flynn, Sean, et al. 2008. "An Economic Justification for Open Access to Essential Medicine Patents in Developing Countries," 37 *Journal of Law Medicine & Ethics* 184.

Frankfurt, Harry. 1987. "Equality as a Moral Ideal," 98 *Ethics* 21.

Frederick, Danny. 2014. "Pro-tanto Versus Absolute Rights," 45 *The Philosophical Forum* 375.

Fu, Pei-jung. 2002. "Tian (T'ien): Heaven," in Antonio S. Cua, ed., *Encyclopedia of Chinese Philosophy*. New York, NY: Routledge.

Fuller, Lon L. 1969. *The Morality of Law*. New Haven, CT: Yale University Press.

1977. *The Morality of Law*. New Haven, CT: Yale University Press.

Gan, Orit. 2015. "The Justice Element of Promissory Estoppel," 89 St. John's Law Review.

Gardner, J. 2017. "The Negligence Standard: Political Not Metaphysical," 80 *The Modern Law Review* 1.

Gaus, Gerald F., and Loren E. Lomasky. 1990. "Are Property Rights Problematic?," 75 *Monist* 493–5.

Gentili, Aliberico. 1933 [1598]. *De Jure Belli Libri Tres*. Oxford: Clarendon Press.

Gibbard, Allan. 1979. "Natural Property Rights," 10 *Noûs* 77.

Glendon, Mary Ann. 1982. "The Transformation of American Landlord-Tenant Law," 23 *Boston College Law Review* 503.

Goldwin, Robert A. 1987. "John Locke," in Leo Strauss and Joseph Crospey, eds., *History of Political Philosophy (Third Edition)*. Chicago, IL: University of Chicago Press.

Gordley, J. 1981. "Equality in Exchange," 69 *California Law Review* 1587.

1991. *The Philsophical Origins of Modern Contract Doctrine*. Oxford: Clarendon Press.

Grotius, Hugo. 1926. *The Introduction to the Jurisprudence of Holland*. Oxford: Clarendon Press.

2005 [1625]. *The Rights of War and Peace*. Indianapolis, IN: Liberty Fund.

2006 [1868]. *Commentary on the Law of Prize and Booty*. Indianapolis, IN: Liberty Fund.

2009 [1609]. *Mare Liberum*. Leiden: Brill.

Haakonssen, Knud. 1985. "Hugo Grotius and the History of Political Thought," 13 *Political Theory* 239.

Halpin, Andrew. 2017. "The Value of Hohfeldian Neutrality when Theorising about Legal Rights," in Mark McBride, ed., *New Essays on the Nature of Rights*. Oxford: Hart.

Harris, J. W. 1996. *Property and Justice*. Oxford: Oxford University Press.

Hart, H. 1972–73. "Rawls on Liberty and Its Priority," 40 *The University of Chicago Law Review* 534.

Hayek, Freidrich A. 1960. *The Constitution of Liberty*. Chicago, IL: University of Chicago Press.

Hegel, Georg Wilhelm Friedrich. 1991 [1821]. *Hegel, Elements of the Philosophy of Right*. Cambridge: Cambridge University Press.

Heller, Michael A. 1998. "The Tragedy of the Anticommons: Property in the Transition from Marx to Markets," 111 *Harvard Law Review* 621.

Hobbes, Thomas. 1991 [1651]. *Leviathan*. Revised Student Edition. Cambridge: Cambridge University Press.

2012 [1651]. *Leviathan*. Oxford: Clarendon Press.

Hohfeld, Wesley Newcomb. 1909. "Nature of Stockholders' Individual Liability for Corporation Debts," 9 *Columbia Law Review* 285.

1913. "The Relations between Equity and Law," 11 *Michigan Law Review* 537.

1913–14. "Some Fundamental Legal Conceptions as Applied in Judicial Reasoning," 23 *Yale Law Journal* 16.

1914. 'A Vital School of Jurisprudence and Law: Have American Universities Awakened to the Enlarged Opportunities and Responsibility of the Present Day?', 14 *Handbook Ass'n Am. L. Schls*. 76.

1916–17. "Fundamental Legal Conceptions as Applied in Judicial Reasoning," 26 *Yale Law Journal* 710.

1923 [1913]. "Fundamental Legal Conceptions, I," in W. W. Cook, ed., *Fundamental Legal Conceptions as Applied in Judicial Reasoning and other Legal Essays*. New Haven, CT: Yale University Press.

Honoré, A. M. 1960. "Rights of Exclusion and Immunities against Divesting," 34 *Tulane Law Review* 453.

Honoré, Tony. 1987a [1961]. "Ownership," *Making Law Bind: Essays Legal and Philosophical*. Oxford: Clarendon Press.

1987b [1977]. "Property, Title and Redistribution," *Making Law Bind: Essays Legal and Philosophical*. Oxford: Clarendon Press.

Hu, Jichuang. 1988. *A Concise History of Chinese Economic Thought*. Beijing: Foreign Language Press.

Huang, Zhongjing 黄忠晶. 2008. "Huang Zongxi jingji sixiang jianlun" 黄宗羲经济思想简论 ["A Brief Discussion of Huang Zongxi's Economic Thought"], 9 *Zhengzhou Qinggongye Xueyuan Xuebao (shehui kexue ban) [Journal of Zhengzhou University of Light Industry (Social Sciences)]* 18.

Huang, Zongxi 黄宗羲. 1985a [17th century]. "Po xie lun" 破邪论 ["Arguments to Defeat Evil"], in Jiasui Sun 孙家遂, ed., *Huang Zongxi quanji: di yi ce* 黄宗羲全集 ： 第一册 *[The Complete Works of Huang Zongxi: Volume 1]*. Hangzhou: Zhejiang Guji Press.

1985b [1662]. "Ming yi dai fang lu" 明夷待访录 ["Waiting for the Dawn: A Plan for the Prince"], in Jiasui Sun 孙家遂, ed., *Huang Zongxi quanji: di yi ce* 黄宗羲全集 ： 第一册 *[The Complete Works of Huang Zongxi: Volume 1]*. Hangzhou: Zhejiang Guji Press.

Huber, Jakob. 2017. "Theorising from the Global Standpoint: Kant and Grotius on Original Common Possession of the Earth," 25.2 *European Journal of Philosophy* 231.

Hunan University Press. 2009. *Wang Chuanshan Yanjiu Zhuzhuo Gaiyao* 王船山研究著作概要 *[Abstracts and Summaries of Various Scholarship on Wang Fuzhi]*. Changsha: Hunan University Press.

Jordan, Pete. 2013. *In the City of Bikes: The Story of the Amsterdam Cyclist*. New York, NY: Harper Perennial.

Kant, Immanuel. 1994. *Ethical Philosophy: Grounding for the Metaphysics of Morals; Metaphysical Principles of Virtue: With "On a Supposed Right to Lie Because of Philanthropic Concerns."* Indianapolis, IN: Hackett.

1996 [1798]. "The Metaphysics of Morals," in Mary J. Gregor, ed., *Practical Philosophy*. Cambridge: Cambridge University Press.

Katz, Larissa. 2008. "Exclusion and Exclusivity in Property Law," 58 *University of Toronto Law Journal* 275.

2012. "Governing through Owners: How and Why Formal Private Property Rights Enhance State Power," 160 *University of Pennsylvania Law Review* 2029.

2013. "The Relativity of Title and Causa Possessionis," in James Penner and Henry Smith, eds., *Philosophical Foundations of Property Law*. Oxford: Oxford University Press.

Kelsen, Hans. 1934. "The Pure Theory of Law," 50 *Law Quarterly Review* 474.

Kemmis, Daniel. 1996. "Barn Raising," in William Vitek and Wes Jackson, eds., *Rooted in The Land: Essays on Community and Place*. New Haven, CT: Yale University Press.

Kennedy, Duncan, and Frank Michelman. 1980. "Are Property and Contract Efficient?," 8 *Hofstra Law Review* 711.

Klimchuk, Dennis. 2013. "Property and Necessity," in James Penner and Henry E. Smith, eds., *Philosophical Foundations of Property Law*. Oxford: Oxford University Press.

Kocourek, Albert. 1920. "Rights in Rem," 68 *University of Pennsylvania Law Review* 322.

Laycock, Douglas. 2010. *Modern American Remedies: Cases and Materials*. New York, NY: Aspen Publishers.

Legge, James. 2006. "*The Chinese Classics, Volume 4*." Chinese Text Project, compiled by Donald Sturgeon. http://ctext.org/book-of-poetry.

Lehman, John Alan. 2006. "Intellectual Property Rights and Chinese Tradition Section: Philosophical Foundations," 69 *Journal of Business Ethics* 1.

Li, Shouyong 李守庸. 1983. "Wang Fuzhi jingji sixiangzhongde jindai tedian pingyi" 王夫之经济思想中的近代特点评议 ["The Special, Modern Characteristics of Wang Fuzhi's Economic Thought"] 9 *Jingji Yanjiu [Economic Research]* 57.

1987. *Wang Chuanshan jingji sixiang yanjiu* 王船山经济思想研究 *[Research on Wang Fuzhi's Economic Thought]*. Changsha: Hunan's People Press.

Lin, Mou-sheng. 1942. *Men and Ideas*. New York, NY: John Day.

Liu, Hanruo 刘含若. 1982. "Wang Fuzhi jingji sixiang san lun" 王夫之经济思想散论 ["Thoughts on Wang Fuzhi's Economic Thought"]. 4 *Qiushi xuekan [Seeking Truth]* 72.

Liu, JeeLoo. 2001. "Is Human History Predestined in Wang Fuzhi's Cosmology?," 28 *Journal of Chinese Philosophy* 321.

2002. "Wang Fuzhi (Wang Fu-chih)," in Antonio S. Cua, ed., *Encyclopedia of Chinese Philosophy*. New York, NY: Routledge.

Liu, Qimei 刘岐梅. 2006. "Huang Zongxi yanjiu bainian shuping" 黄宗羲研究百年述评 ["A Review of the Study of Huang Zongxi in the 20th Century"], 23 *Qingdao Daxue Shifanxueyuan xuebao [Journal of Teachers College, Qingdao University]* 51.

Liu, Sky. 2004. "Contemporary Chinese Studies of Wang Fuzhi in Mainland China," 3 *Dao* 307.

Locke, John. 1695. "Venditio," https://reconstructingeconomics.com/2014/06/06/venditio-by-john-locke/

1975 [1689]. *An Essay Concerning Human Understanding*. Oxford: Oxford University Press.

1988 [1690]. "Second Treatise of Government," in Peter Laslett, ed., *Locke: Two Treatises of Government*. Cambridge: Cambridge University Press.

2003 [1689]. "The Second Treatise of Government," in David Wooten, ed., *John Locke: Political Writings*. Indianapolis, IN: Hackett.

Lou, Yulie. 2012. "Introduction to Volume 4," in Xingpei Yuan, ed., *The History of Chinese Civilisation*. Cambridge: Cambridge University Press.

Lueck, Dean. 2003. "First Possession as the Basis of Property," in Terry L. Anderson and Fred S. McChesney, eds., *Property Rights: Cooperation, Conflict, and Law*. Princeton, NJ: Princeton University Press.

Luo, Langping 骆浪萍. 1987. "Huang Zongxi jingji sixiang zhi wo jian" 黄宗羲经济思想之我见 ["My Views on Huang Zongxi's Economic Thought"], 17 *Hangzhou Daxue Xuebao [Journal of Hangzhou University]* 14.

Ma, Ning 马宁. 2006. "Lun Wang Chuanshan 'E-meng' – wenzhong de jingji sixiang - du Wang Chuanshan 'E-meng' shouji yuangao you gan" 论王船山《噩梦》一文中的经济思想 – – 读王船山《噩梦》手迹原稿有感 ["Economic Thought in Wang Fuzhi's Strange Dream – Impressions after Reading Wang Fuzhi's Strange Dream in his Original Handwriting"], 3 *Chuanshan xuekan [Chuanshan Journal]* 15.

MacCormack, Geoffrey. 2013–14. "Natural Law in Traditional China," 8 *Journal of Comparative Law* 104.

MacPherson, C. B. 1978. *Property: Mainstream and Critical Positions*. Toronto: University of Toronto Press.

Mack, E. 1995. "The Self-Ownership Proviso: A New and Improved Lockean Proviso," 12 *Social Philosophy and Policy* 186.

Mancilla, Alejandra. 2017. "What the Old Right of Necessity Can Do for the Contemporary Global Poor," 34 *Journal of Applied Philosophy* 607.

McFarlane, Ben. 2008. *The Structure of Property Law*. Oxford: Oxford University Press.

McFarlane, Ben, and Roberts Stevens. 2010. "The Nature of Equitable Property," 4 *The Journal of Equity* 1.

McMorran, Ian. 1992. *The Passionate Realist: An Introduction to the Life and Political Thought of Wang Fuzhi*. Hong Kong: Sunshine Book Company.

2000. "Late Confucian Scholarship: Wang Fuzhi," in Wm. Theodore de Bary and Richard Lufrano, eds., *Sources of Chinese Tradition, Volume 2: From 1600 through the Twentieth Century*. New York, NY: Columbia University Press.

Melville, Herman. 1986. "Bartleby," in Frederick Busch and Billy Budd, eds., *Sailor and Other Stories 1*. London: Penguin Classics.

Mendus, S. 2008. "Private Faces in Public Places," in M. H. Kramer et al., eds., *The Legacy of HLA Hart: Legal, Political, and Moral Philosophy*. Oxford: Oxford University Press.

Merges, Robert P., et al. 2012. *Intellectual Property in the New Technological Age*. New York, NY: Aspen Publishers.

Merrill, Thomas W. 1998. "Property and the Right to Exclude," 77 *Nebraska Law Review* 730.

2000. "The Landscape of Constitutional Property," 86 *Virgina Law Review* 885.

2012. "The Property Strategy," 160 *University of Pennsylvania Law Review* 2061.

2014. "Property and the Right to Exclude II," 3 *Brigham-Kanner Property Rights Conference Journal* 3.

Merrill, Thomas W., and Henry E. Smith. 2000. "Optimal Standardization in the Law of Property: The Numerous Clausus Principle," 110 *Yale Law Journal* 1.

2001a. "What Happened to Property in Law and Economics?," 111 *Yale Law Journal* 357.

2001b. "The Property/Contract Interface," 101 *Columbia Law Review* 773.

2007. "The Morality of Property," 48 *William & Mary Law Review* 1849.

Miller, David. 2011. "Property and Territory: Locke, Kant, and Steiner," 19 *Journal of Political Philosophy* 90.

Moller, Dan. 2017. "Property and the Creation of Value," 33 *Economics and Philosophy* 1.

Mossoff, Adam. 2003. "What is Property? Putting the Pieces Back Together," 45 *Arizona Law Review* 371.

2009. "Exclusion and Exclusive Use in Patent Law," 22 *Harvard Journal of Law & Technology* 330.

2011. "The False Promise of the Right to Exclude," 8 *Economic Journal Watch* 255.

2017. "Trademark as a Property Right," available at https://ssrn.com/abstract=2941763

Myers, Peter C. 1995. "Between Divine and Human Sovereignty: The State of Nature and the Basis of Locke's Political Thought," 27 *Polity* 629.

Newman, Christopher. 2011. "Transformation in Property and Copyright," 56 *Villanova University Law Review* 260.

2017. "Vested Use Privileges in Property and Copyright," 30 *Harvard Journal of Law & Technology* 75.

2018. *Hohfeld and the Theory of in Rem Rights: An Attempted Mediation*. Cambridge: Cambridge University Press.

Nozick, Robert. 1974. *Anarchy, State, and Utopia*. Oxford: Basil Blackwell.

Nussbaum, Marta C. 2006. *Frontiers of Justice: Disability, Nationality and Species Membership*. Cambridge, MA: The Belknap Press of Harvard University Press.

Ocko, Jonathan. 2004. "The Missing Metaphor: Applying Western Legal Scholarship to the Study of Contract and Property in Early Modern China," in Madeleine Zelin, Jonathan K. Ocko and Robert Gardella, eds., *Contract and Property in Early Modern China*. Stanford, CA: Stanford University Press.

Olivecrona, Karl. 1971. "The Concept of a Right According to Grotius and Pufendorf,"in Karl Olivecrona, ed., *Law as Fact*. London: Stevens & Sons.

Oliver W. Holmes, Jr. 1991 [1881]. *The Common Law*. New York, NY: Dover Publications.

Oman, Nathan B. 2017. *The Dignity of Commerce: Markets and The Moral Foundations of Contract Law*. Chicago, IL: University of Chicago Press.

Ono, Kazuko 小野和子. 1967. *Kō Sōgi 黄宗羲 [Huang Zongxi]*. Tokyo: Jinbutsu Ōraisha.

Otsuka, Michael. 2003. *Libertarianism without Inequality*. Oxford: Clarendon Press.

2006. "Prerogatives to Depart from Equality," 58 *Royal Institute of Philosophy Supplement* 95.

Ouyang, Kang. 2003. "Wang Fuzhi," in Xinzhong Yao, ed., *Routledge Curzon Encyclopedia of Confucianism*, O-Z. London/New York, NY: Routledge.

Parchomovsky, Gideon, and Alex Stein. 2009. "Reconceptualizing Trespass," 103 *Northwestern University Law Review* 1828.

Parfit, Derek. 1991. *Equality or Priority*. Lawrence, KS: University of Kansas.

Penner, J. E. 1996. "The 'Bundle of Rights' Picture of Property," 43 *UCLA Law Review* 711.

1997. *The Idea of Property in Law*. Oxford: Oxford University Press.

2013. "On the Very Idea of Transmissible Rights," in James Penner and Henry E. Smith, eds., *Philosophical Foundations of Property Law*. Oxford: Oxford University Press.

2018. "Locke on Equality and Inequality: The Consent to Value Money and 'Positional' Goods" (paper on file with the author).

Philbrick, F. S. 1938. "Changing Conceptions of Property in Law," 86 *University of Pennsylvania Law Review* 691.

Platz, Jeppe von. 2013. "Absolute Freedom of Contract: Grotian Lessons for Libertarians," 25 *Critical Review: A Journal of Politics and Society* 107.

Potter, Pittman B. 2012. "Public Regulation of Private Relations: Changing Conditions of Property Regulation in China," in Guanghua Yu, ed., *The Developement of the Chinese Legal System: Change and Challenges*. London: Routledge.

Pufendorf, Samuel von. 1729 [1672]. *Of the Law of Nature and Nations*. London: J Walthoe.

1934 [1672]. *De Jure Naturae et Gentium Libri Octo*. Oxford: Clarendon Press.

Qiao, Liang 乔亮. 2007. "Huang Zongxi he Gong Zizhen jingji sixiang zhi bijiao" 黄宗羲和龚自珍经济思想之比较 ["Comparison between Huang Zongxi and Gong Zizhen's Economic Thought"], 26 *Heilongjiang Jiaoyuxueyuan Xuebao [Journal of Heilongjiang College of Education]* 14.

Rawls, J. 1999. *A Theory of Justice, Revised Edition*. Cambridge, MA: Belknap Press.

2005. *Political Liberalism, Expanded Edition*. New York, NY: Columbia University Press.

Raz, Joseph. 1977. "The Rule of Law and Its Virtues," 93 *The Law Quarterly Review* 195.

1986. *The Morality of Freedom*. Oxford: Clarendon Press.

1990. *Practical Reason and Norms*. Oxford: Oxford University Press.

Ren, Yuhai 任裕海. 2014. "Huang Zongxi yu Luoke zhengzhi zhexue de yizhong bijiao: zhengti jigou de neizai luoji ji qi xingshang liji" 黄宗羲与洛克政治哲学的一种比较 ：政体构建的内在逻辑及其形上理据 ["A Comparison of the Political Philosophy of Huang Zongxi and John Locke: The Inner Logic and Metaphysical Basis of Government Systems and Institutions"], 6

Fujian Luntan: Renwen shehui kexue ban [Fujian Forum: Social Sciences and Humanities Edition] 58.

Ripstein, Arthur. 2006. "Private Order and Public Justice: Kant and Rawls," 92 *Virgina Law Review* 1931.

2009. *Force and Freedom: Kant's Legal and Political Philosophy*. Cambridge, MA: Harvard University Press.

2013. "Possession and Use," in James Penner and Henry E. Smith, eds., *Philosophical Foundations of Property Law*. Oxford: Oxford University Press.

2015. "Means and Ends," 6 *Jurisprudence* 1.

2017. "Property and Sovereignty: How to Tell the Difference," 18 *Theoretical Inquiries in Law*.

Risse, Mathias. 2009a. "Common Ownership of the Earth as a Non-parochial Standpoint: A Contingent Derivation of Human Rights," 17 *European Journal of Philosophy* 27.

2009b. "The Right to Relocation: Disappering Island Nations and Common Ownership of the Earth," 23 *Ethics & International Affairs* 281.

2012. *On Global Justice*. Princeton, NJ: Princeton Univesity Press.

2013a. "A Précis of on Global Justice, with Emphasis on Implications for International Institutions," 54 *Boston College Law Review* 1037.

2013b. "Reply to Abizadeh, Chung and Farrelly," 8 *Les ateliers de l'éthique / The Ethics Forum* 62.

2014a. "The Human Right to Water and Common Ownership of the Earth," 22 *Journal of Political Philosophy* 178.

2014b. "Response to Arneson, de Bres, and Stilz," 28 *Ethics & International Affairs* 511.

Rose, Carol M. 1985. "Possession as the Origin of Property," 52 *University of Chicago Law Review* 73.

1992. "Giving, Trading, Thieving, and Trusting: How and Why Gifts Become Exchanges, and (More Importantly) Vice Versa," 44 *Florida Law Review* 295.

1996. "Property as the Keystone Right?," 71 *Notre Dame Law Review* 329.

Ryle, Gilbert. 2002. *The Concept of Mind*. Chicago, IL: University of Chicago Press.

Salmond, John W. 1972. *The First Principles of Jurisprudence*. London: Stevens & Haynes.

Salter, John. 2001. "Hugo Grotius: Property and Consent," 29 *Political Theory* 537.

2005. "Grotius and Pufendorf on the Right of Necessity," 26 *History of Political Thought* 284.

2010. "Adam Smith and the Grotian Theory of Property," 12 *British Journal of Politics and International Relations* 3.

Sangiovanni, Andrea. 2016. "How Practices Matter," 24 *Journal of Political Philosophy* 3.

Savigny, Freidrich Karl. 1867. *System of the Modern Roman Law*. Madras: J. Higginbotham.

Scanlon, Thomas. 1982. "Nozick on Rights, Liberty, and Property," in Jeffrey Paul, ed., *Reading Nozick*. Oxford: Basil Blackwell.

Shi, Liang 时亮. 2011. "Lun heli keyu de tongzhi: Huang Zongxi yu Luoke zhi zhengzhi pipan jianming duikan" 论合理可欲的统治 ：黄宗羲与洛克之政治批判简明对勘 ["For Reasonable Governance – A Comparative Study of the Critiques of Government between Huang Zongxi and John Locke"], 5 *Zhengzhi sixiangshi [Journal of the History of Political Thought]* 15.

Shimokawa, Kiyoshi. 2013. "The Origin and Development of Property: Conventionalism, Unilateralism, and Colonialism," in Peter R. Anstey, ed., *The Oxford Handbook of British Philosophy in the Seventeenth Century*. Oxford: Oxford University Press.

Simmons, A. John. 1992. *The Lockean Theory of Rights*. Princeton, NJ: Princeton University Press.

Smith, Henry E. 2004. "Property and Property Rules," 79 *New York University Law Review* 1719.

2005. "Self-Help and the Nature of Property," 1 *The Journal of Law, Economics & Policy* 80.

2006. "Property and Property Rules," 79 *New York University Law Review* 388.

2009. "Mind the Gap: The Indirect Relation between Ends and Means in American Property Law," 94 *Cornell Law Review* 959–64.

2012. "Property as the Law of Things," 125 *Harvard Law Review* 1691.

2013. "Emergent Property," in James Penner and Henry Smith, eds., *Philosophical Foundations of Property Law*. Oxford: Oxford University Press.

2014. "Property, Equity, and the Rule of Law," in Lisa M. Austin and Dennis Klimchuk, eds., *Private Law and the Rule of Law*. Oxford: Oxford University Press.

2015. "The Persistence of System in Property Law," 163 *University of Pennsylvania Law Review* 2055.

Smith, Lionel. 2003. "The Motive, Not the Deed," in Joshua Getzler, ed., *Rationalizing Property, Equity and Trusts, Essays in Honour of Edward Burn*. London: LexisNexis UK.

Smith, Noah. 2015. "*The Threat Coming by Land*." www.bloomberg.com/view/articles/2015-09-09/the-threat-coming-by-land

Sreenivasan G. 1995. *The Limits of Lockean Rights in Property*. Oxford: Oxford University Press.

Stapelbroek, Koen. 2014. "Property," in S.-J. Savonius-Wroth, ed., *The Bloomsbury Companion to Locke*. London: Bloomsbury.

Steiner, Hillel. 1987. "Capitalism, Justice, and Equal Starts," 5 *Social Philosophy and Policy* 49.

1994. *An Essay on Rights*. Oxford: Blackwell.

Sterk, Stewart E. 2008. "Property Rules, Liability Rules, and Uncertainty about Property Rights," 106 *Michigan Law Review* 1285.

Stern, James Y. 2013. "Property's Constitution," 101 *California Law Review* 303.

2017. "The Essential Structure of Property Law," 115 *Michigan Law Review* 1177.

Stevens, Robert. 2007. *Torts and Rights*. Oxford: Oxford University Press.

2012. "When and Why does Unjustified Enrichment Justify the Recognition of Propriety Rights?," 92 *Boston University Law Review* 923.

Stilz, Anna. 2014. "On Collective Ownership of the Earth," 28 *Ethics & International Affairs* 501.

Strahilevitz, Lior Jacob. 2006. "Information Asymmetries and the Rights to Exclude," 104 *Michigan Law Review* 1835.

Struve, Lynn. 1988. "Huang Zongxi in Context: A Reappraisal of his Major Writings," 47 *The Journal of Asian Studies* 474.

2002. "Huang Zongxi (Huang Chung-hsi)," in Antonio S. Cua, ed., *Encyclopedia of Chinese Philosophy*. New York, NY: Routledge.

Suárez, Francisco. 1944. "De legibus, ac Deo legislatore," in Gwladis L. Williams, Ammi Brown and John Waldron, eds., *Selections from Three Works*. Oxford: Clarendon Press.

Sun, Baoshan 孙宝山. 2008. *Fangu kaixin: Huang Zongxi de zhengzhi sixiang* 返古开新 ： 黄宗羲的政治思想 *[Returning to the Old and Creating the New: The Political Thought of Huang Zongxi]*. Beijing: People's Press.

Tan, Mingran. 2010. "Crisis and Hermeneutics: Wang Fuzhi's Interpretation of Confucian Classics in a Time of Radical Change from Ming to Qing Dynasties" Ph.D. dissertation, Graduate Department of East Asian Studies. Toronto: University of Toronto.

Thompson, Michael. 2004. "What is it to Wrong Someone? A Puzzle about Justice," in R. Jay Wallace et al., eds., *Reason and Value: Themes from the Moral Philosophy of Joseph Raz*. Oxford: Oxford University Press.

Thomson, Judith Jarvis. 1986. "Self-defense and Rights," in William Parent, ed., *Rights, Restitution, and Risk*. Cambridge, MA: Harvard University Press.

1990. *The Realm of Rights*. Cambridge, MA: Harvard University Press.

Tuck, Richard. 1979. *Natural Rights Theories: Their Origin and Development*. Cambridge: Cambridge University Press.

1993. *Philosophy and Government, 1572–1651*. Cambridge: Cambridge University Press.

Uzgalis, William. 2016. "John Locke," The Stanford Encyclopedia of Philosophy (Spring 2016 Edition), http://plato.stanford.edu/archives/spr2016/entries/locke/.

Vallentyne, Peter. 2000. "Introduction: Left-Libertarianism – A Primer," in Peter Vallentyne and Hillel Steiner, eds., *Left Libertarianism and Its Critics: The Contemporary Debate*. Basingstoke: Palgrave.

Van Ittersum, Martine. 2005–2007. "Preparing Mare Liberum for the Press: Hugo Grotius' Rewriting of Chapter Twelve of De Jure Praedae in November–December 1608," 26–28 *Grotiana* 246.

2009. "Dating the Manuscript of De Jure Praedae (1604–1608): What Watermarks, Foliation and Quire Divisions Can Tell Us about Hugo Grotius' Development as a Natural Rights and Natural Law Theorist," 35 *History of European Ideas* 125.

Van Norden, Bryan W. 2008. *Mengzi: With Selections from Traditional Commentaries*. Indianapolis, IN/Cambridge: Hackett.

Vossen, Bas van der. 2009. "What Counts as Original Appropriation?," 8 *Politics, Philosophy & Economics* 355.

2015. "Imposing Duties and Original Appropriation," 23 *Journal of Political Philosophy* 64.

Waddams, Stephen. 2011. *Principle and Policy in Contract Law: Competing or Complementary Concepts?* Cambridge: Cambridge University Press.

Waldron, Jeremy. 1985. "What is Private Property," 5 *Oxford Journal of Legal Studies* 313.

1988. *The Right to Private Property*. Oxford: Clarendon Press.

2008a. "The Concept and the Rule of Law," 43 *Georgia Law Review* 1.

2008b. "Do Judges Reason Morally?," in Grant Huscroft, ed., *Expounding the Constitution: Essays on Constitutional Theory*. Cambridge: Cambridge University Press.

2010. "Property Law," in Dennis Patterson, ed., *A Companion to Philosophy of Law and Legal Theory*. Chichester: Blackwell Publishing.

2013. "Is Dignity the Foundation of Human Rights?," 12 *New York University Public Law and Legal Theory Working Papers* 73.

Wang, Fuzhi 王夫之. 1964 [1691]. *Song lun* 宋论 *[Discussions on the Song Dynasty]*. Beijing: Zhonghua Press.

1996a [1682]. "*E Meng*" 噩梦 *["Strange Dreams"], in Chuanshan quanshu di shi er ce* 船山全书第*12*册 *[The Complete Works of Wang Chuanshan: Volume 12]*. Changsha: Yuelu Press.

1996b [1687]. "*Du Tongjian lun*" 读通鉴论 *["On Reading Sima Guang's Comprehensive Mirror in Aid of Governance"], in Chuanshan quanshu di shi ce* 船山全书第*10*册 *[The Complete Works of Wang Chuanshan: Volume 10]*. Changsha: Yuelu Press.

Wang, Jinmin. 2012. "Proto-Enlightenment Trends and New Elements in Political Culture," in Xingpei Yuan, ed., *The History of Chinese Civilization, Volume IV: Late Ming and Qing Dynasties (1525–1911)*. Cambridge: Cambridge University Press.

Weinrib, Ernest J. 1995. *The Idea of Private Law*. Cambridge, MA: Harvard University Press.

2011. "Private Law and Public Right," 61 *University of Toronto Law Journal* 191.

2012. *Corrective Justice*. Oxford: Oxford University Press.

Wellman, Christopher Heath. 1995. "On Conflicts between Rights," 14 *Law and Philosophy* 271.

Wenar, Leif. 2013. "The Nature of Claim-Rights," 123 *Ethics* 202.

West, Robin L. 2001. *Re-Imagining Justice: Progressive Interpretations of Formal Equality, Rights, and the Rule of Law Aldershot*, UK/Burlington, VT: Ashgate/Dartmouth.

Wheeler, Samuel C. 1980. "Property Rights as Body Rights," 14 *Noûs* 171.

Widerquist, Karl. 2010. "Lockean Theories of Property: Justifications for Unilateral Appropriation," 2 *Public Reason* 3.

Winstanley, Gerrard. 2009. "The Law of Freedom," in Thomas N. Corns, Ann Hughes and David Loewenstein, eds., *The Complete Works of Gerrard Winstanley*. Oxford: Oxford University Press.

Xiao, Pinghan 萧平汉 and Zhenxi Liu 刘珍喜. 2007. "Wang Fuzhi jingji sixiang xin-lun" 王夫之经济思想新论 ["A New Discussion of Wang Fuzhi's Economic Thought"], 2 *Chuanshan xuekan [Chuanshan Journal]* 5.

Xu, Dingbao 徐定宝. 2009a. *Huang Zongxi ping zhuan* 黄宗羲评传 *[A Critical Biography of Huang Zongxi]*. Nanjing: Nanjing University Press.

Xu, Yanmin. 2009b. "Huang Zongxi," in Linsun Cheng, ed., *Berkshire Encyclopedia of China (Vol. 3)*. Great Barrington, MA: Berkshire.

Yeung, Jason Hing Kau 杨庆球. 2005. *Minzhu yu minben: Luoke yu Huang Zongxi de zhengzhi ji zongjiao sixiang* 民主与民本 ： 洛克与黄宗羲的政治及宗教思想 [People-as-Masters and People-at-the-Root: The Political and Religious Thought of Locke and Huang Zongxi]. Hong Kong: Joint Publishing Co.

Young, Iris Marion. 2011. *Responsibility for Justice*. Oxford: Oxford University Press.

Yu, Peter K. 2012. "Intellectual Property and Asian Values," 16 *Marquette Intellectual Property Law Review* 340.

Zelin, Madeleine. 2004. "A Critique of Rights of Property in Pre-War China," in Madeleine Zelin, Jonathan K. Ocko and Robert Gardella, eds., *Contract and Property in Early Modern China*. Standford, CA: Stanford University Press.

Zelin, Madeleine, Jonathan K. Ocko, and Robert Gardella. 2004. "Introduction," in Madeleine Zelin, Jonathan K. Ocko and Robert Gardella, eds., *Contract and Property in Early Modern China*. Stanford, CA: Stanford University Press.

Zeng, Kunsheng 曾坤生. 1993. "Wang Fuzhi jingji sixiang chutan" 王夫之经济思想初探 ["A Preliminary Exploration of Wang Fuzhi's Economic Thought"], 2 *Guangxi shehui kexue [Guangxi Social Sciences]* 54.

Zhang, Chuanxi. 2012a. "Shang and Zhou: The Patriarchal Clan System and Related Institutions," in Xingpei Yuan, ed., *The History of Chinese Civilization, Volume 1: Earliest Times to 221 B.C.* Cambridge: Cambridge University Press.

Zhang, Huai 张怀. 1997. *Wang Fuzhi ping zhuan: minzu ziliziqiang zhi hun* 王夫之评传 ： 民族自立自强之魂 *[A Critical Biography of Wang Fuzhi: The Soul of Self-Improvement of Nationalism]*. Nanning: Guangxi Education Press.

Zhang, Mo. 2008. "From Public to Private: The Newly Enacted Chinese Property Law and the Protection of Property Rights in China," 5 *Berkeley Business Law Journal* 317.

Zhang, Ru'an 张如安, and Xianchang Huangfu 皇甫贤昌. 1996. "1990–1994 nian guonei Huang Zongxi yanjiu zongshu" 年国内黄宗羲研究综述 ["An Overview of Research done on Huang Zongxi in Mainland China from 1990 to 1994"], 1 *Zhongguo shi yanjiu dongtai [State of Research on Chinese History]* 14.

Zhang, Taisu. 2011. "Property Rights in Land, Agricultural Capitalism, and the Relative Decline of Pre-Industrual China," 13 *San Diego International Law Review* 129.

2014. "Social Hierarchies and the Formation of Customary Property Law in Pre-Industrial China and England," 62 *American Journal of Comparative Law* 171.

Zhang, Yongzhong 张永忠. 2008. "Junzhu biange yu biange junzhu: bijiao Huang Zongxi yu Luoke de zhengzhi zhexue" 君主变革与变革君主 ：比较黄宗羲与洛克的政治哲学 ["Monarch Reform and Reforming Autocracy: A Comparison between Huang Zongxi's and Locke's Political Philosophy"], 4 *Hangzhou Dianzi Keji Daxue Xuebao (shehui kexue ban) [Journal of Hangzhou Dianzi University (Social Sciences)]* 1.

2009. *Huang Zongxi zhengzhi zhexue sixiang yanjiu* 黄宗羲政治哲学思想研究 *[Research on the Political Philosophy of Huang Zongxi]*. Beijing: People's Press.

Zhang, Yuanyuan 张圆圆. 2012b. "Lun Huang Zongxi jingji sixiang" 论黄宗羲经济思想 ["Huang Zongxi's Economic Thought"], 217 *Xueshu Jiaoliu [Academic Exchange]* 116.

Zhao, Yanhua 赵延花. 2005. "Lun Huang Zongxi de shimin jingji sixiang" 论黄宗羲的市民经济思想 ["Huang Zongxi's Social Economic Thought"], 12 *Beifang Jingji [Northern Economy]* 78.

INDEX